lonely 🌏 planet

WEST COAST
AUSTRALIA

Fleur Bainger, Anthony Ham, Ariana Svenson

D1264305

Meander the back roads in search of gourmet treasures. Dare to swim with whale sharks and humpback whales. Listen to ancient stories told through Aboriginal art. Immerse yourself in outback gorges and waterholes. Journey beyond where the paved road ends. Let an Indigenous guide show you the country in whole new ways. Discover beaches and coastal stretches just for you. Experience Perth as locals know and love it.

TURN THE PAGE AND START PLANNING YOUR NEXT BEST TRIP →

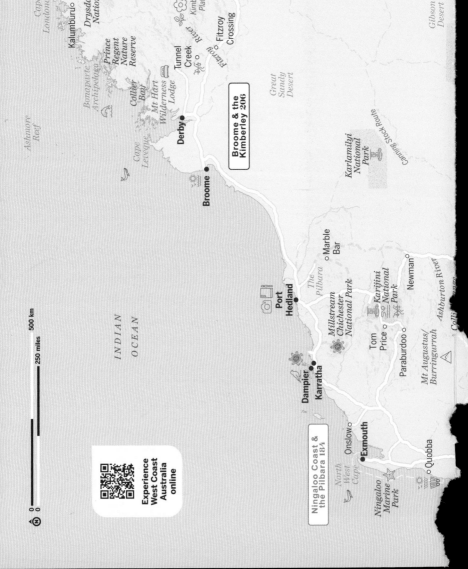

Men of the Karjanarna Jaru getting ready to perform an initiation dance for young adults, Bungle Bungles, Purnululu National Park (p217)

Contents

Kangaroos, Lucky Bay (p140), Cape Le Grand National Park

Acknowledgement of Country

Lonely Planet would like to acknowledge all Aboriginal nations throughout this country, who have nurtured and maintained the land since time immemorial. This guide was written on, and is written about, the lands of many diverse nations.

We recognise the unique and ongoing connection that Aboriginal peoples have to land and waters and thank them for their efforts to preserve them. We pay our respects to Elders past and present and extend this respect to any Aboriginal or Torres Strait Islander people who may be reading this guide.

We also recognise the ongoing efforts of Aboriginal peoples for reconciliation, justice, and social, cultural and economic self-determination. Sovereignty was never ceded. Australia always was, and always will be, Aboriginal land.

Cultural Sensitivity Warning

Aboriginal and Torres Strait Islander readers are advised that this guide may contain names and images of people who have since passed away.

GOURMET
WEST COAST

Australia's southwestern corner is one of the nation's most underrated culinary stars. Margaret River, where the west's reputation for excellence begins, is well-known for its wineries, breweries and much more. But far fewer visitors realise until they're here that Perth also has a richly dynamic eating scene; the Swan Valley is filled with places where you can indulge your taste buds, and Denmark's wine scene is like stumbling on secret treasure.

→ MARGARET RIVER WINES

The Margaret River Wooditchup wine region has more than 150 (mostly boutique) wineries. The most popular grape varieties are chardonnay and cabernet sauvignon.

Left Gourmet lunch, Cullen Wines (p113)
Right Wine tasting, Margaret River/ Wooditchup region (p112)
Below Demonstrating bushtucker, Maalinup Aboriginal Gallery

GOURMET ESCAPE

In November, the Margaret River wine region hosts what may be Australia's leading food and wine festival, the Western Australia Gourmet Escape (p113).

↑ MAALINUP ABORIGINAL GALLERY

The west is fantastic at marrying food and art, which is exactly what Perth's Maalinup Aboriginal Gallery does so well, exhibiting a range of Aboriginal art as well as celebrating native foods and flavours.

Best Food & Wine Experiences

▶ Learn to cook sustainably at One Table Farm in Cowaramup then tour the wineries in Margaret River. (p113)

▶ Choose from 280 wines at The Naked Fox wine bar and shop farmers markets in the Swan Valley. (p86)

▶ Taste little-known native flavours in some of Perth's best restaurants, but especially Wildflower. (p73)

▶ Combine local wines, gourmet foods and art galleries along Denmark's farm-gate trail. (p147)

UNDER
THE SEA

Where the Indian Ocean crashes into Australia's west coast, the sea is a technicolour world of astonishing riches. Whales and whale sharks, turtles and dolphins, corals and the weirdly wonderful stromatolites: they're all here in one of the richest concentrations of marine wildlife anywhere on the planet. Whether you're swimming with sea creatures or diving and snorkelling amid kaleidoscopic underwater colours, this really is one of Australia's best wildlife experiences.

→ DOLPHINS

If Monkey Mia and its dolphins are too much of a scene, stick around to volunteer, or head to Cape Peron (or Bunbury) to escape the crowds.

Left Eagle rays, Hamelin Bay (p122)
Right Volunteer feeding dolphin, Monkey Mia (p176)
Below Breaching humback whale, Ningaloo (p190)

RAYS

There's no better place to widen your marine life checklist than the graceful rays of Hamelin Bay in the South West. Expect smooth stingrays, black stingrays and eagle rays.

↑ WHALE WATCHING

If you can't get enough of whales, head to the calm waters of King George Sound, off Albany along the southern coast, from May to October.

Best Marine Wildlife Experiences

▶ Swim with soulful whale sharks from March to August at Ningaloo. (p188)

▶ Interact with humpback whales at Ningaloo from July to October. (p188)

▶ Watch in wonder the miracle of nesting sea turtles, also at Ningaloo. (p190)

▶ Commune with world-famous bottlenose dolphins at Monkey Mia. (p176)

▶ Go looking for orcas (killer whales) at Bremer Bay on the South Coast. (p143)

ABORIGINAL
ART

One of the best experiences you can have out west is diving into the unimaginably rich world of Aboriginal art. From ancient rock art of the ancestors to modern art centres where you can talk to artists and see their works-in-progress, it's a wonderful introduction to one of the oldest living cultures on the planet.

SUZANNE LONG/ALAMY STOCK PHOTO ©

→ DATING ROCK ART

No one knows how old the petroglyphs of the Pilbara and Kimberley are. Some date back 45,000 years but could be 65,000 years old.

Left Aboriginal rock art, Murujuga National Park (p199)
Right Boomerangs etched into rock, Burrup Peninsula (p198)
Below Aboriginal artist dot painting

ROCK ART

Rock art is the oldest form of human art: some of the most ancient engravings are in the Kimberley where they focus on the Wandjina, the ancestral creation spirits.

RIGHT: CHAMELEONSEYE/SHUTTERSTOCK ©
LEFT: TOTAJLA/SHUTTERSTOCK ©

↑ ART AS CULTURE

Although there's no word in Aboriginal languages for 'art', visual imagery has always served as a connection between past, present and future, and between Aboriginal people and their homelands.

Best Aboriginal Art

▶ **Discover Aboriginal rock art that stretches back 30,000 years at Murujuga National Park.** (p199)

▶ **Enjoy ancient, sophisticated rock art along the Kimberley's King Edward River at Munurru.** (p227)

▶ **Browse works by Wajarri, Noongar, Badimaya and Wilunyu peoples at Geraldton's Yamaji Art.** (p165)

▶ **Admire the work of some of the Pilbara's best artists at Yinjaa-Barni Art in Roebourne.** (p199)

ABORIGINAL
MEETINGS

▰▰ Perhaps more than anywhere else in Australia, Western Australia offers opportunities for genuine encounters with Aboriginal Australian culture. There's nothing staged about sitting with an Aboriginal artist while they work, or being shown the land by an Aboriginal guide working for an Aboriginal-owned tour operator. These are the sorts of memories of which great trips are made.

LEFT: ELEMENTS MARGARET RIVER ©
BOTTOM: DANIJELC/GETTY IMAGES ©

★ WAITOC

The **Western Australian Indigenous Tourism Operators Council** (waitoc.com) should be your starting point in finding Aboriginal-owned tour operators for the areas you'll be visiting.

Best Aboriginal Connections

▸ **Listen to stories as old as time at The Storytellers – Keepers of the Dreaming.** (p165)

▸ **Kayak Shark Bay and learn Indigenous bush skills with Wula Gura Nyinda Eco Adventures.** (p173)

▸ **Walk a local songline with the Goolarabooloo people along the Lurujarri Dreaming Trail, near Broome.** (p231)

▸ **Take a deep dive into Margaret River's Aboriginal food culture on a Koomal Dreaming tour.** (p113)

▸ **Learn about Aboriginal culture at the Avon Valley's Bilya Koort Boodja Centre.** (p97)

Above Koomal Dreaming guided tour (p113)
Left Kayaks, Shark Bay (p173)

The first European to land on Australian soil was Dutch explorer Dirk Hartog in 1616. The island that bears his name looks almost just like it did back then.

The Houtman Abrolhos Islands are the southernmost coral reefs in the Indian Ocean.

LOST
WORLDS

▬▬ You don't have to stray far from the coastal highway to nearly fall off the map. At so many places along this shore, it's possible to leave behind not just the crowds but the modern world, and catch a glimpse of an Australia little changed in the centuries since Europeans first arrived.

Best Remote Adventures

▶ See Australia's wildlife as it once was on **Dirk Hartog Island.** (p177)

▶ **Combine history lessons with wildlife on the gloriously remote Houtman Abrolhos Islands.** (pictured; p165)

▶ **Lose yourself in a paradise of wildlife and blissful isolation in the Dampier Archipelago.** (p199)

▶ **Take the 'road' less travelled as you drive the Kimberley's Duncan Road.** (p216)

Mt Augustus/Burrin-gurrah, inland from Carnarvon, is two times larger than much better-known Uluru.

The Kimberley gorges of Geikie, Tunnel Creek and Windjana form part of an ancient under-sea reef, dating back 350 million years to the Devonian era.

Best Outback Experiences

► Explore the spectacular gorges of the Pilbara's Karijini National Park. (pictured; p195)

► Discover why the Kimberley is such a special place in the remote Mitchell Plateau. (p226)

► Disappear into the labyrinths of the Bungle Bungles in Purnululu National Park. (p229)

► See the dramatic limestone spires of the The Pinnacles at sunset. (p90)

► Marvel at one of Australia's most perspective-altering facades at Wave Rock. (p92)

OUTBACK
VIEWS

The outback presses right up against this remarkable coastline, and these are some of the most beautiful landforms you'll see anywhere. In places, great gorges and epic monoliths rise from the seemingly endless desert. And in this, as in all things, the northwest is very much the jewel of a gem-studded crown.

A DESERTED
SHORE

An extraordinary coast wraps around Australia's west coast, from the wild and windy Great Australian Bight in the south to the soulful Kimberley in the far north, and so many places in between. The beaches here get a fraction of the visitors compared with the country's east coast, and long, lonely stretches of sand are almost guaranteed. Finding a deserted beach is never a problem – choosing which on to visit always is.

LEFT: WENDY JOHNSON/ALAMY STOCK PHOTO ©
BOTTOM: ROBERT MCGILLIVRAY/SHUTTERSTOCK ©

Best Beaches

▸ Enjoy the best of the south's world-famous beaches at gorgeous Shelley Beach. (p155)

▸ Heed the call of the wild at Mandalay Beach in incredible D'Entrecasteaux National Park. (p155)

▸ Hike amid wildflowers and beautiful rock formations from Sugarloaf Rock to Cape Naturaliste. (p121)

▸ Seek out mindblowing rock formations overlooking the Great Southern Ocean in Torndirrup National Park. (p143)

→ HORIZONTAL WATERFALLS

The horizontal falls (actually tides gushing through a narrow rocky defile) near Derby are sacred to the Dambimangari people: you're welcome to visit but not to ride the tides.

← DUNES OF THE SOUTHWEST

WA's most spectacular coastal sand dunes – Yeagarup Dunes – lie in the Pemberton hinterland. Nearby you can see the awesome basalt columns of Black Point.

Above Yeagarup Dunes (p123)
Left Horizontal waterfall, Talbot Bay, Dampier Archipelago (p199)

At last count Perth had a population of just over 2 million people.

Perth often lays claim to being the world's most isolated city: it lies 2104km (a three-hour flight) from Adelaide, the nearest city.

A SECRET
PERTH

Perth is the kind of city where a little inside knowledge makes all the difference, from an octogenarian jazz bar to suburbs like Fremantle and Leederville where the passage of time sits lightly upon the shoulders. Some attractions, such as Cottesloe Beach, are so popular that they simply can't be missed, but you can have it all to yourself if you know when to visit.

→ EUROPEAN COLONISTS

The first Europeans to come ashore at Perth (on Cottesloe Beach) were Dutch sailors in 1697. Modern Perth was not established until 1829.

Left Elizabeth Quay (p79)
Right Cottesloe Beach (p54)
Below Craft-beer tasting

WADJUK COUNTRY

The land on which Perth now sits has been occupied for 40,000 years. This is the land of Wadjuk, a sub-group of the Noongar people.

↑ PERTH'S EVOLVING DRINKING SCENE

Things change. Northbridge, traditionally pubby, brawly and brassy, now sustains a more idiosyncratic drinking scene. Craft beer reigns supreme in formerly hard-drinking Fremantle.

Best Perth Experiences

▶ Get into the swing of Perth's best live music at quirky-cool Jazz Cellar. (p46)

▶ Visit Cottesloe Beach's sculpture festival at dawn and share this fabulous city beach with just a few locals. (p55)

▶ Find your own secluded corner of Bennion Beach, where locals go to escape the crowds. (p67)

▶ Get to the heart of locals-only Leederville by spending a morning at the vibrant Kailis Bros Fish Market. (p58)

Noongar People's Six-Season Calendar

Those who live here know that there are not four European seasons, there are six, and they were identified eons ago by Aboriginal peoples. We recognise their knowledge by using the Noongar people's six-season calendar for some destinations.

Perth Summer

Perth has one of Australia's loveliest summer climates with warm temperatures, clear skies and relatively little rain or humidity.

Scorching Inland

December isn't bad in the desert inland, but it starts to get unbearably hot in January and February.

↑ The Humid Coast

The coast around Monkey Mia and Ningaloo has extremely high humidity, even if it doesn't rain much.

♥ p178

DECEMBER

Average January daytime max:
31.2°C (Perth)
Days of rainfall: 1

JANUARY

West Coast Australia in

SUMMER

Cyclone Season

Keep an eye on weather reports from December to April: this is when cyclones can sweep into the northwest.

← Rain Up North

While much of Australia is on holidays, the northwest can be really humid and thunderstorms can affect travel plans.

FROM LEFT: MARTIN HELGEMEIR/SHUTTERSTOCK ©, MAX.KU/SHUTTERSTOCK ©, MATT JELONEK/GETTY IMAGES ©, ADWO/SHUTTERSTOCK ©, BOTTOM IMAGE: TOTAJLA/SHUTTERSTOCK ©,

→ Perth Music

Late summer sees the excellent Perth Festival and the indie Laneway Festival in Fremantle as live music takes over the city.

● Fremantle (p48)

↑ Fringe World

At Perth's cheekiest arts festival, hundreds of artists perform in parks and pubs across January and February.

● Perth (p40)

▶ fringeworld.com.au

FEBRUARY

Average January daytime max:
32°C (Exmouth)
Days of rainfall: 1

Average January daytime max:
32.3°C (Broome)
Days of rainfall: 8

WEST COAST AUSTRALIA PLAN BY SEASON

🎒 Packing Notes

A hat and sunscreen for warm summer days; a raincoat in the north.

Rain Easing

It can be uncomfortably moist and many 4WD tracks remain closed, but it's lovely and quiet up north.

Central Coast

Rain is always possible and humidity remains high in this subtropical zone, but at least crowds begin to disappear.

↑ Perth in Autumn

With summer in the rear-view mirror, it's lovely to be in Perth, with milder temperatures and generally clear skies.

↖ Red Earth Arts Festival

Over 10 days in March, Karratha and surrounding towns come alive for this Indigenous arts festival.

📍 Karratha (p194)

▶ reaf.com.au

MARCH

APRIL

Average April daytime max:
24.9°C (Perth)
Days of rainfall: 3

West Coast Australia in
AUTUMN

↓ Whale Sharks at Ningaloo

Whale sharks arrive at the Ningaloo Reef in April for one of Australia's greatest wildlife encounters.

📍 Ningaloo (p188)

← Staircase to the Moon

Come to Broome's Town Beach two nights every month from April to October for this stirring natural phenomenon.

📍 Broome (p230)

Ord Valley Muster

Over 10 days in May, Kununurra puts on events such as a huge outdoor concert by the Ord River.

📍 Kununurra (p216)

▶ ordvalleymuster.com.au

MAY

Average April daytime max:
30.6°C (Exmouth)
Days of rainfall: 1

Average April daytime max:
23.8°C (Broome)
Days of rainfall: 2

Outback Cooling

If it's raining on the coast, then rains often linger inland, but temperatures are starting to ease.

🎒 Packing Notes

A jacket for evenings in the south, and light, loose-fitting clothes in the north.

The Perth Winter

Perth in winter is generally warmer than Australia's east coast, but rain is possible and nights are cool.

Inland Oasis

The Western Australian interior is at its best in summer, with dry, mild temperatures and often cold nights.

↑ The Best of Broome & Beyond

Mild temperatures, lower humidity and clear skies make this the perfect time in the northwest.
📍 Broome (p230)

↑ All Good on the Reef

Humidity remains high on the central WA coast but rain is rare and conditions excellent for reef exploration.

JUNE

Average July daytime max:
16.9°C (Perth)
Days of rainfall: 10

JULY

West Coast Australia in
WINTER

Humpbacks at Monkey Mia

The whale sharks may head back out to sea, but whales appear along WA's central coast.

📍 Ningaloo (p189)

↓ Ideal for Hiking

Winter months are perfect for hiking in Kalbarri, Cape Range and elsewhere with milder daytime temperatures.

📍 Kalbarri (p170)

↗ 4WD Happy Days

This is the heart of the dry season and most 4WD trails are open.

Average July daytime max:
23.2°C (Exmouth)
Days of rainfall: 2

AUGUST

Port Hedland Cup

Port Hedland puts on its finest for a day at the races at the annual Port Hedland Cup, on the first Monday in August.

📍 Port Hedland (p203)

Average July daytime max:
28.7°C (Broome)
Days of rainfall: 1

WEST COAST AUSTRALIA PLAN BY SEASON

🎒 Packing Notes

Evenings can be cool and a raincoat may be needed in the south.

Desert Spring

Beyond the coast, spring can be dry and mild, although spring rains are possible late in the season.

Humidity Rising

Early spring is a fine time to explore the central coast, but humidity starts to become uncomfortable as summer nears.

↓ Perth in Spring

The city has a real spring in its step, with warming temperatures and wildflowers close to the city.

↑ Hold on to High Season

Broome and the Kimberley are lovely in September, sticky in October and starting to close in November.

● The Kimberleys (p206)

SEPTEMBER

Average October daytime max:
22.1°C (Perth)
Days of rainfall: 4

OCTOBER

West Coast Australia in
SPRING

Sunshine Festival

October is a great time to visit Geraldton for its Sunshine Festival with much beach merriment.

📍 Geraldton (p164)

▶ sunshinefestival.com.au

↑ Gourmet Escape

Margaret River's culinary celebration is one of Australia's best food-and-wine festivals.

📍 Margaret River (p112)

▶ gourmetescape.com.au

↖ Astro Rocks Fest

Celebrates Mt Magnet's clear outback night skies and unique geology over a mid-September weekend.

📍 Mt Magnet

▶ astrorocks-mtmagnet.com.au

☀

Average October daytime max: 28.5°C (Exmouth) Days of rainfall: 0

NOVEMBER

☀

Average October daytime max: 33.4°C (Broome) Days of rainfall: 1

Spring Wildflowers

WA is fabulous for wildflowers from September to November. They appear as far as the Monkey Mia hinterland.

📍 Monkey Mia (p160)

🎒 Packing Notes

Loose-fitting clothes in the north; both warm and cool clothing in the south.

PERTH & AROUND
Trip Builder

TAKE YOUR PICK OF MUST-SEES AND HIDDEN GEMS

Perth is both a dynamic destination in its own right and the gateway to a world of natural and culinary attractions. This is the west at its most diverse, with a stirring mix of urban and semi-wilderness to nourish the soul.

🗺 Trip Notes

Hub towns Perth, Northam

How long? Allow 10 days

Getting around You won't need a car to get around Perth, but renting a car means you can explore everywhere else at your own pace. Rottnest Island can be visited on a day trip by boat.

Tips Base yourself in Perth, but factor in overnight stays for Rottnest and somewhere close to the Pinnacles so you can enjoy both at sunset and after dark.

Rottnest Island
Stay overnight on Rottnest to get to know secluded, pristine beaches, a hidden history and, of course, the cutest creatures in the west.
🚗 ½–2hr from Perth

Wubin

The Pinnacles
Wait for sunset when the light is perfect for enjoying this unique terrain spotted with limestone spires.
🚗 2½hr from Perth

Bindi Bindi

Wongan Hills

Koorda

Mukinbudin

Chittering Valley

Goomalling

Avon Valley
Enjoy how everything here happens on a cinematic scale, from hot-air ballooning and Australia's longest suspension bridge, to deep-time Indigenous stories.
🚗 1½hr from Perth

Merredin

Toodyay

Northam

Swan Valley
Discover Swan Valley, Perth's quieter alter ego. It's a world of wineries, farmers markets and restaurants set against a pretty backdrop.
🚗 ½–1hr from Perth

York

Perth
Begin in feel-good Perth and you'll quickly understand the breadth of the city's charm, from its abundant sunshine and eclectic neighbourhoods to fabulous food, wine and historical offerings.

Kondinin

Hyden

Bannister

Kulin

Wave Rock
Drive east for one of the grandest and more perspective-altering rock formations you'll find anywhere.
🚗 4hr from Perth

Narrogin

● **Collie**

Darkan

Darling Range

DOWN SOUTH
Trip Builder

TAKE YOUR PICK OF MUST-SEES AND HIDDEN GEMS

From Perth to the wild south, it can feel as though there's a whole continent full of diversity on this odyssey through the south. It has all the hallmarks of the west's magnificence: dramatic landscapes, a passionate food-and-wine focus, and quiet roads that lead to a real sense of discovery.

Trip Notes

Hub towns Perth, Margaret River, Albany

How long? Allow two weeks

Getting around You really need your own vehicle to explore this vast region; the reward is being able to take all those enticing back roads.

Tips Plan to stay at least a couple of nights in each place. Otherwise, you'll feel like you're spending much of your time on the road.

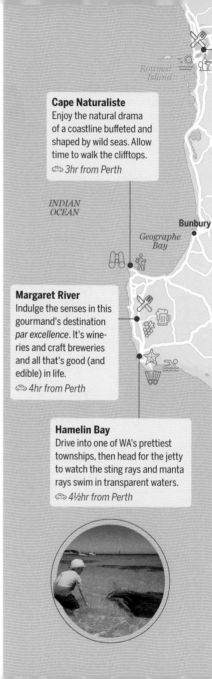

Rottnest Island

Cape Naturaliste
Enjoy the natural drama of a coastline buffeted and shaped by wild seas. Allow time to walk the clifftops.
🚗 3hr from Perth

INDIAN OCEAN

Bunbury

Geographe Bay

Margaret River
Indulge the senses in this gourmand's destination *par excellence*. It's wineries and craft breweries and all that's good (and edible) in life.
🚗 4hr from Perth

Hamelin Bay
Drive into one of WA's prettiest townships, then head for the jetty to watch the sting rays and manta rays swim in transparent waters.
🚗 4½hr from Perth

Perth
Dive into Perth's vibrant cultural and culinary life. This is one beautiful city and it's usually bathed in sunshine.

Narrogin

Lake King

Wagin

Walpole-Nornalup National Park
Lose yourself in the rivers and ancient forests of giant eucalypts at Walpole-Nornalup National Park.
🚗 7½hr from Perth

Katanning

Kojonup

Albany
Feed both body and soul in Albany, an emerging destination for foodies as much as it is a haven for historians.
🚗 9hr from Perth

Lake Magenta Nature Reserve

Ravensthorpe

Jerramungup

Hopetoun

Manjimup

Pemberton

Cranbrook

Stirling Range National Park

Wellstead

D'Entrecasteaux National Park

Mt Barker

Walpole

Fitzgerald River National Park
Go on an adventure in Fitzgerald River with its wilderness feel, incredible floral diversity and inspiring views from East Mt Barren.
🚗 11hr from Perth

Denmark
Discover Denmark with its fair share of wineries and surrounding country that takes in glorious coastline and forests.
🚗 8hr from Perth

SOUTHERN OCEAN

100 km
50 miles

PERTH TO MONKEY MIA

Trip Builder

TAKE YOUR PICK OF MUST-SEES AND HIDDEN GEMS

■■■■ You don't have to travel too many kilometres north of Perth to realise that West Coast Australia is one wildly beautiful shore. The traffic thins, the distances between towns grow, and the views just get better the further north you go.

🗺 Trip Notes

Hub towns Perth, Geraldton, Denham

How long? Allow two weeks

Getting around You could get from A to B by bus, and there are flights (handy for getting back to Perth). But there's really no substitute for having your own vehicle.

Tips Don't be too ambitious about how far you travel each day. Distances are vast, and you'll enjoy it more if you take it slowly.

Francois Peron National Park
Explore beyond where the paved road ends and enjoy the unmistakeable wilderness feel of Shark Bay's Francois Peron National Park.
🚗 *9hr from Perth*

Shark Bay Road
Go kayaking with an Aboriginal guide and drive the storied Shark Bay Rd to get a taste of this superb World Heritage–listed area.
🚗 *8hr from Perth*

INDIAN OCEAN

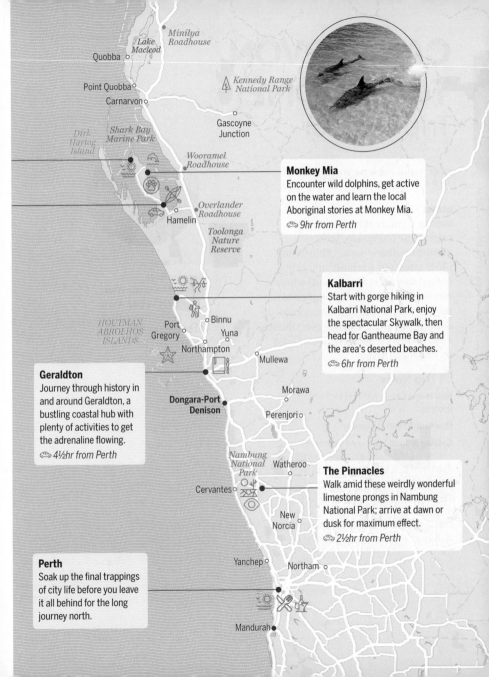

Quobba

Minilya Roadhouse

Lake Macleod

Point Quobba

Carnarvon

Kennedy Range National Park

Gascoyne Junction

Dirk Hartog Island

Shark Bay Marine Park

Wooramel Roadhouse

Monkey Mia
Encounter wild dolphins, get active on the water and learn the local Aboriginal stories at Monkey Mia.
🚗 9hr from Perth

Overlander Roadhouse

Hamelin

Toolonga Nature Reserve

Kalbarri
Start with gorge hiking in Kalbarri National Park, enjoy the spectacular Skywalk, then head for Gantheaume Bay and the area's deserted beaches.
🚗 6hr from Perth

HOUTMAN ABROLHOS ISLANDS

Port Gregory

Binnu

Yuna

Northampton

Mullewa

Geraldton
Journey through history in and around Geraldton, a bustling coastal hub with plenty of activities to get the adrenaline flowing.
🚗 4½hr from Perth

Morawa

Dongara-Port Denison

Perenjori

Nambung National Park

Watheroo

The Pinnacles
Walk amid these weirdly wonderful limestone prongs in Nambung National Park; arrive at dawn or dusk for maximum effect.
🚗 2½hr from Perth

Cervantes

New Norcia

Perth
Soak up the final trappings of city life before you leave it all behind for the long journey north.

Yanchep

Northam

Mandurah

CARNARVON TO BROOME
Trip Builder

TAKE YOUR PICK OF MUST-SEES AND HIDDEN GEMS

▬▬▬ This stretch of coastline is a special combination of incredible marine life (Ningaloo Reef), glorious outback parks (Millstream Chichester and Karijini), and gritty coastal towns (Port Hedland) where mining and Aboriginal communities rub shoulders. Put together, it's an opportunity to experience everything good about the northern West Coast on one long drive.

🗺 Trip Notes

Hub towns Carnarvon, Port Hedland, Broome

How long? Allow two weeks

Getting around You'll need your own vehicle to get around, and make it a 4WD if you want to fully explore the parks of the interior.

Tips It can be fiercely hot at any time, but the summer months (November to April) can be unbearable; consider skipping the inland portion of this route if travelling at this time.

0 — 200 km
0 — 100 miles

INDIAN OCEAN

Ningaloo Reef
Swim with whale sharks and encounter humpback whales in this technicolour world of dazzling marine life.
🚗 3¼hr from Carnarvon

Montebello Islands Conservation Park

Barrow Island

Muiron Islands Onslow

● **Exmouth**

○ Learmonth

Coral Bay

Gnaraloo ○

Quobba ○

Point Quobba ○

Gascoyne Junction ○

Monkey Mia ○

Port Hedland

Mingle with miners and take in the photogenic industrial skyline against a blood-red sunset in this fascinating coastal outpost.

🚗 9hr from Carnarvon

Bidyadanga

Eighty
Mile
Beach ☼

Murujuga National Park

Step back in time at Murujuga National Park, close to Karratha and home to tens of thousands of ancient Aboriginal rock engravings.

🚗 7hr from Carnarvon

Broome

Go to the drive-in, learn the Indigenous story of Roebuck Bay, look for dinosaur footprints and watch the sunset from Gantheaume Point.

🚗 15hr from Carnarvon

Dampier

Roebourne

Karratha

*Fortescue
Roadhouse*

Whim
Creek

Marble Bar ○

*Millstream-
Chichester
National
Park*

Pannawonica

*The
Pilbara*

Hillside

○ Nullagine

*Cane
River*

*Hamersley 〰
Gorge*

○ Wittenoom

Karijini National Park

Disappear off the map and into Karijini, with its gorges, waterfalls, spinifex plains and other-wise stunning landscapes.

🚗 8½hr from Carnarvon

*Nanutarra
Roadhouse*

Tom
Price ○

Paraburdoo

Newman ○

*Mt Augustus
(Burringurrah)* △

Quobba Coast

Leave well-travelled routes and head for deliciously remote Quobba Blowholes and Gnaraloo Bay, an easy day trip from Carnarvon.

🚗 1hr from Carnarvon

Carnarvon

Start this epic journey in Carnarvon, an appealingly provincial coastal town that's a base for exploring the remote Quobba Coast and journeys inland to Mt Augustus National Park.

KIMBERLEY TRAVERSE
Trip Builder

TAKE YOUR PICK OF MUST-SEES AND HIDDEN GEMS

▬▬▬ The Kimberley is one of Australia's true frontiers, at once Indigenous homeland filled with storied rock art dating back millennia and a simply beautiful landscape of remote rivers and red-rock escarpments. It's an adventurous destination custom-made for those with an explorer's spirit.

🗺 Trip Notes

Hub towns Broome, Kununurra, Halls Creek

How long? Allow at least two weeks

Getting around If you're doing the Gibb River Road, you'll need a 4WD; book months in advance to make sure you get one.

Tips The Gibb River Road (and anywhere off the Kimberley's paved roads) are inaccessible during the wet season; plan to come here between June and September.

Crocodiles can inhabit all waterways in tropical areas. Swimming is not recommended.

0 — 100 km
0 — 50 miles

TIMOR SEA

BONAPARTE ARCHIPELAGO

Heywood Islands
Augustus Island

Adele Island
Kuri Bay °

BUCCANEER ARCHIPELAGO

Doubtful Bay

Cape Leveque

Horizontal Waterfalls

King Sound

Beagle Bay °
Dampier Peninsula

Derby ●
Gibb River Road

Tunnel Creek National Park

Willare

Broome
●

Fitzroy Crossing
Learn about Indigenous art from the Aboriginal art centres in this classic crossroads town of the outback.
🚗 *12hr from Kununurra*

Emma Gorge
Rest by the waterhole for one last hurrah along the Gibb River Road before you return to the paved road.
🚐 *10hr from Derby*

Wuggubun
Visit an Aboriginal community and stay long enough to go fishing and learn about local life.
🚐 *45min from Kununurra*

Kununurra
Rest for a while in the capital of the east Kimberley, a pleasingly remote yet agreeable pit stop in the midst of stunning country.
🚐 *12hr from Derby*

Mornington Wilderness Camp
Go on an adventure deep into the Kimberley at this wildlife-rich sanctuary where the night sky is utterly incredible.
🚐 *5hr from Derby*

Mimbi Caves
Venture underground in search of fish fossils and ancient rock art in the company of an Aboriginal guide at Mimbi Caves.
🚐 *11hr from Kununurra*

Purnululu National Park
Drive off-road and into one of the strangest landscapes anywhere in Australia: the Bungle Bungles are utterly unforgettable and turn deep red at sunset.
🚐 *5hr from Kununurra*

Map labels: TIMOR SEA · Cape Londonderry · Cape Bougainville · Cape Voltaire · Bigge Island · King George Falls · Kalumburu · Drysdale River National Park · Home Valley Station · Wyndham · Gibb River Road · El Questro Wilderness Park · Doon Doon · Lake Argyle · Charnley River Station · Mt Barnett Roadhouse & Manning River Gorge · King Leopold Ranges Conservation Park · Mt Hart Wilderness Lodge · Chamberlain River · Durack Range · Warmun · Purnululu National Park · Mt Ord (937m) · Bedford Downs · Ord River · Leopold Downs · Fitzroy River · Mueller Range · Duncan Rd · NORTHERN TERRITORY · Geikie Gorge National Park · Margaret River · Mt Amhurst · Halls Creek · Tanami Rd · Yiyili · Wangkatjungka · Larrawa Station

7 Things to Know About
WEST COAST AUSTRALIA

INSIDER TIPS TO HIT THE GROUND RUNNING

1 Wild Winds

If you are travelling anywhere north of the continent's westernmost point (Steep Point near Monkey Mia), watch out for cyclones. Cyclone season runs from November to April, although a November cyclone is rare. When a cyclone is on the way, you'll be encouraged to travel away from the area in the days before the cyclone makes landfall. In this, as in all things, listen to the locals.

▶ See more about travel essentials (p242)

2 Perth Prices

The mining boom transformed WA (particularly Perth) into one pricey destination. Petrol prices in the outback will make your eyes water.

▶ See more about managing your money (p243)

3 Patchy Comms

Mobile (cell) phone coverage is generally fine in the South West and in most coastal towns. But don't expect any signal at all in between. Internet can also be slow, unreliable or non-existent outside medium-sized towns.

4 High Humidity

It begins up north in October with what's known as the 'build-up'. Then come the rains. When it's not raining, it can be so humid that you'll be drenched in sweat after undertaking the smallest of tasks. Many tourist operators shut down for the season. Yes, it can be lovely and quiet. But consider if this outweighs the considerable discomfort?

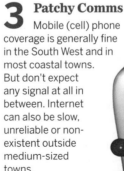

HUMIDIT
-100
90
80

5 This is a BIG Country

Western Australia's south is relatively compact, but take the coastal road north out of Perth and the country's scale can be staggering.

By the time you reach Broome, you'll have driven almost 2500km. That's roughly the distance from Madrid to Oslo or from New York City to Denver. With that in mind, be realistic about what you can achieve.

▶ See more about getting around (p240)

6 Covid Isolation

Western Australia has always been a place apart from the rest of the country. But this went to a whole new level during the Covid-19 pandemic, and it remains a common conversation starter in the west.

For nearly two years, Western Australians lived inside what was known as a 'hard border', with extremely tight restrictions governing who could (and, far more often, couldn't) enter the state. The restrictions were eventually eased and the state opened its borders on 3 March 2022.

For all its inconveniences, the strict border policy was hugely popular among Western Australians: at the height of the pandemic, the left-leaning state government won an electoral landslide with an unprecedented 70% of the vote. And from a public health perspective, it's not difficult to see why: only 10 people died from Covid in WA during the first two years of the pandemic.

▶ See more about safe travel (p242)

7 Tipping the Waiter

Tipping around 5% to 10% in restaurants and upmarket cafes (if the service warrants it) is common, especially in Perth and the wine regions. But it's by no means obligatory. Taxi drivers also appreciate you rounding up the fare. Tipping is not usually expected at hotels.

▶ See more money tips (p243)

WEST COASAT AUSTRALIA LOCAL TIPS

Read, Listen, Watch & Follow

 READ

Welcome to Country (Marcia Langton; 2019) A travel guide to Indigenous Australia.

Cloudstreet (Tim Winton; 1991) Classic Aussie novel about two Perth families by a master storyteller.

Title Fight (Paul Cleary; 2021) David-vs-Goliath story of how one Aboriginal community took on the mining companies.

Batavia (Peter FitzSimons; 2011) Rollicking true story of an infamous 17th-century Dutch shipwreck off Geraldton.

 LISTEN

Human Design (Birds of Tokyo; 2020) Sixth studio album by this award-winning alternataive rock band from Perth.

Welcome Stranger (The Blackeyed Susans; 1992) Showcases the early work of this highly regarded band who hail from Perth.

The West Live (thewest.com.au/the-west-live) Podcast on Western Australian life with a focus on Perth.

We Sing Until Sunrise (The Merindas; 2020) The latest from up-and-coming pop duo Candice Lorrae and Kristel Kickett.

DANIEL KNIGHTON/GETTY IMAGES ©

The Slow Rush (Tame Impala; 2020) Award-winning fourth album by psychedelic indie-rock group from Perth (pictured above).

WATCH

Rabbit-Proof Fence (pictured top right; 2002) Three young stolen Aboriginal children try to reach home in the 1930s.

Red Dog (2011) A quirky outback tale about a man and his dog from Dampier.

Paper Planes (2014) Heart-warming story of small-town Australia.

Australia (pictured bottom right; 2008) Baz Luhrmann's sweeping tale with the outback and Kimberley as a glorious backdrop.

Bran Nue Dae (2009) Coming-of-age story of WA Aboriginal teens.

TOP: PENNY TWEEDIE/ALAMY STOCK PHOTO ©
BOTTOM: TCD/PROD.DB/ALAMY STOCK PHOTO ©

FOLLOW

Perth Blogs (destinationperth.com.au/blog) Collection of blogs covering Perth attractions and festivals.

Hello Perth (helloperth.com.au/blog) Good, high-level articles on life in the city.

WAITOC (waitoc.com) The best resource for Aboriginal-run operators and experiences.

Pilbara News (pilbaranews.com.au) Local news and life from a fascinating stretch of coast.

Kimberley Travel Guide Blog (kimberleyaustralia.com/kimberley-australia-blog.html) Travel tips, updates from the Kimberley.

Sate your West Coast Australia dreaming with a virtual vacation at lonelyplanet.com/west-coast-australia# planning-a-trip

PERTH

BEACHES | OUTDOORS | CITY LIFE

**Experience
Perth online**

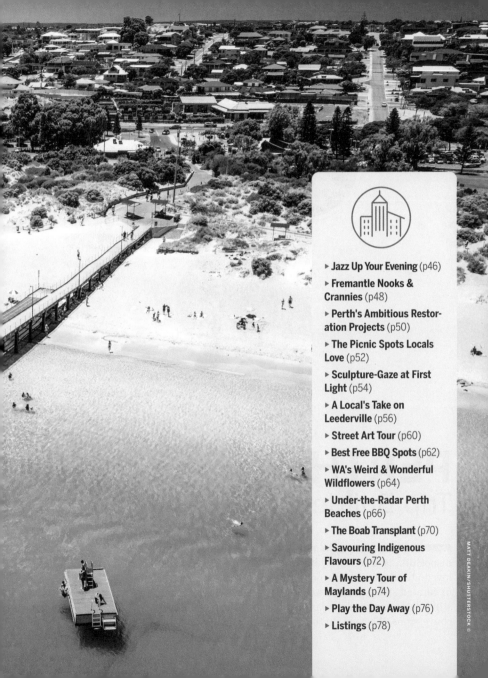

```
    0        0        5 km
(N) 0 ═══════════════════ 2.5 miles
```

INDIAN OCEAN

Seek out the underground **Jazz Cellar** run by octogenarians (p46)
🚃 *15min from Perth City Station*

Tour a curated open-air **street art gallery** on a walk through the city, spotting works like Amok Island's *Sugar Glider* (p60)
🚶 *central Perth*

Admire the 750-year-old tree that arrived with police escort in **Kings Park** (p70)
🚃 *6min from central Perth*

Rottnest Island

Find a secluded picnic spot at the **Coombe Reserve** off Perth's most expensive street (p53)
🚗 *20min from central Perth*

PERTH
Trip Builder

▬▬▬ Basking in ridiculously good weather, Perth's sunny disposition is reflected by its lifestyle-oriented locals. People love to hit the beach, picnic in leafy parks and wander streets of curated street art. After dark things are less sedate, but still select: think upbeat jazz haunts, small bars and heritage conversions. Welcome to the good life.

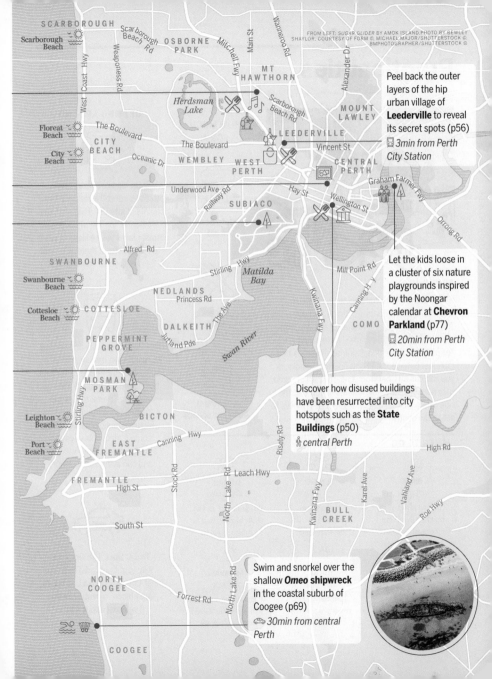

Peel back the outer layers of the hip urban village of **Leederville** to reveal its secret spots (p56)

🚊 *3min from Perth City Station*

Let the kids loose in a cluster of six nature playgrounds inspired by the Noongar calendar at **Chevron Parkland** (p77)

🚊 *20min from Perth City Station*

Discover how disused buildings have been resurrected into city hotspots such as the **State Buildings** (p50)

🚶 *central Perth*

Swim and snorkel over the shallow *Omeo* shipwreck in the coastal suburb of Coogee (p69)

🚗 *30min from central Perth*

Practicalities

BEEBOYS/SHUTTERSTOCK ©

ARRIVING

✈ **Perth International Airport** is located in Terminal 1. Some domestic flights also use Terminal 1, as well as Terminals 3 and 4, which are located about 15 minutes' drive away. Terminal 2 is for regional airlines. There's a taxi rank just outside the T1 and T3 sliding doors, or you can call an Uber from a nearby parking area; they usually take a few minutes to come to the ride-share pick-up bays. It's about 25 minutes to get to the centre.

HOW MUCH FOR A

Cold beer
A$11

Burger
A$25

Ice cream
A$5 (per scoop)

GETTING AROUND

Train Many of Perth's train stations are still a distance from points of interest. That said, the Fremantle line will whisk you to most places you're likely to want to see, and from there, it's most enjoyable to walk.

Bus Perth inner city and central Fremantle run free loop services called CAT (Central Area Transit) buses, with giant black cats on the side. Several routes run past many visitable spots. Regular public buses can be complicated, unless you're staying close to the inner city and can avoid connections.

Taxi & Uber The simplest way to get around. From an inner-city suburb like Leederville or Subiaco to central Perth, it will cost about A$10.

WHEN TO GO

BIRAK
DEC–JAN

The start of summer's cloudless skies, when the coast beckons.

BUNURU
FEB–MAR

Hot, dry, sun-drenched days made for beach-going.

DJERAN
APR–MAY

A shift to milder days and cooler evenings ideal for outdoor pursuits.

MAKURU
JUN–JUL

Rains fall, arctic winds blow and temperatures drop for winter.

DJILBA
AUG-SEP

Crisp, clear nights give way to sunshine and showers.

KAMBARANG
OCT–NOV

Mother Nature reawakens with warmer airflow and wildflower carpets.

EATING & DRINKING

Perth's food is influenced by its location: being isolated from Australia's east coast, and looking more to neighbouring Asia, you'll find an inventiveness to its modern-fusion fare, often spiked with authentic oriental flavours. In recent years, native and indigenous ingredients have had a moment. Marron (freshwater crayfish) is a regular on upmarket menus, perhaps garnished with the citrus twang of Geraldton wax, while kangaroo (pictured top right), served rare for its leanness, may be dusted with pepperberry or quandong (native peach) powder. To drink, try the classic flavours of a Negroni cocktail (pictured bottom right).

Best Negroni cocktail
Darling Darling (p49)

Must-try marron
Wildflower (p73)

CONNECT & FIND YOUR WAY

Wi-fi The inner city and busy urban villages such as Leederville, Fremantle and Subiaco have free hotspots, as do most cultural institutions. However, it's simplest to buy a prepaid SIM card so you can connect on-the-go.

Navigation Perth is split by the Swan River and edges the Indian Ocean. Most places you'll visit will be on or between the two.

CYCLING

Many hotels now offer free bikes; Perth's bike paths have been well developed in recent years, with good lighting and safety.

WHERE TO STAY

Perth is ranked as an affordable city, but accommodation can be pricey. Staying central means more hotels and easier public transport; if hiring a car, go suburban.

Area	Pros/Cons
Central Perth	New, flashy, overlooking the river. Shopping, nightlife and dining pockets. Easy transiting. Mid- to high range.
Northbridge	Nightlife, small bar buzz, Chinatown, some trashy streets. Fast access to cultural hubs and transit links, neighbours Perth CBD. Affordable.
Leederville	Cafe strip, hip neighbourhood, street art, walkable. Midrange.
Subiaco	European vibes, leafy streets, quiet with some night activity. Inner city. Pricey.
Cottesloe	Beach frontage, posh-casual, cafes. Car required. Expensive.
Fremantle	Characterful port town, backpacker magnet, historic streets, away from centre. All price points.

MONEY

Almost anything can be paid for with card in Perth, mainly via smartphone. Carry some cash for emergencies and small items. Many parking zones offer first hour free, with ticket.

01 Jazz Up Your **EVENING**

MUSIC | CULTURE | DISCOVERY

Hidden off a quiet suburban street, out the back of a car park, the Jazz Cellar is an underground – literally – institution that, despite 20 years of fun, has remained a closely kept secret. Embark on a musical exploration of it, and its contemporaries, with three excellent options dotted around the city.

How to

Getting here From the city, take the No. 15 bus all the way to Mount Hawthorn; get off outside the IGA. It's a 10- to 15-minute walk to Jazz Cellar from there. Uber to the other jazz clubs.

Tickets Ideally, book a ticket at least two weeks in advance (at jazzcellar.net.au). This secures your spot, but you'll still need to pay $30 in cash at the door, on the night.

When to go Doors open at the Jazz Cellar at 5.45pm and the band starts at 7pm; the night wraps up around 10.30pm.

Enter through the red phone box Every Friday night a team of 70- and 80-somethings play upbeat, swing, Charleston and vintage styles of jazz on a tiny corner stage. Sounds sedate? It's anything but. The energy and enthusiasm from these lively senior citizens is inspiring. It feels intimate, too: only about 80 people can fit into the small room and the atmosphere is electric – with dancing guaranteed.

Tracking down the entry is half the fun. Find the Salvation Army opportunity shop on Buxton St; look to the right of the building where you'll see an open gate leading to a rear car park. Walk in and enter the red phone box, go down narrow stairs and discover a small, windowless cavern decked out with vintage posters and signs – you have arrived.

Rub shoulders with the best Head to **The Ellington Jazz Club** for far more serious, seated viewing. This is where Perth's jazz aficionados mingle with lecturers and students

JAZZ CELLAR ©

Hot Tips

The Jazz Cellar allows BYO (bring your own) food and drinks, making for an affordable night.

Rather than ordering pizza at the convenient hole-in-the-wall a half-block away, grab takeaway from **Neighbourhood Pizza**, an alleyway warehouse off the bustling Scarborough Beach Rd strip. Find it down light-strung Anvil Lane, between the Vinnies store and Tsukaya restaurant; it's just 10 minutes on foot from the Jazz Cellar.

For libations, hit **The Mezz**, a shopping centre with a Woolworths supermarket and a BWS liquor store. If pizza ain't your thing, there are good takeaway options in the leafy courtyard here.

from the highly regarded Western Australian Academy of Performing Arts – it has turned out jazz artists who are globally esteemed, including Jamie Oehlers. Expect low lighting, small round tables and minimal chatter.

Try a two-fer For dinner and a show, try the **Duke of George** in East Fremantle.

This basement haunt in a former broom factory offers a revolving line-up of styles, performed as multicourse meals are delivered to your table. While the jazz is top-notch, there's a light-hearted feel to this venue; we can't promise anything, but there may be dancing in the aisles, depending on the night's vibe.

Above Jazz Cellar

02 Fremantle Nooks
& CRANNIES

SECRET SPOTS | LOCAL PICKS | ENTERTAINMENT

Freo, as it's affectionately referred to by locals, is Perth's characterful port town and a well-trodden traveller fave, but there are still a few secret spots. Let us lead you to a hidden-in-plain-sight rooftop bar, a tiny drinking den that evokes 1800s-era seafaring and the place for the tastiest 'cheap cut' of fish you may ever try.

DOMONABIKE/STOCKIMO/ALAMY STOCK PHOTO ©

🗺 How to

Getting here If you're not already staying in Fremantle, take the Fremantle train line in. The train station is close to everything and it's a joy to wander around on foot, at your own pace.

When to go Fremantle enjoys beautiful weather year-round. Weekends are twice as busy as weekdays, and there's a change in shift from days to nights, when families give way to evening revellers.

Good to know Freo is a hotspot for buskers, especially around the covered markets, so keep a few loose coins handy.

JASON KNOTT/ALAMY STOCK PHOTO ©

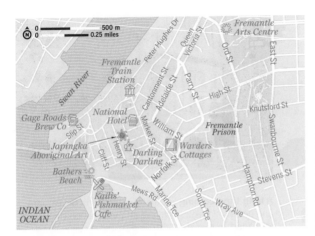

Left National Hotel
Below Kailis' Fishmarket Cafe

PERTH EXPERIENCES

A rooftop secret You'll hear the **National Hotel** before you see it. The multi-level Federation-era pub usually has live music playing in the main bar, but don't stop there. Go in the narrow side entrance and up the stairs. Take them slow, not only so you don't puff, but so you notice the gallery of art the owners have curated on the colourful walls. Reaching the summit, you'll walk out onto a sun-drenched deck with clusters of couches and tables, where locals converge to take in Fremantle's rooftop, ocean and working port views.

A merchant vessel on land As the sun goes down, slip in to the 25-seat, walk-ins-only **Darling Darling** and be transported to another time. The bijou bar seems to reek low-lit, mahogany-hued history from every surface, but it's all a carefully created illusion. Marvel at the weathered ropes, the wooden ship wheels, the barrels topped with free, crack-'em-open peanuts and the chainlink light fittings. There's atmosphere in spades. Expect a queue on the weekend.

A cheap feed For the best-value bites in Freo, head directly to **Kailis' Fishmarket Cafe** on the pretty harbourfront and order the $6 fish wings. Forget any ideas you have about fillets, this is better. It's a cut from around the fish fin and is one of the most tender, sweetest parts you can savour. The more adventurous will also try the fin, deep fried to resemble a potato crisp. Trust us, you'll never go back.

☀ Tips from a Freo Fan

Gage Roads Brew Co
This brewery faces onto Fremantle Harbour; you can watch tug boats and cargo ships pass by.

Japingka Aboriginal Art
Support Aboriginal artists at this High St gallery.

Fremantle Arts Centre
Catch a free outdoor concert on Sunday in the warmer months.

Warders Cottages This is where prison guards used to live in central Fremantle. You can spend the night or have a wine in micro-bar Gimlet (p51) or grab a bite from Emily Taylor restaurant, all in the one precinct.

Bathers Beach Take a dip where the first European settlers of the Swan River Colony came ashore in August 1829.

■ Tips by Ryan Mossny
Tour guide with Two Feet & a Heartbeat walking tours
@twofeetperth

JASON KNOTT/ALAMY STOCK PHOTO ©

Perth's Ambitious Restoration Projects

IF ONLY THE WALLS COULD SPEAK

Once a city prone to knocking heritage buildings down to rebuild in glass and steel, Perth has been reimagining its historic bones over the past 20 years or so, dusting off old haunts and creating them anew. Get to know the hotels, bars and restaurants that now flourish inside elderly structures.

Left State Buildings, Barrack St
Centre Rechabite Hall, William St
Right Fremantle Market

A long time coming For many years, Perth developers and decision makers held the attitude that only new was good. In the late 1960s and 1970s, in particular, a slew of Perth's architectural beauties were demolished, from tall, gothic masterpieces to grand, gold-rush-era hotels. Notably, the State Heritage Act was only brought into law in 1999. It helped to preserve some examples of late-19th- and early-20th-century architecture that poke between skyscrapers and marked the dawning of a new psyche: that there's value in historic buildings. The adaptation of heritage buildings also had practical merits: as Perth's population surged, there was a need to increase density and rein in urban sprawl. More recently, arguments for greater sustainability in the built environment – for social and environmental reasons – have also weighed in.

From dust to darling Perth's majestic Treasury building, which dates back to 1874, is one of the city's most awarded and impressive conversions. It lay dormant for nearly two decades before one of the founding members of the Little Creatures (p81) brewing empire – today a property developer – embarked on its multimillion-dollar reinvention. Before reopening in 2015 as the State Buildings, it housed the WA capital's original General Post Office, its treasury and government offices and a police cellblock. An impressive 95% of the original buildings were retained, now filled with a chic collection of bars, restaurants, boutiques and a five-star hotel.

Secret society space In nearby Northbridge, the looming, whitewashed Rechabite Hall was formerly the headquarters for a secret society known as

The Independent Order of Rechabites. Over its 100-year lifespan, it was used for church services, school productions and as an election polling station, eventually becoming Perth's most popular dance hall. For decades, it fell into disuse, before its sweeping wooden staircase, yawning ceilings and ornate tile floors were thoroughly resuscitated, reopening in 2019. Nowadays, it's a neon-lit live performance space with both basement and rooftop bars and a mess-hall-style restaurant. The most amusing thing about the number of drinking nooks is that the Rechabites of old were firmly focused on fighting the evil influence of liquor. Take the glass elevator up through the four floors and appreciate the layers of construction left deliberately exposed.

> The State Heritage Act was only brought into law in 1999.

Ghosts make way At the port end of the city, Warders Hotel in Fremantle has shrugged off its former life as housing for the nearby Fremantle Prison's guards. The 1851 limestone row has been transformed into 11 hotel rooms, opening in 2020. They have the city's smallest bar at their feet, Gimlet, and an alfresco Asian restaurant named Emily Taylor, after a spice trading ship that came to grief off Fremantle in 1830. So persistent was the belief that ghosts may lurk between the heritage walls, that a ghost buster was called to clear the space. Guests still report seeing apparitions, though. The friendly staff at the boutique hotel, which neighbours the bustling Fremantle Market, tend to welcome anyone who asks for a stickybeak.

🗐 Heritage Conversions

Freo's West End precinct contains over 250 heritage buildings, many from the late-19th-century gold-boom era.

Amid its narrow streets are some of my all-time favourite experiences to be had in heritage conversions. **PSAS** is a contemporary art space in a converted shipping warehouse.

Across the road is the **Republic of Fremantle**, a boutique distillery and cocktail bar and, nearby, is the excellent **Bread in Common**, one of the most architecturally awarded heritage conversions in WA. Pop into **Compendium Design Store**, especially if you've got a thing for pens, and **Paperbird**, a stunning children's bookshop with an upstairs gallery dedicated to illustrations and home to the Woylie Aboriginal Story Festival.

■ **Tips by Marcus Canning**
Founder of Fringe World, Rooftop Movies and the man behind The Rechabite reinvention; @therechabitehall

03 The Picnic Spots
LOCALS LOVE

OUTDOORS | LOCAL SECRETS | LEISURE

■■■ In a city blessed with more sunny days than any other Australian capital, picnicking is a popular pastime. Here are three places in-the-know locals love best, from a nook in a ritzy suburb to a riverside idyll and a free-to-roam beach estate.

PAUL KANE/GETTY IMAGES ©

🗺 How to

Getting here These three destinations are best reached by car or Uber.

When to go Perth's cloudless, blue skies are present for most of the year, so anytime is picnic time – even some winter days. During hot spells,

go around 10am or just before sunset.

Top tip If you have kids in tow at Cottesloe's Civic Gardens, head down the southern steps and discover a secret slippery dip and, just beyond, a grassy playground shrouded in tree canopy.

JASON KNOTT/ALAMY STOCK PHOTO ©

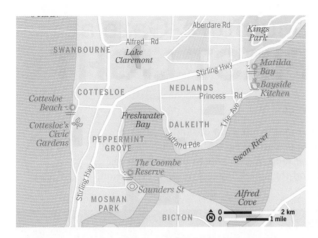

Left Matilda Bay
Below Bayside Kitchen, Matilda Bay

Family fun Mention **Matilda Bay** to any local and their eyes will light up, but few visitors are aware of this little sandy beach along the Swan River that's shaded by native gums. Groups of picnickers, families in particular, flock here on weekends with boogie boards, lilos and eskies in tow. It's not uncommon for them to spend the entire day dipping in and out of the water, doing bombies off the twin platform jetties, observing the (harmless) jellyfish, watching for dolphins and resting on rugs and deck chairs under the trees. For those who don't have picnic gear, there's a nice cafe at the water's edge called **Bayside Kitchen**.

Your own private Idaho For a far more secluded picnic spot, drive further around the river to the **Coombe Reserve**, which is found at the toes of Perth real estate's most expensive street (Saunders St) – glimpsing the multi-million-dollar mansions justifies the trip alone. Venture beyond the immediate grassy park to the tiny beach beyond. So long as there's not a wedding in play, you'll likely have this quiet nook all to yourself.

Grassy enclave Finally, **Cottesloe's Civic Gardens** are unfairly overlooked for the neighbourhood's iconic sandy stretch. Walk in to the free-to-visit, estate-like grounds and find a place on the west-facing lawn beneath the pines. With gorgeous ocean views, it's almost criminal that barely another soul will be there. As you roam freely, it's great fun leaning in to that feeling of old-money opulence.

☀ Be Sun Smart

The Australian sun is very harsh. Before you head outdoors, you'll need to follow the local mantra of 'slip, slop, slap'. It stands for 'slip on a shirt, slop on some sunscreen and slap on a hat'.

The saying comes from the Cancer Council's 1981 sun-smart campaign, using a board-short-wearing, tap-dancing cartoon seagull named Sid. The rise in public awareness around skin cancer risk was so successful, you'll frequently hear Aussies rolling out the saying, some three decades later. Take the advice and avoid being out in the heat of the day or seek out a tree to picnic under. Happily, many of Perth's playgrounds are shaded.

04 Sculpture-Gaze at
FIRST LIGHT

OUTDOOR SPACES | ART | BEACH

Perth's most popular and iconic strip of sand, Cottesloe Beach, gets more packed than normal each March, with dozens of huge sculptures dotting the sand. Here's how to beat the crowds and stroll peacefully around the state's biggest outdoor exhibition, Sculpture by the Sea.

JARROD TAYLOR, STRUCTURAL WAY SCULPTURE BY THE SEA, COTTESLOE 2021. PHOTO: RICHARD WATSON ©

🗺 How to

Getting here Take the Fremantle train line from Perth to Cottesloe. In summer there's a free beach bus that departs from near the train platform. Otherwise, it's a 15-minute walk to the coast.

When to go Cottesloe is lovely at any time of the day, but our tip for viewing the sculptures minus the masses is to arrive at sunrise.

Top tip Walk to the end of the rocky groyne – there's always an interesting sculpture at its end. On the return journey, you'll notice artworks that can only be seen from that angle.

MERLE TOPS DAVIS, SEA ANOMALIES 3, SCULPTURE BY THE SEA, COTTESLOE 2022 ©. PHOTO: MARTINE PERRET ©

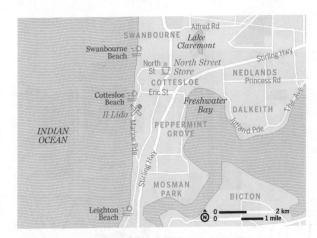

Left *Structural Wave* by Jarrod Taylor, Sculpture by the Sea 2021
Below *Sea Anomalies 3* by Merle Topsi Davis, Sculpture by the Sea 2022

Artfully dodge the crowds Cottesloe Beach is always – and deservedly so – busy. But when **Sculpture by the Sea** is on, beachcomber numbers swell by tens of thousands (which, by Australian standards, is seriously packed). It's one of the largest free-to-the-public sculpture exhibitions in the world, showing works by international and local artists. The sculptures, often standing several metres tall, run along the sea wall, as well as up grassy terraces and under Norfolk pine trees. To view the art without a dozen smartphones held up in front of you, set the alarm and go at the time locals believe is the most beautiful part of the day: dawn.

Breakfast with views Give yourself an hour to roam around the sculptures, which are sprinkled over a fair distance. Consider jumping in for a swim – there's a shark-proof net that forms an ocean-safe haven many swimmers enjoy. Afterwards, climbing 20m up the hill for breakfast at **Il Lido**, an Italian cantina that has an alfresco dining square, from which you can gaze over the Indian Ocean. Walk off your indulgences (particularly if you had the duck waffle) by joining the conga line of fitness-loving locals as they power walk along the beachfront path.

Worth the walk Head northward until you reach North St, then puff up the hill and past a couple of roundabouts until you reach the far end of the road. There you'll see the unrelentingly popular **North Street Store**, usually identifiable by its wrap-around queues. The only place to sit is on the verge outside, yet people do it because the baked goods inside are addictively delicious. Surely enough time has passed for you to fit in a burger or the speciality cinnamon scroll.

Public Art Fund

In a city sometimes teased for its lack of art and culture, it's interesting to note that back in 1989, the WA state government enacted an initiative to ensure all new developments would involve a piece of public art.

These days, that means any development over A$2 million has to invest 1% of the total cost in public art. The Percent for Art Scheme has seen a growing collection of large-scale sculptures, wall murals, street patterning, artistic lighting and more pop up around Perth. Keep your eyes peeled and you'll spot plenty.

05 A Local's Take on LEEDERVILLE

URBAN | NEIGHBOURHOOD | CULTURE

Inner-city Leederville is one of Perth's most idiosyncratic neighbourhoods, loved for its eclectic mix of boutiques and bars, its approachable but distinctive restaurants and its light-strung laneways and street art. Here's our insider's guide to Leederville.

JACK LOVEL ©

🗺 How to

Getting here From Perth centre, take the Joondalup train line (often named as Butler on live signs) one stop to Leederville, or catch the No. 15 bus; both will drop you on Leederville's main cafe strip, Oxford St. From there, stick to walking.

When to go Leederville is fun year-round. During the day it's all about the shopping and people watching, whereas at night the bars, big pub and restaurants bustle.

Top tip If you're driving, there's a huge car park hidden behind Oxford St; access is via the Good Grocer store.

BIG STATE IMAGES/ALAMY STOCK PHOTO ©

At first glance, **Leederville** looks like an easy-to-read, eclectic inner-city suburb. Its streetscape is dotted with stripy red and white umbrellas, alfresco dining nudges out onto car parking spaces and every shop front is individual. But there's even more to it than that. In fact, peeking behind the facade is exactly how to get to know Leederville's authentic heart.

Take **Babylon Cafe**, a narrow coffee house that's found down a side street and behind a rug shop. Its sign gives nothing away, saying, simply, 'Babylon'. But walk past the forest of potted plants and miss-matched garden chairs, duck your head under the low, vintage brick doorway and you will find a buzzing den scented with caffeine. Many claim it does the area's best coffee, but with plenty of competition, that's a debate for another day.

MAURITIUS IMAGES GMBH/ALAMY STOCK PHOTO ©

🗺 Electric Lane

A disused Leederville laneway has been reimagined as a social thoroughfare, branching off to bars, businesses and office buildings. Named in 2021, Electric Lane honours the Leederville Hotel's history as being the area's first business to get electric lights in 1905.

Above left Servo
Above Train heading towards Joondalup Train Station
Left Street signs, Leederville

A short wander away is one of main drag Oxford St's long-timers. **Urban Records** does what it says on the label: it sells racks and racks of vinyl, with the odd stack of discounted CDs slotted in. There are street clothes, watches and record players, which all seems pretty standard. But edge further down the aisles and you'll find **Urban Depot**, a shop within a shop. It's a haven of the unlikely, with mind-tickling books by The School of Life sitting alongside joke ice trays, risqué greeting cards and chic women's fashion. If you need a gift, this is your place. The scruffy-haired owner, Paul, has been selling curiosities for decades and is always ready to hand out local tips.

If you're fascinated by fresh seafood – with an enormous coastline, WA has an abundance of it – stop in at **Kailis Bros Fish Market**. If you ask, staff will join you at the open tank and carefully pick up the state's freshwater crayfish, known as marron, for you to get

◎ Leedy's Must-Dos

Secret community garden
Go to the end of Muriel Pl, walk through the park and spot the vegetable gardens. What's better than unlimited organic herbs?

Luna Cinema An iconic cinema, showcasing international and Australian films in nostalgic surrounds. It even has an outdoor rooftop cinema!

Bunn Mee A foodie escape to Vietnam, via authentic *banh mis* and Vietnamese ice coffees. You can smell the grilled pork belly from 50m away and you'll be well fed for $10 to $20.

Roberts on Oxford A quaint, small bar that is homey yet upmarket. Rob, the owner, built the bar himself.

■Tips by Jenny Lam
Former MasterChef contestant and the whiz behind Bunn Mee and Phat Lon in Leederville
@jennylamau

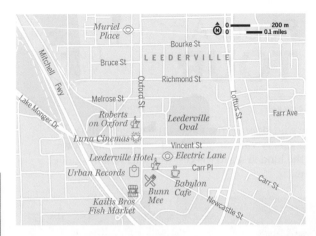

Left Luna Cinema
Below Black marron (crayfish)

a closer look. Occasionally, they'll offer up the tongs, so if you're game, have a try.

From there, cross the street to the sprawling landmark **Leederville Hotel**, which had a makeover in 2021. Bypass the main bar as well as the main restaurant. Instead, order a craft brew from the beer bar, **Sandgropers** (it's the name of a local dune-loving insect and what Western Australians affectionately call themselves). Every month, a different small-batch brewery takes over the taps, so you never know what you'll get to try.

Head to the back of the Leederville Hotel and find **Servo**, an energetic new restaurant that edges the rear laneway. Its food is perhaps the most adventurous around: think mussels with fennel pollen on squid ink baguette. It has a secret weapon: just outside the glass doors and off the alfresco dining zone is a garage space. Inside is a cubby house, chalkboard wall and plastic building blocks: the kids are happy, and the parents get to eat adult food and finish their sentences. Win-win.

06 Street Art **TOUR**

ART | WALKING TOUR | DISCOVERY

■■■ Fancy a walk on the wild side? Perth's street art has been deliberately curated, giving it an urban gallery vibe. Sneak behind bars and edge down alleys to glimpse some of the hidden masterpieces, with this walking guide through some of the best parts.

SUGAR GLIDER BY AMOK ISLAND. PHOTO BY BEWLEY SHAYLOR, COURTESY OF FORM ©

🗺 How to

Getting here The walk kicks off in the city centre, so take a train or bus to Perth Central Station and go from there.

When to go Perth is rarely rainy, so anytime of year suits. By day you'll see more detail in the art, but by night the bars are open – while on Nicks Lane you'll see people in search of a secret bar, Toots (p81).

Cost It costs nothing to view this street art, but we recommend you visit some of the bars or eateries en route, so budget for that fun.

↑ **Look up!**

Tabitha McMullan runs the nonprofit cultural body, FORM. She says, 'Look up! Some of Perth's more dynamic pieces of public art hang high above sight lines, so they're playfully out of view. At night when you pass through Perth's Cultural Centre, look upwards along the alleyway that runs adjacent to Alex Hotel and see Joshua Webb's neon *Blue Sun* illuminating the path to some of the city's hidden bars and watering holes.'

■ **Tips from Tabitha McMullan**
Head of FORM
@formwa

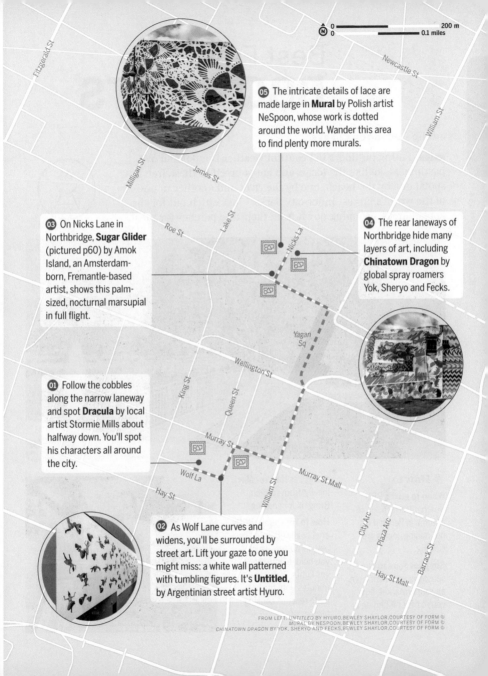

0 200 m
0 0.1 miles

05 The intricate details of lace are made large in **Mural** by Polish artist NeSpoon, whose work is dotted around the world. Wander this area to find plenty more murals.

03 On Nicks Lane in Northbridge, **Sugar Glider** (pictured p60) by Amok Island, an Amsterdam-born, Fremantle-based artist, shows this palm-sized, nocturnal marsupial in full flight.

04 The rear laneways of Northbridge hide many layers of art, including **Chinatown Dragon** by global spray roamers Yok, Sheryo and Fecks.

01 Follow the cobbles along the narrow laneway and spot **Dracula** by local artist Stormie Mills about halfway down. You'll spot his characters all around the city.

02 As Wolf Lane curves and widens, you'll be surrounded by street art. Lift your gaze to one you might miss: a white wall patterned with tumbling figures. It's **Untitled**, by Argentinian street artist Hyuro.

FROM LEFT: UNTITLED BY HYURO.BEWLEY SHAYLOR.COURTESY OF FORM ©
MURAL BY NESPOON.BEWLEY SHAYLOR.COURTESY OF FORM ©
CHINATOWN DRAGON BY YOK, SHERYO AND FECKS.BEWLEY SHAYLOR.COURTESY OF FORM ©

07 Best Free
BBQ SPOTS

PICNIC | OUTDOORS | FREE

Eating outdoors in beautiful weather is a popular WA pastime. Make like the locals and get yourself to these free BBQ spots: one by the beach, one by the river and another in one of the world's largest inner-city parks – just watch out for the kookaburras swooping down from their tree perches for meat.

JASON KNOTT/ALAMY STOCK PHOTO ©

🗺 How to

When to go It's BBQ weather from spring to autumn in Perth; if it's not raining, locals are sizzling.

Supplies You can buy sausages and meat from any supermarket, but you're best off finding a local butcher that makes

'snags', as they're called locally, from scratch. Bring oil for cooking.

How to Free public BBQs are usually operated by a push-button, which you hold in until the gas lights. Wait a few minutes until the hot plate reaches cooking temperature.

BELLE HUNG/SHUTTERSTOCK ©

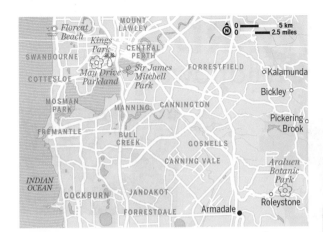

Left May Drive Parkland
Below Public BBQ

Ocean views Groups of extended families and friends come to **Floreat Beach** for the ocean-view BBQs that lie to the left of The Kiosk cafe. They face a lush lawn and an excellent playground – it's a sprawling octopus made from soft wood, which kids can scramble up, then slide down the slippery dip into sand. Duck to the ocean for a dip or lean on the viewing platform that looks over the water. Happily, the seagulls aren't too much of a bother.

Park BBQs Most travellers only make it to the city view section of Kings Park (p70). Drive in to its heart and find the **May Drive Parkland** (on the park's western side off Saw Ave or Poole Ave), where there are huge replicas of WA megafauna, an island playground with misting plant sculptures and lakeside BBQs. Beware the winged wildlife when you're cooking – kookaburras, whose call sounds like a cackle, are particularly good at stealing sausages. Alternatively, the entry fee to **Araluen Botanic Park** in Roleystone is well worth it; the 59-hectare valley garden, which is carpeted in tulips from August to October, also has electric and wood-fired BBQs.

Local etiquette If all BBQs are in use, don't worry. It's customary to say hello and ask if you can share the hot plate. If there's room, Australians are generally very happy to share and will often help you cook if you're a novice or forget your tongs. You are expected to clean up after yourself, so the hot plate is gleaming and ready for the next person.

Sir James Mitchell Park

For the best view of the Perth city skyline, take the commuter ferry across the Swan Valley to Sir James Mitchell Park, a huge green space that edges the foreshore in South Perth.

The first thing you'll see are two enormous canopy sculptures of Australian wildlife: a 10m-high frill-necked lizard and a numbat – WA's mammal emblem – in yellow and orange perforated steel.

Look out for the smaller sculpture of an emu and its chicks. From there, head in an easterly direction and spot the free BBQs, close to the playgrounds and surrounded by shady trees.

WA'S WEIRD &
Wonderful Wildflowers

01 Sexual predator
This carousel spider orchid (*Caladenia arenicola*) impersonates native wasps so convincingly – pheromones and all – that male insects try to mate with them.

02 Scented blossom
The *Eucalyptus kingsmillii* can be seen in Kings Park (p70) in Perth, as can all the flowers described here. Australia has loads of perfumed, flowering trees.

03 Grevillea variifolia
There are hundreds of types of grevillea variifolia, known as the spider plant. This drought-hardy shrub grows happily in the sand and gravel along the Ningaloo Coast.

04 Sun worshipper
The scented sun orchid (*Thelymitra macrophylla*) pops up everywhere during wildflower season, which runs from June (in the mid-north) to late October (in the south).

05 Bug beater
The wily triggerplant (*Stylidium araeophyllum*) dusts visiting insects with pollen by smacking them with a hidden swat, triggered by the touch of tiny legs.

06 Fringed lily
The edges of the leafless fringed lily are like the fine lace used in *haute couture*. It's delicate purple petals open at dawn and are closed by the afternoon, like a shy beauty.

07 Donkey orchid
Let's be honest, the donkey orchid looks like an ass. As it's name suggests, it's perky petals resemble donkey ears. They're a delight to spot and their bright colours are an easy tell-tale.

08 Bird's-eye view
This is the top view of a firewood banksia (*Banksia menziesii*). The woodland species seems dry and scratchy until its intricate details are seen up close.

08 Under-the-Radar Perth
BEACHES

BEACH | OUTDOORS | SHIPWRECK

When you see a Perth beach, you'll be ruined for life: few other city beaches globally compare. But it's not only silky white sand and crystal-clear waters you'll find here. Why not seek out rock pools, dusk swims and fire twirlers at these alternative options?

MICHAEL WILLIS/ALAMY STOCK PHOTO ©

📷 How to

Getting here These beaches are most easily accessed by car. A bike route also links most coastal destinations.

When to go Perth beach lovers hit the sand from October to June. Only the truly dedicated make it all the way through winter.

Top tip Hit the coast prior to 10am for best water clarity and becalmed waters, before the 'Fremantle Doctor' breeze blows in.

FAITHIE/SHUTTERSTOCK ©

The privacy-lovers' beach If gazing into rock pools and sheltering in eroded rock caverns sounds like your kind of adventure, make your way to **Bennion Beach** in Perth's north. The tiny stretch is wedged between popular Trigg Beach and Mettams Pool, the latter a much-loved snorkelling and annual abalone diving spot. Go exploring and find your own private nook facing a soft reef and calm, shallow waters. This beach is open to dogs; it can be great fun watching joyful pooches bound about. Those in the know come here for the tranquillity – it pays to bring a good book.

The hippy haven What **South Beach** lacks in pristine sand (it's a mix of caramel and black grains) it makes up for in eye-catching entertainment. By day, there's a grassy park for picnics and a playground shaded by Norfolk pines leading to calm water that

DYLAN ALCOCK/SHUTTERSTOCK ©

✅ Beach Etiquette

Perth beach-goers are accustomed to having plenty of sand to themselves, so be careful not to sit too close, or set up directly in front of your fellow sun worshippers – it won't be appreciated. Beach thievery is rare; be relaxed about your belongings, but keep them within eyesight.

Above left Bennion Beach
Above City Beach
Left South Perth foreshore

seems knee-deep forever – perfect for paddling. As dark approaches, out come fire twirlers, hacky sack players, buskers and all manner of eccentric visitors. It's busy in a laid-back kind of way. On Saturdays in summer, from 5pm to 9pm, sunset markets fill the park. Various stalls, a pop-up bar and live entertainment deliver a festive atmosphere. Few travellers venture south of Fremantle, but those who do are well rewarded.

The sunset spot Closest to Perth's centre, **City Beach** is one of few beaches to be floodlit at night, allowing for delightful dusk swims on steamy evenings. It's also a prime sunset-watching spot, with groups of friends and families sharing hot fish and chips from the nearby **Clancy's Fish Pub** beach cafe as that giant orb plunges behind the horizon line. WA delights in its seaside sunsets.

☼ CY O'Connor Beach

Mix beauty and history with a visit to CY O'Connor Beach in North Coogee. The vast ruins of the 1950s South Fremantle Power Station loom in the sand dunes, providing a dramatic backdrop.

Look out for the statue of CY by WA artist Tony Jones out in the ocean, most visible at low tide. It marks the site where the state's hugely impactful chief civil engineer rode his horse into the ocean and shot himself in 1902, in despair that his goldfields water pipeline wasn't going to work. It did, and it is today celebrated as one of the great engineering feats of the early 20th century.

■ **Insider knowledge by Marcus Canning**
Founder of Fringe World, Rooftop Movies and the man behind The Rechabite reinvention
@therechabitehall

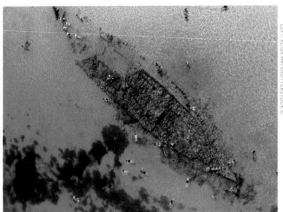

The submerged shipwreck The newly developed coastal suburb of **Coogee** is in Perth's far south, and when you see its glass-clear waters and blindingly white sand, you'll wonder why it took so long for the estate builders to arrive. Off a nondescript street, find a steel staircase that descends over a rock groyne into the shallow ocean.

Just beyond it is the **Omeo shipwreck**, a cargo steamer that ran aground here in 1905 and has since become a snorkellers' exploration site. If you have kids or aren't a confident swimmer, check the tides before you come, and arrive at low tide, when part of the wreck is accessible by wading in on foot, in just over a metre or so of water. Otherwise, splash in and consider following the **Coogee Maritime Trail**, an underwater snorkelling route that runs from 2–7m deep. Look out for the golden sea lion – its nose peeks above the waterline.

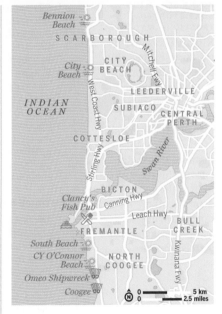

Left CY O'Connor statue, CY O'Connor Beach
Above Omeo shipwreck

The Boab Transplant

**HOW A BEGUILING
BOAB STOPPED
TRAFFIC IN WA**

Kings Park is one of the largest inner-city parks in the world, home to a sacred tree that can live for up to 1500 years. Brought there in one of the world's longest distance transplant efforts, the story of its fraught journey, from the state's far north to south, is as fascinating as its stately presence.

Left Gija Jumulu
Centre Gija Jumulu arriving in King's Park
Right Stilt walkers, Fairyland Festival

A Global Feat

A police escort, the removal of multiple traffic lights and 3200km of travel. Shifting the Kings Park boab, known as Gija Jumulu, was an almighty effort – one much greater than first imagined. It all began with a phone call to the Botanic Gardens & Parks Authority in 2008. The boab, sacred to the Gija people of the East Kimberley and only found in the state's tropical north, had to be moved to make way for a significant new motorway near the community of Warmun and its Aboriginal custodians wanted to know how to transplant it. A decision was made to send it to Kings Park, launching a world-first translocation that same year. Never before had a mature tree such as this been transported across such a distance, on land. When uprooted, it was estimated to be 750 years old. Before departing, the Gija performed a cultural farewell ceremony.

Touch & Go

The first hurdle came when, on moving day, it was discovered that the tree trunk and root ball were dramatically larger and heavier than calculated. A new truck trailer had to be sourced within a day or two if all the pre-arranged road blocks across the entire length of the state were to be accessed. Stress levels rose, but at the 11th hour, a new trailer capable of transporting the 36-tonne specimen was volunteered. Next began six days of travelling through outback and regional Australia. As word spread, entire town communities came out to wave and honk as the boab passed through.

Quite the Spectacle

Wide and rounded like a tall bottle, sprouting green tufts and tangled branches from its top, the tree measured 14m from top to bottom, its trunk spanned 2.5m and its branches reached 8m wide – after pruning. It took up two lanes of the highways it travelled on, and when it arrived in Perth, parked cars had to be moved and traffic lights uprooted to allow it to fit down city roads.

> The tree acts as a signpost to the plants and flowerbeds of the Botanic Garden, each representing different parts of the vast state.

After a long, slow journey through the city complete with news-crew helicopters buzzing overhead, it arrived in Kings Park to cheers and applause. A huge crane lifted it into its new home, in a climate far cooler than what it was used to. No one was sure if it would survive, but eventually, green shoots began to emerge.

The year 2021 marked a decade since the boab was planted in Kings Park. It continues to bloom, standing regally at the Two Rivers Lookout, where the Swan and Canning Rivers meet. It has the best views in town. The tree acts as a signpost to the plants and flowerbeds of the Botanic Garden, each representing the environment of different parts of the vast state. They are most breathtaking in spring, when the wildflowers bloom, heralding the annual Kings Park Festival each September.

How the Regal Park Became

For at least 40,000 years, the land where Kings Park now stands was a significant space for the Noongar people. They called it Mooro Katta or Kaarta Gar-up. European settlement in 1829 saw that change. John Septimus Roe, the first surveyor general of the Swan River colony, protected the wooded area two years after the land was forcibly seized from Aboriginal people.

Its preservation was overturned by Perth's early inhabitants only six years later, using the area for logging. The timber mill continued for 36 years until a large tract of bush was successfully preserved. By 1890, the parkland was extended and soon after, officially opened.

It was called Kings Park in 1901 to mark King Edward VII's ascension to the British throne.

09 Savouring Indigenous **FLAVOURS**

INDIGENOUS | CULTURE | FOOD

From Perth's fanciest restaurant to time with an Aboriginal Elder, here are some of the ways to taste bush flavours found only in Australia. Wrap your mouth around lemon myrtle, lilly pilly, tree ants and more as you dive deeper into WA's culinary diversity.

THE RITZ-CARLTON PERTH ©

🗺 **How to**

Getting around Uber or walk you way around the city.

When to go Each season delivers new flavours and fresh ingredients. Look up the six-season Noongar calendar and decide which is for you.

Top tip Native ingredients aren't necessarily singled out on menus, so ask your waitstaff to tell you which ones they are, and to describe how each one tastes.

CLEARVIEWIMAGES RF/ALAMY STOCK PHOTO ©

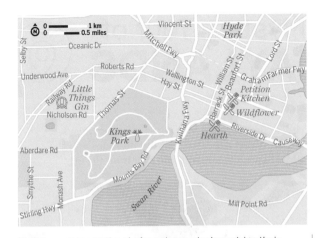

Perth's most innovative chefs are increasingly centring their menus around native foods that have long been overlooked in professional kitchens. The wealth of Australia's endemic bounty has always been known and valued by WA's Aboriginal peoples, and now those with a curious palate are diving into the fresh and unique flavours. Savour the mineral twang of crisped salt bush, the zing of lemon aspen and the crunch of beach spinach at some of Perth's most refined restaurants.

Fine-dining twists Go all out at **Wildflower**, the city's classiest fine diner, which sits in a glass box atop Como The Treasury boutique hotel. Its multicourse tasting menus change in harmony with the Noongar people's six-season calendar, reflecting the indigenous ingredients available in each period. Marron, a freshwater crayfish and local delicacy only found in WA, is almost always featured. Wildflower's opening chef Jed Gerrard took his ethos to **Hearth**, the flagship restaurant at the nearby Ritz-Carlton. Although he's since moved on to Margaret River winery restaurant Wills Domain (p115), it continues to permeate the carte in a more subtle way, much like it does at **Petition Kitchen**, a chic restaurant with an energetic vibe inside the State Buildings. Look out for pipis, an endemic shellfish, and native spinach.

Small-batch gin Native flavours are also increasingly infused into locally distilled sprits. At **Little Things Gin**, lemon myrtle, native river mint and Australian thyme make up the botanical mix, best savoured in its distillery bar. When in other watering holes, look out for **Giniversity**'s Australian Native Gin, made from Geraldton wax (which tastes similar to kaffir lime leaf), lemon myrtle and emu plum.

Left Hearth at the Ritz-Carlton
Below Bunya nut

🍴 A Dining Experience

Perhaps more than anyone else in WA's cooking scene, pop-up dining company **Fervor** deeply and meaningfully embraces indigenous Australian flavours.

Chef and founder Paul Iskov goes foraging with Aboriginal people before each degustation-style dining event, working the finds into the night's always-surprising menu. Think green tree ants, desert lime, bunya nut, boab tubers and an A-to-Z of things you've never heard of.

Most of Fervor's events are held in remote destinations around WA, but occasionally they bring their talents to Perth. Check the website events calendar and book well ahead for an unforgettable experience.

10 A Mystery Tour of MAYLANDS

URBAN | DISCOVERY | BARS

Meet Maylands, a gritty neighbourhood that mixes street-art alleys with community-centric bars, specialist delicatessens with op shops and the best cupcakes for miles – all just an eight-minute train ride from the city.

ISTETIANA/SHUTTERSTOCK ©

🗺 How to

Getting here The Midland train line drops you opposite Maylands' cafe strip on Whatley Cres. It's very handy. Walking is best from that moment on.

When to go Maylands buzzes most in the late afternoon and evening, on Friday and Saturday. Come hungry and allocate more time than you expect to spend here. There are plenty of treasures.

Top tip There are good op shops here, if you go searching.

🍺 A Maylands Microbrewery

Most of Maylands' finds run along Whatley Cres. But if you venture to traffic-jammed Guildford Rd, you'll discover the **Seasonal Brewing Co**, which opened in 2019. Powered by renewable energy, composting all waste and recycling water, this craft beer haven is as authentic as the former mechanic's garage it inhabits.

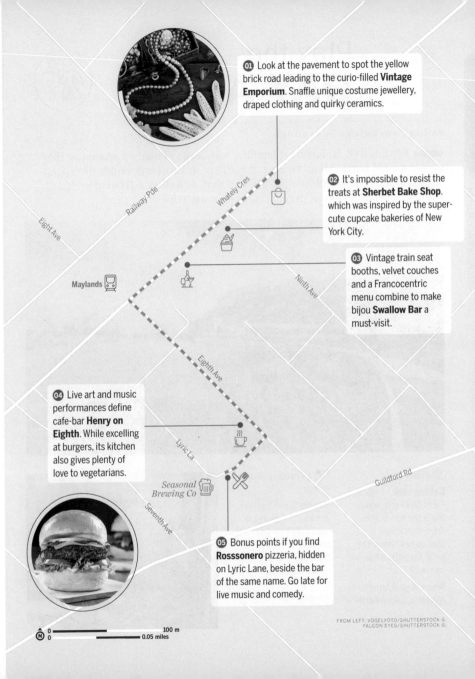

01 Look at the pavement to spot the yellow brick road leading to the curio-filled **Vintage Emporium**. Snaffle unique costume jewellery, draped clothing and quirky ceramics.

02 It's impossible to resist the treats at **Sherbet Bake Shop**. which was inspired by the super-cute cupcake bakeries of New York City.

03 Vintage train seat booths, velvet couches and a Francocentric menu combine to make bijou **Swallow Bar** a must-visit.

04 Live art and music performances define cafe-bar **Henry on Eighth**. While excelling at burgers, its kitchen also gives plenty of love to vegetarians.

05 Bonus points if you find **Rosssonero** pizzeria, hidden on Lyric Lane, beside the bar of the same name. Go late for live music and comedy.

Railway Pde

Whately Cres

Eight Ave

Maylands

Ninth Ave

Eighth Ave

Lyric La

Seasonal Brewing Co

Seventh Ave

Guildford Rd

0   100 m
N 0   0.05 miles

11 Play the DAY AWAY

FAMILY | ADVENTURE | OUTDOORS

▬▬ Perth is well designed for families, with loads of outdoor spaces, be they green, shaded parks, urban farms and markets, or vast playgrounds incorporating the state's unique wildflowers. Find all that, as well as a 314-step bridge climb and 75km/h zipline, during this on-foot day trip.

MICHAEL WILLIS/ALAMY STOCK PHOTO ©

🗺 How to

Getting here To reach Perth City Farm, where this adventure begins, drive, take a train to Claisebrook Station or jump aboard the free yellow CAT bus.

When to go A farmers market is held at Perth City Farm each Saturday morning.

Top tip Supervised kids are free to explore the whole of Perth City Farm, so venture behind the buildings to discover chooks and crops of leafy greens.

LUKE RILEY CREATIVE ©

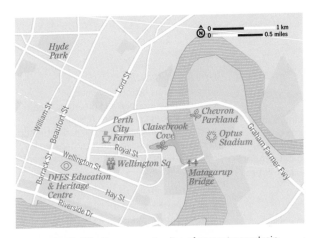

Left Optus Stadium and Matagarup Bridge
Below Perth City Farm

Start at **Perth City Farm**, a rustic slice of green among train lines, a student campus and assisted accommodation flats. It's free entry; say hello to any volunteers you see as you roam the veggie patches and watch the chooks. There's a good cafe on-site with raised sandpits filled with toy trucks for the kids. A five-minute walk away, a A$17.5-million playground opened in **Wellington Square (Moort-ak Waadiny)** in early 2021. It has landscaped bush, water fountains and parkour zones. Kids love climbing up towers shaped like banksias, zipping down steel tube slides and jumping on mini trampolines.

Stroll to Royal St for lunch and follow the duck-dotted waterway leading to **Claisebrook Cove**, where kids can run across the footbridge and roam around Victoria Gardens. Towards the river is a steep hill ideal for body rolls. Walk another 10 minutes to **Matagarup Bridge**, designed to look like swans, and Perth's **Optus Stadium** (judged the world's most beautiful sports facility in 2019). Consider harnessing up for the bridge climb, which reaches a 72m-high, glass-bottom SkyView Deck. It's open to kids aged eight and up who bring their 'big person' along. The zipline here is for 10 year olds and above.

Follow the river to **Chevron Parkland**, home to six nature playground zones (ignore the playground near the bridge). It was created with the Whadjuk community and connects to the six seasons recognised by WA's Noongar people. Scale towers modelled on quandong trees, run through numbat burrows, find hatching emu eggs and build stick cubbies. There are free BBQ facilities here, too.

A Mini Fire-fighter's Dream

The Department of Fire and Emergency Services (DFES) Education & Heritage Centre is housed in the original Perth Central Fire Station and grants free entry to those keen to try on firefighting uniforms, don hard hats and hoist themselves up into a fire truck. There's also a firefighters' pole to swing on, and a relics gallery (more for big kids). The centre is part of Hibernian Place, a cluster of restaurants edging a public lawn.

Listings

BEST OF THE REST

In the Open Air

Somerville Auditorium

Encircled by pine trees that point to the starry night, this outdoor cinema on the beautiful University of WA grounds shows international films from November to April. Bring a cushion to avoid deck-chair bot-rot and order on-site pizza.

Rooftop Movies

Atop a six-storey car park is an unlikely scene: vintage caravans, palm trees and bean bags pointed at a screen suspended on shipping containers. Food trucks provide sustenance. Open over summer.

Esplanade Park

This big green space opposite Fremantle Port has a rope-climbing pyramid, a tall slippery dip, an all-ages skate park and a parkour activity zone. You'll be there for hours.

Hyde Park

A large, leafy square where walking paths are overhung by enormous Moreton Bay fig trees, all encircling a tranquil lake. Look over the edge and spot native turtles.

The World's Oldest Living Culture

Go Cultural

Walk through Perth's waterfront precinct, Elizabeth Quay, and feel as though the pavement and buildings have been lifted, revealing the cultural use of this land before European settlement. Your Noongar guide shares the meeting places, hunting areas and gathering spaces once frequented by Aboriginal people.

Nyungar Tours

Kings Park has historically been an important ceremonial and dreaming area for WA's Aboriginal people. A Noongar woman will guide you over the park's treetop bridge and through its bush gardens while telling rarely heard Whadjuk Yorga (women-focused) stories.

Djurandi Dreaming

Explore Perth's southern lakes by torchlight with a Noongar man, as he shares how these fresh water sources were once vital connections to the ocean for local Aboriginal people, as well as tribal community meeting places and food sources.

The Great Outdoors

Heirrison Island

Don't expect to see kangaroos within sight of skyscrapers? Ride, walk or drive to Heirrison Island, facing the city. A small group of roos lives in a fenced sanctuary on the isle's southwestern side. If you go early in the day, or around sunset, you're almost guaranteed to spot them grazing in the wetlands or grasses.

DAVID STEELE/SHUTTERSTOCK ©

Hyde Park

Whale watching

The world's longest whale migration passes Perth's coastline, with playful humpbacks putting on a show for boat tours that run from September to November. Several companies run whale-watching expeditions.

Hike Collective

The eco-minded guided hikes focus on connecting with nature and one another. Each adventure is held within an hour of the city centre. Explore Rottnest Island's lakes and bays or wander through the landscaped gardens at Araluen Botanic Park.

GoGo Active Tour

Discover secret cliff hideaways even locals don't know are there with a guided kayak of the Swan River. Kayak journeys explore waterbird habitats, limestone caves and even visit a winery.

Perth Waterbike Adventures

Pedal past city dolphins while drinking in the best view of Perth's city skyline, on an aquatic bike on the Swan River. Eco-friendly, near-impossible to capsize and far easier than push bikes, you can paddle at your own pace, alone or on a tour.

 Family Fun

Scitech

Kids love the interactive, hands-on science centre with a planetarium dome on top. See fluro material travel through wind tunnels in the dark, race water boats, control electronic arms and much more.

Elizabeth Quay Water Park

Running through the jets of water as they rise and fall, brushing hands over the mosaic floor and, at dusk, marvelling at the colourful lighting display are all part of the fun at this water park. Find it opposite the Elizabeth Quay Train Station.

Perth Zoo

Perth Zoo

The native wildlife sections include rarely seen cassowaries and tree kangaroos; there's also a reptile enclosure full of venomous snakes and a nocturnal house revealing Australia's furry night animals, such as the bilby and quokka.

 Caffeine Hit

Telegram Coffee

Join the daily queues at this petite cafe contained in a wooden box – the eucalyptus panels are opened via a hand-powered pulley system each morning. Find it hidden inside the grand, heritage-listed State Buildings.

Lil' Toastface

Arguably Perth's tiniest cafe, this literal hole-in-the-wall pumps out excellent coffees and great toasties. Pull up an old school chair or milk crate and watch Northbridge's parade of odd and intriguing personalities go by.

Pixel Coffee Brewers

Where all the cool kids get their caffeine buzz for the day. The sage and white subway tiles and greenery inside are lovely, but the 'parklet', an upcycled seating space taking up a car bay out front, is where it's at. Found north of Leederville's cafe strip.

Breakfast of Champions

Odyssea $$

Overlook the ocean as you sip on a fresh juice or get stuck into smashed avocado with chorizo and poached eggs. Tie in your trip with a swim.

Hylin $$

A cute, narrow cafe with lots of seating under the trees beside the road. They do huge, filling breakfasts and excellent coffee. Brisket Benny is a highlight dish. Watch out for the parking meters.

Moore & Moore $$

This popular breakfast and brunch spot with an art gallery and garden seating is a characterful Fremantle icon in the historic West End. Note: they use a hot plate to cook everything, so they only do poached or fried eggs – never scrambled.

Dining Out after 9pm

Vincent Wine $$

A very European corner wine bar serving French classics until late – whether you're perched on the brass bar or seated on the outside deck. The wine list is impressive, best teamed with chicken liver parfait.

Bar Rogue $$

It's walk-ins-only and snack-focused at this wine bar in Highgate, opened in 2021, but don't let that put you off. Flavour punches are thick and fast; think cold fried chicken on waffles, or miso-glazed pork belly skewer.

Tiny's $$

Tucked back from the road in the city's west, Tiny's has a cult following for its rotisserie chicken, housemade gravy and duck fat potatoes. But honestly? Anything you order will be top-notch.

Natural Wine Hubs

Wines of While $$

A young wine-loving doctor opened this 50-seat wine store and bar in Northbridge with the aim of sharing his passion for chemical-free wines. The sustainable drops are one thing, but the food is quite another.

Casa $$$

This hip but friendly neighbourhood bar opened in Mt Hawthorn in 2021, with a long, expensive list of minimal intervention wines. Arrive late afternoon and sit at the sidewalk tables, or lean on the narrow bar out back.

Nieuw Ruin $$

With 300 wines on the list and a penchant for the unusual, this cottage-feel Fremantle bar charms with its drinks savvy and its atmosphere welcoming. They do small batch and hyper local so well you won't want to leave.

Best in Chinatown

Good Fortune Duck House $

The name says it all. The boneless roast duck is other level, with its only competition the Peking duck pancakes.

Elizabeth Quay Water Park (p79)

Viet Hoa $

Here's where to fill up on a steaming bowl of *pho* (noodle soup) in Northbridge. Go traditional and get the raw beef, with fresh mint and crisp bean sprouts on the side.

Tak Chee House $

The home of Hainan chicken rice, cooked the authentic way. This Malaysian eatery bears cheap and cheerful interiors and service is brash, but it's good value and seriously tasty.

Sip & Fizz

Republic of Fremantle

Gin is the speciality at this warehouse-feel distillery that has a bustling bar, fun outside seating and excellent eats. Hear how the base spirit is batch-stilled from locally grown grapes using traditional processes.

Little Creatures

Once a microbrewery, now a global name, the original harbourside tank sheds still exist, forming the backdrop for a hectic kitchen (try the roo skewers and prawn pizza), long sampling bar and lively beer garden.

Gage Roads Brewery

Picture a 100m-long beach-shack-style brewpub in a former cargo shed perched on a working port. That's what you get at Fremantle's A Shed. Views include Rottnest ferries wrapped in quokka imagery.

Secret Bars

Toots

This late-night disco haven is all '70s mirror balls and pastel hues. It's found inside another secret bar in Chinatown, for which you'll need a password to gain entry on Friday and Saturday nights. Once you've worked out where to start, go up to the bar to order and ask the bartender if you can speak to Toots.

Little Creatures

BELLE HUNG/SHUTTERSTOCK ©

Astral Weeks

Vinyl lovers have found their happy place in this 2022 opening. The bar is dedicated to a high-quality listening experience, fitted with a Line Magnetic sound system. Lo-fi wines are served in the former Chinese herbalist's shop, which bears no sign.

Ripper Rooftops

QT Hotel

Reach the pinnacle of QT Hotel and marvel at the view: the city stretches out around you in all directions. Best seen at night when the lights are glittering, with a cocktail on hand.

Songbird

Shoot up to this flash, open-air, open-to-all bar on the 1st level of The Ritz – it's not exactly a rooftop, but it feels like one. The best seats are on the balcony overlooking Elizabeth Quay.

Mechanics Institute

Found down a laneway and up some stairs, this shabby-chic, hipster-vibe bar on the 2nd floor is loved for its open deck, slick cocktails and edgy bar staff. Bonus: they'll deliver burgers up from the ground-level diner.

 Scan to find more things to do in Perth online

PERTH REGION

NATURE | ADVENTURE | OUTDOORS

Wander through the surreal **Pinnacles** desert domes at golden hour (p90)

🚌 *2hr from Perth*

Green Head

Jurien Bay

Cervantes

Nambung National Park

Lancelin

INDIAN

OCEAN

Watheroo National Park   Wubin

Badgingarra   Watheroo

Moora   Bindi Bindi

Cataby

Moore River National Park

Guilderton

Yanchep

Hillarys

PERTH

Fremantle ●**Armadale**

Rockingham   Jarrahdale

Mandurah Pinjarra   Bannister

Kalannie

Pithara

Koorda

Wyalkatchem

Avon Valley Toodyay

Northam   Cunderdin

●**York**

Shop at family-run fruit and vegetable stalls in Perth's most accessible winery region, the **Swan Valley** (p86)

🚗 *30min from Perth*

Hit the **Perth Hills** when fruit trees are blossoming, dropping carpets of petals (p102)

🚗 *30min from Perth*

Spend a night on quokka-dotted **Rottnest Island** and mix wildlife adventures with deep relaxation (p98)

⛴ *30min from Perth*

Settle in for an off-menu, ultra-sustainable meal made entirely of leftovers at **Millbrook Winery** (p105)

🚗 *1hr from Perth*

Kondinin   Hyden

Climb to the top of 15m-high **Wave Rock**, made entirely of eroded rock (p92)

🚌 *4hr from Perth*

PERTH REGION
Trip Builder

A wealth of Perth's treasures are right at its fingertips: the quokka-land of Rottnest Island is 19km across the water, and the dips and plunges of the Perth Hills are only 30 minutes from its centre. Surreal rock formations found no where else in Australia – the Pinnacles, Wave Rock – are further afield, but you'll find all WA exploring is worth the effort.

0   100 km
0   50 miles

Practicalities

ARRIVING

 Perth International Airport Most visitors to this region will arrive at Perth Airport, from where it's just a quick taxi or share-ride to the Swan Valley or Perth's centre. A number of car-rental companies are located near Terminals 1 and 2.

CONNECT

Internet service in the bush is often patchy and even phone service can drop out between towns, especially for smaller service providers. Limited free hotspots.

MONEY

Generally things are cheaper in the country. Pay pass is common, but internet-based systems are often down. Always carry cash; ATMs are few and far between.

WHERE TO STAY

Town	Pros/Cons
Rottnest Island	Options from cottages to hotel rooms, self-contained tents and BYO camping sites.
Swan Valley	Quiet and family run, with farmstays, B&Bs and a few sophisticated options.
Perth Hills	Tranquil at night. Some lovely B&Bs on produce properties, plus retreats and spas.
Cervantes	Mostly camp sites or beach-houses. RAC Cervantes Holiday Park ticks many boxes.
Northam	Limited choice beyond Airbnbs, but one pearler: the Farmers Home Hotel.

EATING & DRINKING

Country pub meals are seen as a throwback to the days when WA was more of a frontier state, tucking into lamb chops (pictured bottom right) and steamed veg that spilled off the plate. If you have the opportunity to go old-school, do it. Winery regions are largely more highbrow now, so you might find, say, hollandaise asparagus or confit duck with mixed grain salad. Always try the local vino or join the locals in a pint of WA beer.

Best winery lunch
Millbrook Winery (p105)

Must-try chicken parmigiana
Sandpiper Tavern (p91)

GETTING AROUND

Car By far the easiest way to get off the beaten track and explore properly.

Train The Transwa AvonLink train travels from Midland to Northam, passing through the picturesque Avon Valley.

Coach tours Visit the most popular destinations but tend to stick to the key sights.

BIRAK	**BUNURU**	**DJERAN**	**MAKURU**	**DJILBA**	**KAMBARANG**
DEC–JAN	FEB–MAR	APR–MAY	JUN–JUL	AUG–SEP	OCT–NOV
The mercury rises in line with the breeze. Time for water activities.	Temperatures inland are much hotter than at the coast.	Sunny days with gentle breezes – a favourite time of year for local travellers.	Cold with intermittent rain that generally doesn't last long. The off-season for many.	Night-sky clarity makes for ultimate stargazing; days are cool but sun-kissed.	Fresh, light-flooded days and cool nights as summer approaches.

12 SURPRISES
in the Swan Valley

WINE | MARKETS | CURIOSITIES

▬▬▬ Rows of grapevines rake the landscape only a 30-minute drive from Perth, a scene that has greeted the eyes for more than 180 years. European migrants kicked off winemaking in these parts, and their descendants continue the vinous bent. It's what makes the region special: you bypass big-name wineries for rustic, familial options.

🗺 How to

Getting around Unless you're joining a tour, it's simplest to drive yourself around the Swan Valley. There's a pleasant 32km Swan Valley Food & Wine Trail loop drive around the region which passes most attractions.

When to go Anytime works, but spring heralds festival time, with **Entwined in the Valley** (entwinedinthevalley.com.au) held each October.

For something different You can hire a horse-drawn wagon, or do a guided tasting tour via river cruise or kayak (try GoGo Active Tours).

Map of the Swan Valley region showing: 0–5 km / 0–2.5 miles scale; Upper Swan; Great Northern Hwy; Henley Brook; John Kosovich Wines; Gnangara Rd; Baskerville; Old Young's Kitchen; The Naked Fox; Whiteman Park; West Swan Rd; Herne Hill; Toodyay Rd; Oakover Grounds; Dayton; Kellers Farm; Reid Hwy; Caversham; Kato's at 3000; Guildford; Museum of Natural History; Tonkin Hwy; Rusty Old Boat; Great Eastern Hwy; Roe Hwy.

Digging up hidden gems Opened early in 2022, **The Naked Fox** wine bar is run by a young couple who threw in their day jobs to pursue their ardent love of local wine. The menu features 280 bottles sourced from independent WA vineyards – impressive, especially given the venue only fits 100 people. Beyond the bar, there are picnic rugs ready to be rolled out on the grass beneath old trees, metres from the vines that the pair use to make their own blends under their Beneath the Vines label.

Farm-gate trails Wine grapes are just the beginning. Fresh fruit and vegetable stalls are dotted along the Valley's roadsides. Source table grapes from **Kato's at 3000**, where the family grows some 15 varieties, harvesting from January to late March. In Dayton, **Kellers Farm** sets up weekend stalls selling seasonal produce, preserves and free-range eggs as chickens and goats mill about. Swiss-born Philipp

KEVIN OSBORNE/FOX FOTOS ©

🥂 Explore Further

John Kosovich Wines
(Baskerville) This winery celebrated 100 years of sensational family winemaking in 2022. Some of my earliest memories are running around in the cellar. I love the bottle-aged chenin and the MPV – but do not, on any account, miss tasting the rare muscat.

Oakover Grounds (Middle Swan) There's wine, cider and coffee tasting as well as a marketplace full of local and imported gourmet treats. Jump on the free paddle boats for a potter around the lake.

Museum of Natural History (Guildford) A 1920s theatre now houses a cornucopia of taxidermied curiosities. You'll find emus, armadillos, dinosaurs and dolphins.

Keller bakes Swiss chocolate bread while his wife Marija, of Croatian heritage, wood-fires an incredible cheddar and jalapeño sourdough.

Countering all that freshness Treat yourself to 'fancy' fish and chips at the fun at Guildford's **Rusty Old Boat** restaurant. Unlike the usual takeaway, this maritime-themed diner has a wine and cocktail list to pair with sustainably caught fish. Or, enjoy a long lunch at **Old Young's Kitchen**. This newcomer is elevating the native culinary bar with its crocodile chorizo dusted in rosella leaf, kangaroo tartare with endemic youlk shrub and brined kingfish with salty samphire and tangy Geraldton wax leaves.

■ **Recommendations by James Young**
Distiller and CEO at Old Young's
@oldyoungsdistillery

Above The Naked Fox

13 The Pinnacles
BY SUNSET

GEOLOGY | NATURE | NATIONAL PARK

■■■■ The Pinnacles are like nowhere else in Australia, and yet many people visit them at times when they're far from their best. Be intentional about your experience: choose to tour these limestone formations – which rise from the desert sand like thousands of knobbly fingers – at sunset, when they beam and glow, before silhouetting against the pink and purple sky.

BENNY MARTY/SHUTTERSTOCK ©

🗺 How to

Getting there The Pinnacles are a two-hour drive north of Perth. Cervantes and Jurien Bay are the nearest towns.

Know the wind This is one of WA's windiest areas; plan your activities in harmony with it, along with the swell, tide and moon. Light winds from an easterly direction are prime for the beach and boating. When the wind switches to a southerly in the afternoon, you'll want to go caving.

Good to know Nambung National Park is open 24 hours; Pinnacles Desert Discovery Centre until 4.30pm. Entry costs $15 per vehicle.

SAMMAX CHONG/SHUTTERSTOCK ©

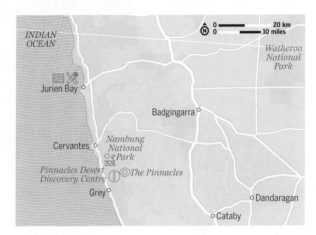

INDIAN OCEAN

Jurien Bay

Badgingarra

Watheroo National Park

Cervantes

Nambung National Park

Pinnacles Desert Discovery Centre

The Pinnacles

Grey

Dandaragan

Cataby

0 — 20 km
0 — 10 miles

Left The Pinnacles
Below Night sky, the Pinnacles

The best time of day Most visitors drive through the 25,000- to 30,000-year-old, space-like limestone spires known as **The Pinnacles** during the day, on their way to somewhere else. They turn off the Indian Ocean Drive, roll slowly through the karst formations on the loop route, and head off again. Don't make the same mistake. Timing your visit for golden hour, when the setting sun drenches the landscape in warm yellow hues, makes for an incomparable experience. It's also likely to be a much cooler one, with the heat of the midday sun softened, allowing you to follow walking trails through native bush and to boardwalk lookouts, rather than just touring in your car. The tallest columns are 5m high and about 1m wide – it's worth getting out of the car to study them up close. There's another bonus, too: if you stay late enough, the region's dark skies deliver sharp, bright stargazing.

When you're done, head to the nearby rock lobster fishing town, Jurien Bay, and grab a feed from **Sandpiper Tavern** (just bear in mind, it shuts at 8.30pm, as do most country eateries). It's within walking distance of a rather unusual glow-in-the-dark art gallery. The lights-off **Sea Spray Art** gallery only opens for around two hours in the evenings, so check ahead.

◎ Local Knowledge

A lot of the best experiences in this region are advertised locally on the Jurien Bay Community Chat page on Facebook. Through it, you'll know when the sound healing group or the astro photography group hold occasional sessions in the Pinnacles. It is an incredibly spiritual place even after sunset. The most moving experience, held once a year, is the opera in the Pinnacles. Tickets sell out fast – it is truly a once-in-a-lifetime experience.

On the Jurien Bay Crayz Facebook page you'll see when a local rock lobster fishing boat is selling live crays to the public.

■ **Tips by Kiera Wuillemin**
Artist and gallerist at Sea Spray Art
Instagram @sea_spray_art

14 The Oddities & Curiosities
OF WAVE ROCK

OUTBACK | ADVENTURE | ROCK FORMATIONS

▬▬▬ Imagine a monster wave, poised just as it's about to crash. That's the scene that greets you at Wave Rock, a 15m-high, 2.7-billion-year-old slab of granite that stretches 110m long. Here's how to do it right.

🗺 How to

Getting here Wave Rock is a four-hour inland drive east from Perth. Coach tours come here, but for ease of exploration, it's best to drive.

Go via The historic cafe town of York, the quirky Tin Horse Highway, the 182m-long community water slide at Kulin and Corrigin's poignant dog cemetery are all along the way.

When to go Avoid summer, when temperatures soar.

Top tip Park by the Wave Rock village to avoid the pricey parking tickets in car bays closer to the rock.

Some 300km east of Perth, surrounded by scrub and dry, sun-baked earth flushed the shade of sienna, is **Wave Rock**. The formation – naturally eroded by wind and water hollowing out its softer underside – achieved global notoriety in the 1960s, when *National Geographic* magazine published a photograph of it. It's vertically striped, a result of rain flushing iron oxide and carbonates down the curved surface in a rainbow of earthy stains.

Most visitors come during the day, when piercing light mutes its colours. Instead, go at sunset. As the bruising sun softens, the wave's scale becomes more apparent, and it's vastly more enjoyable to walk around. Edge along its base (be sure to snap a playful pic of you 'surfing' the wave) and carefully across its peak, where you're gifted endless views of bush and farmland.

👁 Tin Horse Highway

Detour 15 minutes from the main road to take in the Tin Horse Highway. With their tongues in their cheeks, local farmers have welded and painted more than 70 characterful horses from bits of tin and metal, dotting them along a 15km stretch. Most are on the Gorge Rock-Lake Grace Rd.

Above left Wave Rock
Above View from summit, Wave Rock
Left Tin Horse Highway

The Curiosity: Float like an Astronaut

Only 800m away is the **Lake Magic Swimming Pool** with water so saline you bob about weightlessly, as though you have zero gravity. Take the steps gingerly – they can be slippery – and expect squishiness underfoot. Limestone cabanas with hammocks and showers have been built around its perimeter, adding a desert day-spa vibe. It's part of the Wave Rock Resort site, but the pool is open to anyone. The water comes from **Lake Magic**, a gypsum-rich expanse next door that provides beautiful reflections at dusk.

Hippo's Yawn

Meet another rock formation, standing almost 13m tall and reached via a 1.7km loop walking trail from the Wave Rock car park. You can crawl to the back of the gaping jaw and scramble up its tumble of boulders. It really does look like a hippo yawning. Kids bound through the gaps, whereas for adults, it's more of a twist and slide.

✿ WA's Most Inland Winery

About one hour's drive south of Wave Rock (a small distance in these parts) is **Walkers Hill Vineyard**.

To any wine buff, it shouldn't be possible to grow grapevines this far east, but the owners of this establishment are not wine people. The former truckie and hairdresser were desperate to buy land; this piece came with a vineyard. The wine tastes of its terroir – flinty, dusty ironstone – but they do the best food for miles (bookings essential).

Tip: the owners hold a community grape pick each February/March. Anyone can join in. Exact dates are announced on Facebook, with about one week's notice.

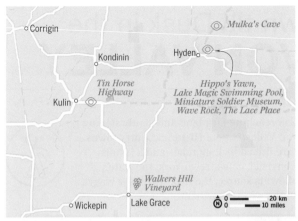

Left Red-wine grapes
Below Noongar paintings, Mulka's cave

Mulka's Cave

This cave holds the largest collection of Noongar paintings in the south west of WA, yet few have even heard of it. While most other sites bear fewer than 20 works, Mulka's Cave counts more than 450 pieces on its cool, dark walls. Look carefully and you'll see hundreds of Aboriginal handprints captured with ochre spray, plus other art motifs depicted in seven different colours. It's worth taking the 18km graded dirt road out – drive carefully.

The Oddities: Niche Collections

Now for something you'd never expect to find in the outback. The **Miniature Soldier Museum**, only metres from Wave Rock, assembles at least 10,000 army characters into detailed war scenes, with large ships made from sardine tins, spam cans and bottle tops. Both world wars have been recreated, along with the Napoleonic and American Civil Wars, and others. Sharing the same roof, **The Lace Place** houses a vast collection of delicate creations under protective low light. Each 2.5cm of lace represents an hour of embroidery. As you exit into the adjoining cafe, gaze upwards or you'll miss the huge, butterfly-shaped dried flower creations the owner made in the 1980s, to act as insulation.

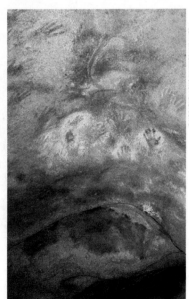

15 Dawn till Dusk in the
AVON VALLEY

CULTURE | HISTORY | NATURE

████ Scrubby bush, horizon-reaching farmland and gently sloping valleys greet you in the Avon Valley region. Historic country towns encircling grand old pubs are linked by long roads and a joyous sense of space. Stop in at convivial, cafe-strewn York, the state's oldest inland town, and follow its source, the Avon River (or Wagyl, in Ballardong Noongar), all the way to Northam.

RIC JACYNO/SHUTTERSTOCK ©

🗺 How to

Getting here & around The AvonLink train travels to Northam but you'll need a car to explore the area properly. In town, park and follow the Dorntj Koorliny Track, a looping walking path tracing the edge of the Avon River. The name is Noongar for 'walking together', and it was laid by volunteers. The mix-and-match of pavers made the community project affordable.

When to go Canola fields flower from mid-August into September, illuminating the landscape.

📖 The Stolen Generation

Many Aboriginal people living today are part of what is called the Stolen Generation, whereby children were forcibly removed from their families by the state and federal governments between 1910 and 1970.

Northam's **Bilya Koort Boodja Centre** (pictured) has an important 'sorry space' dedicated to healing through sharing this traumatic history, the impact of which continues to linger.

01 Hot-air ballooning just out of **Northam** is a standout experience. Coast at low elevation above the region's submarine-yellow canola fields before rising above the clouds for an eagle's-eye view.

02 Wander thoughtfully through **Bilya Koort Boodja Centre** for Nyoongar Culture and Environmental Knowledge, where you may meet and learn from Aboriginal people.

Goomalling Rd

05 Spend time at **Laura's Wine Bar**, the town's only small bar, a rustic, crafted brick design built by the Northam-born architect and builder Brian Kloppers (1937–2020).

Peel Terrace

03 At 117m-long, Northam's pedestrian **suspension bridge** is the longest in Australia. Look for the town's imported white swans on the Avon River below. Swans indigenous to WA are black.

Fitzgerald St

04 Take a look at two 1970s brutalist buildings designed by lauded architect Iwan Iwanoff in the town centre. One is **Northam Library**, where artistically placed concrete blocks cast patterns in the sunlight.

0   1 km
0   0.5 miles

16 Overnighting on ROTTNEST

ISLAND | WILDLIFE | BEACH

Want to understand the creature behind the thousands of grinning selfies with celebrities? Rottnest Island's quokkas are known for their photogenic poses, but a simple snap sells them short. Experience the transformative nature of spending a night – or three – on Perth's holiday haven, surrounded by curious wildlife, peaceful coves and oodles of natural beauty.

BENNY MARTY/SHUTTERSTOCK ©

📖 How to

Getting here Rottnest-bound ferries depart from Perth's city centre, Fremantle and Hillarys Boat Harbour. There are also light plane and helicopter options.

Getting around Most people hire bicycles. You can also get about on foot or e-bike, take the shuttle, or buy a ticket for the hop-on, hop-off bus, which loops around the 11km-long island.

When to go The days are warm and skies are blue from September to May.

GRAKHANTSEV NIKOLAI/SHUTTERSTOCK ©

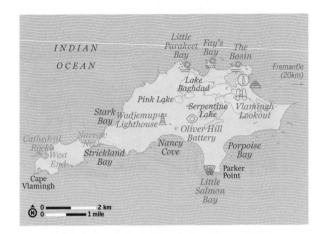

Left Little Salmon Bay
Below Quokka

Gone are the crowds Departing on the day's last ferry, tens of thousands of visitors to Rottnest Island never see it at its best – as the sun softens and the bustle calms, or as the native marsupials emerge. They leave with quokka selfies, the slick of sunscreen and the crunch of salt in their hair. It's fun, sure, but you can do better. Those that stay over night get an entirely different experience. As night nears, quokkas – which are nocturnal – come out in droves. In the dark they are most active, bouncing across walking paths and around anyone wandering by. They scramble up trees, tussle with one another and nibble on grasses. It's a significant contrast from daytime, when they barely move, appear stunned or lazily scavenge. These quokkas are only there because of people – and that's why feeding them is a no-no. If you see a quokka sleeping during the day – they curl up while seated and rest their heads on their tails – don't bother them; they need their shut-eye.

Relax into 'Rotto' pace While you're here explore beyond the main settlement to little-used hiking trails and boardwalks and have enchanting beaches all to yourself. Paradisiacal **Little Parakeet Bay** is flanked with eroded limestone formations and faces an ocean pool of blue colour swirls. At **Fay's Bay**, a curving, flat beach gives way to craggy rocks with leafy seagrasses and rock pools at their base; it's an ideal spot for children to explore and amateur fishers to drop a line. For snorkelling head to sheltered and calm **Little Salmon Bay**, where an excellent snorkel trail is dotted with underwater panels.

🐾 A Few Fun Quokka Facts

When 17th-century Dutch sailors explored the craggy, limestone island, they mistook its resident fur-balls for large rats. The quokkas' presence resulted in the island's name, Rottnest, translating to rat's nest.

Quokkas get most of the water they need from eating native greenery, such as grasses, succulents and seedlings, so they rarely drink water.

Quokka joeys poke their little heads out of their mother's pouch each September, and the island holds a public, weekend-long Quokka Birthday party for all the newborns. They're ultra cute, but should never be touched.

Beyond the Quokkas

ROTTNEST ISLAND'S LAYERED AND COMPLEX BACKSTORY

Rottnest Island – also known as Wadjemup – is outshone by its famous quokkas. But look beyond the cuteness and you'll find an isle of living history, where the heritage buildings you might be staying or playing in tell stories of lonely colonial settlement, world war efforts and hard-knocks farming.

Left Thomson Bay
Centre Vlamingh Lookout
Right Salt Store

JON ARNOLD IMAGES LTD/ALAMY STOCK PHOTO ©

Early Origins

Perth's playground, 19km across the Indian Ocean, wasn't always an island. Some 7000 years ago, Rottnest Island formed part of the WA mainland. Artefacts found, such as a 27,000-year-old cutting tool made of chert, suggest Rottnest's traditional owners, the Whadjuk Noongar people, walked across the land bridge well before sea levels rose, using it as a meeting place and ceremonial site.

It was in 1831 that Rottnest's European residents set up here. Robert Thomson, with his wife and children, are believed to be the first Euroepans to live on Rottnest Island. Along with other settlers, they farmed everything from livestock to grains, tobacco and fruit, as well as harvesting salt from central saline lakes.

Parts of the Thomsons' homestead and water well can still be viewed. There's also a 4km walking trail weaving through the area that the Thomsons farmed. Follow it from Vlamingh Lookout, a hilltop perch that descends, eventually reaching a raised boardwalk with pink-hued salt lakes and samphire carpets on either side, leading to Little Parakeet Bay (p97).

A Hidden History

The Thomson family was the last to privately own land on Rottnest – in 1839, private ownership was prohibited. Around the same time, the island was transformed into an Aboriginal penal colony. Over the next century nearly 4000 men and boys were imprisoned here.

Prisoners undertook brutally hard labour, quarrying stone and constructing most of the colonial buildings still standing in Thomson Bay, the island's main settlement. Hundreds are believed to have perished and are still buried in grounds that were, until the 1980s, unknown to the

public. The many Aboriginal lives lost on Wadjemup means the island holds special significance for WA's Aboriginal peoples. The prison, known as the Quod, was closed in 1904 and the last inmates left in the 1930s. A project is underway to recognise and preserve the sites that are connected to the Aboriginal prison era. It's worth noting that Wadjemup translates as 'place across the water where the spirits are'.

A New Era Dawns

The closure of the prison made way for leisure pursuits. Rottnest's buildings, washed with white lime that reflected harshly in the lucid light, were slapped with a peach ochre hue that continues to be synonymous with Rottnest's historical cottages today. During the two world wars, Rottnest was repurposed as a prisoner-of-war camp and military defence base. When the global conflicts ended, the remnant cannons and army barracks became tourist attractions, the Boys' Reformatory was turned into accommodation, and the governor's summer residence was converted into a pub. The heritage buildings are continuously preserved in harmony with their ongoing, everyday use.

> The only people allowed to live on the island are long-serving staff members.

Today the only people allowed to live on the island are long-serving staff members, numbering around 200. While upgrades have been made to the settlement holiday houses, they remain blissfully basic. To put you in the picture, saltwater showers were only switched to freshwater in the 1990s, and TVs were first introduced to rooms in 2006. There was such enraged push-back that surveys were subsequently conducted to check people still wanted them (they did). Rottnest's sandy-footed simplicity is highly valued by its regulars. There are plenty of them, too: another survey found that nearly half of all Rottnest's visitors have been 10 times or more.

WA's Most Sustainable Destination

In 2018 Rotto became the first WA tourism destination to score sustainability certification from **EarthCheck**.

Solar panels and a wind turbine provide about 45% of the island's energy needs. Water comes from a desalination plant that filters some 150 million litres per year, while treated wastewater is used for irrigation. A volunteer-managed nursery produces 30,000 seedlings annually for constant revegetation projects, mulched by green waste. The only cars on the island are service vehicles.

The island was declared a Class A nature reserve back in 1917 – the same year quokka hunting was outlawed.

17 Easy-Access Roo SPOTTING

WILDLIFE | NATURE | OUTDOORS

▬▬▬ The thrill of seeing your first kangaroo bound effortlessly through tall grasses, illuminated by the day's last light, is hard to beat. Here's where to find creatures in the wild, with a little patience and local know-how. Mix in a bit of luck and you'll also spot echidnas and bandicoot, plus a special colony of koalas.

KEVIN LEBRE/GETTY IMAGES ©

📷 How to

Getting around Public transport is tricky in these semi-rural areas, so it's simplest to drive yourself.

When to go Australian wildlife is most active at dawn and dusk.

A caveat Go just before dawn or dusk to minimise driving during risky periods, when creatures may bounce and run unexpectedly from roadsides. Be mindful as you head back in the dark.

DAVID STEELE/SHUTTERSTOCK ©

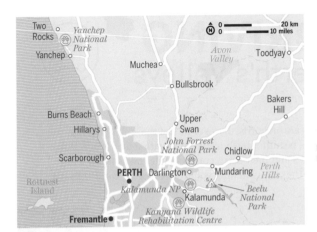

Left Kangaroos, Yanchep National Park
Below 28 parrot

Wildlife hotspot Depending on the day, there might be less than a handful, or huge groups of relatively tame, yet wild, roos at **John Forrest National Park** in the Perth Hills. You'll see western greys, kookaburras and '28s', a local parrot with vibrant green colours, close to the park's paved walkways, near the car-park area. In September and October, prolific native wildflowers bloom – look closely at the bush to spot their astonishing details.

Backyard stickybeaking Drive around the semi-rural fields surrounding the hills townships of **Darlington** and **Kalamunda**, and park on the roadside. You'll spot roos naturally grazing in open paddocks, in vineyards (like Darlington Estate Winery), or in bush inside Kalamunda National Park, where there are also echidnas, bandicoot and native birds.

Dusk and dawn discoveries To explore on foot, consider camping at the Perth Hills Discovery Centre inside **Beelu National Park**. Take any of the bushwalking trails and keep an eye – and an ear – out for wildlife.

Easy viewing Big packs of smaller roos are reliably seen nibbling on the lawn near the pub within **Yanchep National Park**, in Perth's north. There's also a wheelchair-accessible boardwalk through a thicket of trees where a group of koalas live. You won't see them in the wild, though – koalas are not native to Western Australia. This colony was first started in 1938, for residents' enjoyment.

◎ Getting up Close

There's a certain excitement about observing wild creatures, whereas holding one is a guaranteed heart-melter.

Given that most of Australia's wildlife is nocturnal, the **Kanyana Wildlife Rehabilitation Centre** in the Perth Hills district of Lesmurdie runs all-ages night tours as well as daytime discovery programmes, including intimate, hands-on encounters.

In all, it looks after more than 3000 displaced, injured and orphaned creatures at the **Wildlife Hospital** each year. You might see echidnas, bilbies, red-tailed black cockatoos, possums and a range of other wildlife. The not-for-profit organisation also breeds threatened species that you'd struggle to see otherwise.

18 DRIVING
Perth's Valleys

FOOD | HIKING | NATURE

Go fruit picking in leafy orchards, discover one of the smallest cellar doors in WA and hike along beautiful bush trails – one with a food truck at its entry. The bucolic Perth Hills and their artsy, country-style townships are an easy 30-minute jaunt from the city, switching you from urban to rural with the vibe as well as the outlook.

BMPHOTOGRAPHER/
SHUTTERSTOCK ©

🗺 How to

Getting around Public transport is limited; it's best to drive.

When to go Spring and autumn are best for dramatic colours and blooms.

Bush magic There are dozens of excellent bush walks to explore, from the **Kalamunda Railway Heritage Trail** to the **Carmel Walk** and **Victoria Reservoir Trail**.

⊘ Insider Intel

Kookaburra Cinema (Mundaring) Fantastic outdoor movies under the stars.

Kishi (Kalamunda) A 20-seat, traditional-looking Japanese restaurant with great fresh fish.

Lions Lookout (Korung National Park) A 4km loop walk with city views and the Travelling Snack Restaurant food truck Friday to Sunday. Best at sunset.

■ **Recommendations by Nicolas Smeets**
Owner of the Travelling Snack Restaurant food truck; @travellingsnackrestaurant

0   2 km
0   1 mile

Kalamunda
National Park

02 Step inside the corrugated
shed and find a tiny cellar door
and restaurant known as **The
Vineyard Kitchen** in Bickley
Valley. Sit outside if you can –
the gardens are beautiful.

03 Locals describe the
Whistlepipe Gully hike as
like being in a magical fairy
playground. The 3.5km return
trail is relatively easy, with a
few rocky climbs.

o Kalamunda

Bickley

01 Book in to pick-your-own fruit block at
Carmel Cherry Farm. The small local orchard
grows delicious, exotic fruit, from cherries to
lychees. Other orchards may take drop-ins.

04 Follow the trail to the platform
lookouts at **Lesmurdie Falls**, then
descend into the bush and arrive
at the waterfall's feet.

Pickering
Brook
o

05 The fruit tree blossoms
at **Core Cider** in Pickering
Brook from September to
November are so prolific
they look like snow. Join a
tractor tour then grab a
tasting paddle.

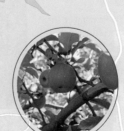

19
Eco Eats, Unicorns &
WATERFALLS

FOOD | SUSTAINABILITY | WINERY

▬▬ Psst! Want to know a little secret? This is perhaps Perth dining's best deal – for so many reasons. Here's how to tuck in to a genuinely sustainable, home-grown, hyper-seasonal, multi-course meal in Perth's forested outskirts. No Waste Monday lunches are arguably the best leftovers you'll ever eat.

🗺 How to

Getting here A car is the only way to go. It'll take about one hour from the city centre.

When to go Anytime of year is great, but the changing colours of the grapevine leaves and European trees in autumn makes for great eye candy.

Top tip Remember, the food served is strictly governed by the seasons, so if you love stonefruits and fresh herbs, go in summer, whereas in winter you'll see more root vegetables on the menu.

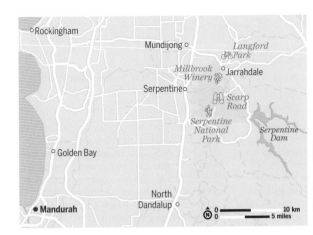

Left Serpentine Falls
Below Heirloom tomatoes

There aren't many restaurants that book out on a Monday. Nor are there many that use up the entire week's leftovers with one banging-value lunch sitting. Enter **No Waste Mondays** at Millbrook Winery in semi-rural Jarrahdale, where the eco-minded chef-gardener goes off-menu to leverage every bit of produce in his kitchen, before closing on Tuesday and Wednesday. He and his team fashion multi-course creations that often differ from table to table, delivering an environmentally friendly, bespoke dining experience.

The chef, who lives locally, tends an extraordinary kitchen garden and farm. There's fresh honey, free-range eggs, olives, orchard fruit and more than 100 varieties of **heirloom vegetables**. So while he creates dishes from odds and ends, they're no less exceptional. He's a restaurant industry **unicorn**, reaching the holy grail of zero waste (something, happily, many more are now striving for). You might expect to pay a pretty penny for this, but it's only A$50 (wine is extra) – one of many reasons it books out weeks in advance, despite still being an in-the-know experience.

Work off the indulgence with a hike through **Serpentine National Park**, part of the Darling Scarp, where waterfalls spill over sheer, jet-black rocks. Go beyond the main attraction and hike up the steep hill to discover rock pools and serene clusters of native bush, often with no one else around. While hopping wildlife is rarely seen during the day, there are some 70 species of birds twittering in the trees – look out for western rosellas, black cockatoos and yellow robins.

Do the Darling Range Like a Local

Mundijong Markets Hit the market on the first and third Wednesday of each month. There's heaps of random junk, but I always score at least one great rare find in the auction.

Langford Park I love the mountain bike track here. Don't fall off too bad, though – it's a long drive to the nearest hospital.

Jarrahdale Tavern Sip a perfectly poured pint of Guinness. The tavern's history dates back to 1894.

Scarp Road Go bush bashing through Scarp Road. At the top of the hill you can look back over the valley and see the farmhouse where I live at Millbrook.

■ **Recommendations by Guy Jeffreys**
Executive Chef at Millbrook Winery in Jarrahdale; @veg_guy

Listings

BEST OF THE REST

 ## Wine Time

Mandoon Estate

The options are copious at this sprawling Swan Valley property: choose from pizzas and pub grub at the Homestead Brewery, go fancy at Wild Swan restaurant or keep it simple with a bought-on-site picnic on The Llawn, where there's an art gallery for adults and a playground for kids. Head indoors to the cellar door to sample Mandoon's wines.

Upper Reach Winery

A new TreeHouse Bar, wine appreciation classes, a restaurant facing the vines and even a behind-the-scenes vineyard and winery tour chased with a wine tasting and two-course lunch...all available at this charming, family-run estate in the Swan Valley.

Plume Estate Vineyard

Expect boutique wine and designed-to-share seasonal dishes, while overlooking a gently sloping valley at this intimate Perth Hills estate.

Lancaster Wines

The outdoor tasting tin shed is cleverly positioned in the middle of the vineyard, making for a very scenic, but also very approachable, cheese and wine tasting. Bonus: it's opposite a chocolate factory.

 ## Pick-Your-Own Farms

Bickley Valley Asparagus Farm

Asparagus of all hues is picked each spring, usually from August, at this bucolic Perth Hills property with valley views. If you want to join the harvest, you should you stay overnight at the on-site B&B cottage as it starts early.

Otherwise drop in to the farm shed and pick up some snap-fresh organic produce.

The Orchard Perth

Citrus is on offer nearly year-round at this farm in the pretty Chittering Valley, a 45-minute drive from Perth. Besides picking oranges and mandarins, you can jump aboard a tractor tour, take part in occasional stargazing nights with pizza and live music, or even have a private picnic complete with freshly squeezed juices. Kids love feeding the farm animals.

S&R Orchard

From roughly December to March, you can pluck apples from the trees, but in September, the branches blossom and the orchard rows become selfie heaven. S&R runs tractor tours, has an animal farm and there's usually a food truck on-site and ice cream for sale.

Wanneroo Strawberry Picking Farm

There are a lot of strawberry farms on Perth's outskirts, all giving regular Facebook updates when they open for punters to come and pick (and you're allowed to munch as you go). Picking usually happens September to November and you pay by the box.

FERNANDA PHOTOS/SHUTTERSTOCK ©

Strawberry picking

Charming Drives

Yalgorup National Park

Unexpectedly beautiful lakes, woodlands and billabongs peel off the road that winds through Yalgorup National Park, which holds wetlands of international importance. Watch for waterbirds as you follow marked nature trails through the scrub.

Lake Clifton

Take the Old Coast Rd from Mandurah (rather than the newer, faster Forrest Hwy) and stop at Lake Clifton, where there's a boardwalk to rarely seen, early life forms known as thrombolites. They're not particularly pretty, but they are fascinating, and this is the largest living thrombolite reef in the southern hemisphere.

Destination Dining

Lontara $$$

Defiant Asian flavours ripple through the menu at Samphire resort's signature restaurant, overlooking the ocean on Rottnest Island. Always check the chilli factor with the staff, just in case.

Mistelle $$

Perched on a slope above grapevines at Hainault Vineyard in the Perth Hills, this balconied French restaurant serves delicate dishes overlooking leafy vineyard rows. It does classic dishes exceptionally well.

Luxe Island Seafood Cruise $$$

Savour a surprisingly good-value seafood degustation aboard a private vessel, with Rottnest Cruises. Before your white tablecloth, wine-matched lunch begins, try to catch a coveted western rock lobster in the boat's pots – are you game to pick one up?

Lake Clifton

 Pies, Hot Dogs & Burgers

Alfred's Kitchen $

Outdoor fire pits, rustic red bricks and old-school burgers have delivered Alfred's serious longevity. Located in Guildford, it's the city's longest-running roadside burger kitchen, with everything cooked on the grill until late.

Joey's Swan Valley Diner $

This cute pink and white eatery doubles as a drive-through hot dog and burger joint. That's a fun option, but most prefer to park the car and sit on the alfresco picnic tables to nosh down while the food is hot. They do breakfast, too.

Miami Bakehouse $

This bakery is a popular pit stop on the Forrest Hwy, loved for its award-winning pies, coffee and treats like raw raspberry and chocolate slice. Dozens of life-size, painted kangaroo sculptures decorate the alfresco area.

MARGARET RIVER & THE SOUTH WEST

BEACHES | FORESTS | WINERIES

Experience Margaret River & the South West online

MARIE HENSON / SHUTTERSTOCK ©

MARGARET RIVER & THE SOUTH WEST
Trip Builder

Pristine white beaches, thrilling surf breaks, gorgeous swathes of unique eucalyptus forests, epic hiking and biking trails, glittering underground caves and charming rural villages – this foodie and nature lovers' heaven is known worldwide for good reason.

Find a foodie paradise in the rolling green hills of **Ferguson Valley** (p128)
🚗 2hr from Perth

Discover more than 40 large-scale murals around the revitalised port city of **Bunbury/ Goombarup** (p131)
🚗 2hr from Perth

Be blown away with the world-class surf in **Yallingup**, literally the place of holes (p121)
🚗 30min from Margaret River

Base yourself in **Busselton/ Undalup** for a lively foreshore, white beaches and fun for the whole family (p126)
🚗 45min from Margaret River

Satisfy your senses around **Margaret River/Wooditchup**, the epicentre of a world-famous gourmet food and wine industry (p112)
🚗 3hr from Perth

Witness the annual northward migration of whales at **Flinders Bay** in Augusta as they pass long the coast (p122)
🚗 30min from Margaret River

INDIAN OCEAN

Stratham
Mumballup
Cape Naturaliste
Geographe Bay
Capel
Dunsborough
Donnybrook
○ Wilyabrup
Gracetown
○ Cowaramup
Nannup ○
Blackwood River
○ Karridale
○ Augusta
D'Entrecasteaux National Park
Cape Leeuwin
Flinders Bay
Leeuwin-Naturaliste
Northcliffe

0 ___ 25 km
0 ___ 10 miles
N
SOUTHERN OCEAN

Practicalities

ARRIVING

 Busselton Jetstar has direct flights from Melbourne to Busselton Margaret River Airport. Hire a car at the airport or join a tour.

 Bunbury Twice-daily trains arrive from Perth. From here, coaches run to destinations such as Margaret River and Augusta.

FIND YOUR WAY

Reliable maps are available from the visitor centres – never travel without one and don't rely on phone reception or GPS in remote areas.

MONEY

Card payment is common, especially in major centres, but carry some cash for out-of-the-way places and things like roadside stalls.

WHERE TO STAY

Town	Pros/Cons
Busselton	Luxury resorts, pet-friendly caravan parks and family spots. Short drive from Margaret River's attractions.
Yallingup	Exclusive luxury spas and spectacular private views through to rustic camping and glamping options.
Bridgetown/ Balingup	Glamping, farmstays and forest retreats in the rolling hills of the South West.
Pemberton	Cute forest cottages and lakes edged by elegant eucalyptus.

EATING & DRINKING

Famous for its food and wine scene, Margaret River is home to gourmet restaurants, wineries, craft breweries, innovative distilleries and artisanal providores selling chocolate (pictured above left), cheese, lavender ice cream (pictured below left) olive oil and more. Caves Rd, running from Cape Naturaliste to Cape Leeuwin, is dotted with many tempting culinary stops. You won't go hungry here.

Best farm experience
One Table Farm (p113)

Must-try lavender ice cream
Cape Lavender Teahouse (p137)

GETTING AROUND

Car Your best bet is to drive; if you are a confident driver, hire a 4WD and experience divine secret spots.

Bus The public-transport system is reliable and buses connect most towns, but it is limited by infrequent schedules.

Tours A plethora of tour options, from wineries to canoeing, can give you unique insights.

MARGARET RIVER & THE SOUTH WEST FIND YOUR FEET

| **BIRAK** DEC–JAN Busiest time of year, warming up, great for outdoors. | **BUNURU** FEB–MAR The hottest season and best time to get wet. | **DJERAN** APR–MAY Clear days and crisp nights; best for whale watching. | **MAKURU** JUN–JUL Cool, wet and wild, exhilarating storms. | **DJILBA** AUG-SEP Windy but getting warmer. | **KAMBARANG** OCT–NOV Spring wildflowers in full bloom. |

20 A Margaret River TASTER

FOOD | WINERIES | TOURS

As a leading Australian wine-growing region, you can be fairly certain you'll taste some exquisite wines, from cabernet sauvignon to chardonnay, and gourmet food while in the Margaret River/Wooditchup area. But don't miss out on getting your hands dirty – learn how food is grown and made, follow an organic wine trail or join an innovative tour to get up to date on lo-fi winemaking.

MICHELLE MORRISON PHOTOGRAPHY ©

How to

Getting around Pick a designated driver when visiting the wineries and breweries, and if no one's willing to put their hand up, join a bus tour.

Farm-gate food Roadside stalls around Manjimup offer the freshest produce – look out for seasonal stone fruit, berries, apples, asparagus and avocados.

Top tip Buy directly from the farmers themselves every Saturday morning at the **Margaret River Farmers Market**. Fresh and delish!

PHIL HILL/ALAMY STOCK PHOTO ©

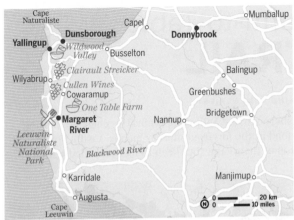

Left Wildwood Valley cooking school
Below Wine tasting, Cullen Wines

Cook up a feast On an organic farm in Cowaramup, the community-focused **One Table Farm** cooking school, run by Tim and Cree, teaches visitors about generative farming through a number of workshops and tours. Join the popular one-day sourdough class, a paddock-to-plate cooking class or the sustainable living farm tour. Thirty kilometres north in Yallingup, the **Wildwood Valley** cooking school, run by a trained chef, also offers classes that highlight fresh, local produce inspired by an interesting mix of Tuscan and Thai flavours.

Wineries With over 200 wineries in the region, there is certainly a lot of choice. **Cullen Wines** in Wilyabrup is known for impeccable organic and biodynamic wines, including the cabernet-based red Diana Madeline and chardonnay Kevin John wines. At **Clairault Streicker** create your own cabernet sauvignon or shiraz blend using real-deal equipment and under the expert guidance of a winemaker; you'll expand your knowledge of wine blending, what makes your palate zing, and then take your creation home. You even get to name your own drop.

A foodie festival The hugely popular **Western Australia Gourmet Escape** (gourmetescape.com.au), held in late November, combines the Margaret River region's pristine landscapes with an extravaganza of fresh, innovative food. Considered the premium showcase of Western Australia's food and wine, the star-studded guest list usually includes some of the biggest international and Australian names in the foodie world. It's not just for the elite gastronome but for people who simply love great food.

The Best Winery & Cultural Tours

Koomal Dreaming
Learn about the native ingredients used by many chefs in the Margaret River region on a tour led by Wadandi custodian Josh Whiteland. You'll forage for native bush foods, discover their cultural uses then gather around the campfire for a seasonal lunch – dishes might include kangaroo, emu, abalone, coastal herbs or quandong.

Margaret River Discovery Tour A handpicked winery and gourmet experience, plus exciting 4WD and canoeing adventures, led by tour guide Sean Blocksidge – and all in a day.

Walk Talk Taste Meet locals working in the food and beverage scene and hear about the produce that inspires them on an intimate evening tour of Margaret River town.

21 Farm-to-Table
TRALL

SUSTAINABILITY | FINE DINING | BREWERIES

In and around Dunsborough and Yallingup, innovative chefs are putting seasonable, locally grown food at the forefront of their menus. Visit a few fine-dining restaurants at the top of their game, but keep things grounded with a few casual brews.

JESSICA WYLD ©

🗺 How to

Getting around If you're not joining a tour, having a car is the best way to experience this trail – you never know what might take your fancy as you travel along.

When to go Many restaurants and wineries have grassy areas where you can sit outside and take in the views while kids burn energy on the playground. But many also have cosy wood fires and make for a great winter escape. If you want to visit farms, March–April and October–November are the driest months.

ⓘ What's up?

In southern WA, many place names end with *-up*, which, in the Bibbulmun language, literally means 'place of.'

'One of the biggest misconceptions is that Yallingup is the place of lovers, an early tourism idea because, 100 years ago, historic Caves House was popular for honeymooners. Yallingup is, in fact, the place of caves and holes, which makes sense given it's above the limestone ridge.'

■ **Insider knowledge by Iszaac Webb**
Wadandi Cultural Custodian & Knowledgeholder
@undalup.com

01 At **Eagle Bay Brewing Co** near Dunsborough, enjoy preservative-free brews, ridiculous views and a hearty modern Australian menu using ingredients direct from the kitchen garden.

02 Book a table at **Yarri** in Dunsborough for a modern Australian small-plates (pictured p114) or fine-dining menu inspired by local growers and paired with wines from Snake + Herring.

03 Everything about **Arimia** in Yallingup is driven by sustainability and a deep respect for the land. Produce grown at the on-site farm (from marron to olives) features on head chef Evan Hayter's fine-dining, seasonal menu.

04 Sustainable and wild harvested food is the focus of head chef Jed Gerrard's fine-dining degustation at award-winning **Wills Domain** in Yallingup – and the recipe is working. The wine's not bad either.

05 Settle in with a tasting paddle and a few share plates at the family-friendly **Wild Hop Brewing Company** in the Yallingup Hills. On summer Sundays, there's live music.

Cape Naturaliste

Bunker Bay

Eagle Bay

Meelup

Geographe Bay

Leeuwin-Naturaliste National Park

Dunsborough

Quindalup

INDIAN OCEAN

Yallingup

Wyadup

Wilyabrup

Leeuwin-Naturaliste National Park

Cowaramup

Gracetown

0   5 km
0   2.5 miles
Ⓝ

The Biggest, Tallest
& QUIRKIEST

01

02

03

04

05

01 Longest jetty
Busselton's endless wooden jetty is a whopping 1.8km long, making it the longest wooden jetty in the southern hemisphere and the second longest in the world.

02 Quirkiest
Yes, it's true: there's a town here completely populated by garden gnomes. Gnomesville (p129) has got to be seen to be believed.

03 Delicate wonder
With over 350 terrestrial orchid species in the South West, keep an eye out for the delicate spider orchids genus: the widespread *Caladenia* or the bright-yellow cowslip *Caladenia flava*.

04 Snorkelling joy
The natural pool known as the Aquarium (p121) off Smiths Beach Road is good for snorkelling.

05 Tallest trees
The cream-barked karri (*Eucalyptus diversicolor*) is the 14th-tallest tree in the world and the fifth-tallest eucalyptus.

06 The most south-westerly point
Cape Leeuwin Light-house (p132) stands where the Southern and Indian Oceans meet – a powerful blustery spot where you feel the might of the ocean.

07 Falling leaves
The Golden Trees Park in Balingup is the largest arbore-tum in the state and comes alive with amazing colours when the weather turns cool.

08 White wonder
In October Donny-brook is surrounded by trees awash with magnificent pink and white apple fruit blossom.

09 Natural rush
Injidup Natural Spa (p121) is created when waves crash over the rocks into a natural pool.

22

Go Forest
BATHING

FORESTS | WATERFALLS | HIKING

When you visit the South West region, you'll discover endless forests – unique, remote and pristine – making this the perfect spot for forest bathing, plus canoeing, fishing and bushwalking. Enter the forest and match the pace of the slow-moving rivers that wind through this region, taking in even the smallest details as you go.

AGEN' WOLF/SHUTTERSTOCK ©

🧭 How to

Getting around Having your own wheels is a wonderful way to explore.

When to go Cool and often enshrouded in a veil of mist, the Southern Forests grow here due to an especially wet climate; even in summer prepare for cool nights and frequent rain, especially June through September.

Tours If you are short of time or want to get off road, **Margaret River Exposed** can help maximise your time. For environmentally aware adventure tours, check out **Pemberton Hiking & Canoeing**.

LKONYA/SHUTTERSTOCK ©

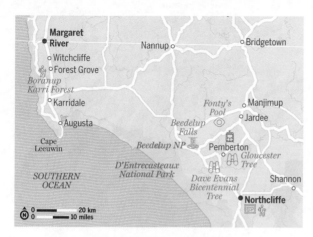

Margaret River
Nannup
Bridgetown
Witchcliffe
Forest Grove
Boranup Karri Forest
Karridale
Fonty's Pool
Manjimup
Jardee
Augusta
Beedelup Falls
Beedelup NP
Cape Leeuwin
Pemberton
Gloucester Tree
D'Entrecasteaux National Park
Dave Evans Bicentennial Tree
Shannon
SOUTHERN OCEAN
Northcliffe
0   20 km
0   10 miles

Left Gloucester Tree lookout
Below Beedelup Falls

Get grounded, be mindful The idea of forest bathing, a Japanese concept which emerged in the 1980s, encourages you to tune in to all of your senses when you go to the forest. And what better place a get a taste of forest bathing – or, indeed, just to appreciate the beauty of tall trees – than in the vast expanses of karri, marri and jarrah forests in the South West. Listen to the harmonious sound of waterfalls and birdsong, fill up your lungs with the rich earthy aroma of petrichor after a good rain – it's a welcome recalibration from busy beeping lives.

Zen-like beauty There are plenty of walks for forest bathing – just choose a spot and go. The **Beedelup Falls** in the Greater Beedelup National Park are spectacular in winter and the suspension bridge adds to the adventure. The zen-like beauty of **Boranup Karri Forest**, with its elegant, tall pale pink karri trees, is an earthly balance to the other attractions of the Margaret River region. The even size and symmetry of the karri trees is, ironically, due to logging here 100 years ago. Boranup Drive is a wonderful experience for people of all abilities.

All aboard! The charming and rickety **Pemberton Tramway** meanders through spectacular karri forest, crossing rickety trestle bridges until you arrive at the gorgeous Cascades in Gloucester National Park. This is a romantic and fun way to experience the Southern Forest, especially for those with limited mobility and kids, who love the ride. From Pemberton, you can also take the 86km **Karri Forest Explorer Drive**, which offers many chances to get out and smell the rich forest, including the 12km Heartbreak Trail.

Fire Look-out Trees

In the 1950s fire lookout towers were installed in the tallest trees to provide an early warning system for spotting smoke in the dry summers.

As the fifth-tallest eucalypt species, the karri towers over the forest canopy, providing a truly bird's-eye view.

The network of lookout towers have long been replaced by spotter planes, but you can still climb the metal rungs of the 53m **Gloucester Tree** in Gloucester National Park and the purpose-built 65m **Dave Evans Bicentennial Tree** in Warren National Park to get incredible views across the forest. Be warned – most people have pretty sore legs the next day.

23 An Almighty
COAST

BEACHES | SURFING | MARINE LIFE

From incredible rock formations to natural spas, aquariums and ocean creatures of all kinds, it's impossible to visit this region without spending time on the coast. While the area is known for its world-class surf and famous championships, there is plenty to experience if surfing isn't your style.

SARA BIANCARDI/SHUTTERSTOCK ©

📷 How to

Getting around All the places listed here are accessible with 2WD, but be aware that these are narrow and winding country roads, so watch out for wildlife. Always drive to the conditions.

When to visit Between June and December whales pass along this coast during their annual migration north to warmer waters.

Swim safe The ocean here is powerful and dangerous; observe warnings and be careful at all times, especially on rocky coastal areas. If a sign says 'No Swimming', then this is what it means.

NEXXT FRAME PHOTOGRAPHY/SHUTTERSTOCK ©

Rockin' Rocks & Natural Havens

The unique rock formations of the Leeuwin Naturaliste coast have been formed by the granite gneiss rocks being weathered over eons by the powerful movement of the waves. Some of the more notable are **Canal Rocks** near Yallingup and **Sugarloaf Rock** at Cape Naturaliste (also an incredible spot to watch the sunset).

A short drive from Sugarloaf Rock, to the other side of the cape, is **Meelup Beach**, with clear aquamarine waters and pure white sand – it's perfect for a tranquil swim. If a bit more froth has you bubbling, then **Injidup Natural Spa** is a hidden rock pool where waves crash over the rocks to form a spa-like sensation. For protected snorkelling head to the **Aquarium** near Smiths Beach.

AGENT WOLF/SHUTTERSTOCK ©

🏄 Yallingup Surfing

The WA surfing scene took hold in Yallingup in the early 1950s, with pioneer surfers making the long trek down south in search of waves. Yallingup Main Break can be OK for beginner surfers, but better for those with some experience. **Margaret River Surf School** offers lessons at Redgate Beach, while **Josh Palmateer's Surf Academy** runs out of Gnarabup Beach.

Above left Injidup Natural Spa
Above Sugarloaf Rock
Left Canal Rocks

Short Coastal Walks

There's nothing more invigorating than short walks to appreciate this coast. An easy and fully accessible option is the 4km walk from Cape Naturaliste Lighthouse (p132) to Sugarloaf Rock, while the 4km return hike to **Quinninup Falls** from Moses Rock car park takes you along part of the Cape to Cape Track (p136) for a true wilderness experience.

Hiking is best from September through November when wildflowers dot the coastal heath and you might spot the thrilling sprays of whales as they migrate northward. Plus it shouldn't be too hot, though keep a lookout for snakes.

Spotting Graceful Rays

Beautiful **Hamelin Bay**, to the south of Margaret River, is another beachside getaway. It's best known for its frequent

The Whale Highway

Flinders Bay in Augusta is where humpback, southern right and blue whales first reach land after crossing the ocean from Antarctica.

Between June and August, whale-watching cruises here enable you to get a close, though respectful, look. From September to November you can also take whale-watching trips from Dunsborough as the whales and calves return during the southerly migration after birthing in warmer waters in the north.

The **lighthouses** at Cape Naturalise and Cape Leeuwin also both provide great vantage points for whale-watchers, as does Sugarloaf Rock.

visitors – three different species of wild sea creatures: smooth stingrays, black stingrays and eagle rays. On calm mornings these locals can be seen around the picturesque old Hamelin Bay jetty and along the shallows of the beach. Remember these are wild creatures – keep a safe distance, don't touch them and definitely don't feed them.

4WD Adventures

The pristine **Yeagarup Dunes** form one of the largest land-locked dune systems in the world. Driving along the top of the dunes, with karri forest on one side and pure sand on the other, is awe-inspiring. Equally incredible are the towering hexagonal basalt columns of **Black Point**, formed 135 million years ago, as is nearby **Lake Jasper**, the largest natural freshwater lake in WA. These are true adventures for the experienced 4WDers. Alternatively, contact Pemberton Discovery Tours for its unique options.

Left Breaching whale
Above Basalt coast, Black Point

Iszaac Webb
*Wadandi Cultural Custodian &
Knowledgeholder*
@undalup.com

Living on Country

**TREAD SOFTLY WHEN
YOU VISIT, LEAVING
ONLY FOOTPRINTS**

Iszaac 'Zac' Webb is filled with an incredible passion and energy for sharing his culture and the traditions of the Wadandi people. Not only does he teach the significance of – and respect for – the traditional custodians of the land, he also partners with community and government organisations to increase knowledge and understanding.

Left Undalup Mob Wadandi people
Centre *Gnuraren* (western ringtail possum)
Right Spring-flowering willow myrtle

MATT DUNBAR/GETTY IMAGES ©

A Common Creation Story

Zac is a Wadandi Pibulmun man. His forefathers, the Wadandi (Saltwater people), lived on the land from Bunbury/Goombarup in the north, over the Capes area and through to the Blackwood River/Goribilyup. His grandmother is from the Pibulmun (the people of plenty where the forest meets the sea) whose family lived on the southern side of the river through to Nannup/Nanninup.

There are 14 clans that make up the larger Bibbulmun tribe, which loosely covers the area from Jurien Bay in the north to Esperance in the south. They share a common creation story: the people were camped around Lake Jasper/Yoondadadup. The basalt rock at Black Point/Bohlganup was a volcano, emitting gases that made the old people fall asleep. The earth shook and, when they woke, they split into the different clan groups who went in separate directions, eventually speaking distinct dialects though sharing similar customs but the same beliefs.

Teaching Traditional Ways

Zac works on multiple projects through the Undalup Association, all with one end: reigniting the knowledge of traditional ways, demystifying his culture and teaching the importance of Boodja (Country).

At the heart of one of these projects is working with local business, scientists and government organisations to up-skill young Aboriginal people. Through this

programme, students gain conventional certifications, as well as a valuable additional layer of cultural knowledge. For example, they might learn about the peppermint tree, but with Zac and his team they also learn it is the Wannang, from which women can make a *Wanna* (digging stick).

> When the Elders tell us off, they are teaching – we shouldn't take it personally, we should take it on board.

'*Gnuraren* (western ringtail possum) will eat the new leaves and build their *Drey* (nest) in a symbiotic relationship. The existing model of education teaches that the tree grows in *silicous* (sandy) soil; with cultural education we teach to look at the plants around it for context. In the most practical sense,' Zac says, 'having their classes on Country keeps young people more engaged and, most of all, proud of who they are.'

There are always some challenges. 'People don't know the right steps; they are scared of making mistakes. We all make mistakes; this is how we learn. When the Elders tell us off, they are teaching it – we shouldn't take it personally, we should take it on board.'

Zac's hope for the future is that we can all work hand in hand, as custodians of the land, find deeper connection to Country and also to reach an understanding that we are all connected.

♡ Everything is Connected

Kaya Nala Maat Kaya Noonduk (Hello Our Family Welcomes You) to Wadandi Boodja (Saltwater People's Country).

We are the country, and country is us. Everything is connected – every tree, rock or stone. When we visit the ocean, we greet it, we say hello. When we arrive at fresh water, we take a mouthful of water and hope to create a rainbow spray, and in doing so, pay homage to the rainbow serpent of the freshwater.

You don't have to call out greetings to the ocean or freshwater spirits like we do. Instead, you can give quiet gratitude in your head. You can pay respect silently; you can be present in the country. This is what we would like visitors to do.

24 Fun for All Ages in
BUSSELTON

FAMILY FRIENDLY | ADVENTURE | PLAYGROUNDS

▬▬▬ With family-oriented resorts and a fun foreshore area, Busselton/Undalup is a solid option for your first visit to the South West. In fact, the whole region is extremely child friendly – plan on making day trips along the coast, including to Dunsborough or Margaret River, and expect everyone to be happy.

ARIANA SVENSON/LONELY PLANET ©

🗺 How to

Getting arund Set yourself up in Busselton and then make day trips with a car.

Where to stay Busselton is the quintessential family resort town; accommodation options feature waterslides, bouncing pillows and endless pools.

Alternatively, farmstays and forest retreats often include playgrounds and animal feeding.

Make lots of stops In Myalup, the **Crooked Carrot** has a fun playground and restored vintage Melbourne trams, while the **Old Coast Road Brewery** has a WA-themed mini-golf course.

KAI EGAN/SHUTTERSTOCK ©

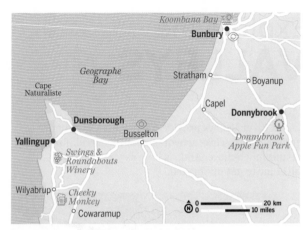

Koombana Bay
Bunbury
Geographe Bay
Cape Naturaliste
Stratham
Boyanup
Capel
Donnybrook
Dunsborough
Donnybrook Apple Fun Park
Busselton
Yallingup
Swings & Roundabouts Winery
Wilyabrup
Cheeky Monkey
Cowaramup
0 20 km
0 10 miles

Left Donnybrook Apple Fun Park
Below Fish beneath Busselton jetty

Busselton jetty & foreshore Kids of all ages will love taking the cute solar-powered train out to the end of the 1.8km-long Busselton jetty where the Underwater Observatory enraptures with a glimpse of what lies below. Back on land, there's an awesome playground, a seasonal fairground and the **Shelter Brewery Company** on the foreshore. At sunset take an easy walk, salt in your hair, ice cream in your hand, and there's really nothing quite like it. This place is pure family fun.

Kid-friendly wineries and breweries At most dining establishments in these parts, you'll find children's menus and kid-friendly playgrounds. A good choice is **Swings & Roundabouts Winery** in Yallingup, a 30-minute drive west of Busselton; everyone loves the yummy pizzas and swings here. Just 10 minutes further south along Caves Rd, the **Cheeky Monkey Brewpub** in Wilyabrup has an awesome family atmosphere and pours top brews with lake views.

The biggest there is Around 60km east of Busselton is the revamped **Donnybrook Apple Fun Park**, the long-time holder of 'the biggest free fun park in Australia' title. Combine your trip here with some fruit picking in season and Donnybrook makes a great day out.

Detour to Cowtown Cowaramup gets its name from the Aboriginal word 'cowara'. meaning purple crowned lorikeet – but at some point it was dubbed 'Cowtown' due to the area's thriving dairy industry. The town's main street features 40 life-sized black and white Friesian cows. Say hello to these quirky residents, stop in at the **Candy Cow** lolly shop, then head out of town for a scoop or two at **Millers Ice Creamery**.

Fun & Adrenaline in the South West

A Maze'n (Margaret River) One of the largest hedge mazes in Australia.

Discover Deadly (Carbunup River) An interesting introduction to snakes and other reptiles.

Koombana Bay (Bunbury) Extremely cool foreshore playground. Next door the **Bunbury Dolphin Discovery Centre** has a state-of-the-art interpretation centre and tours that get you up close to the dolphins that come to the bay most mornings in the warmer months (October to April).

Manjimup Timber Park Rad adventure playground with a mega slide that can be combined with the interactive Power Up Electricity Museum.

25

Explore the
VALLEYS

BIKING | FORESTS | MURALS

The Ferguson and Collie River Valleys provide the ultimate weekend getaways with rolling green hills, world-class artworks, pristine jarrah forest, adrenaline-filled adventure and much more. And, as long as you're in the know, you don't have to travel far to get unplugged.

DOMONABIKE/ALAMY STOCK PHOTO ©

📖 **How to**

Getting around The Collie River Valley is to the northeast of Bunbury while the Ferguson Valley is to the southeast. You'll be best off exploring the region with your own car.

Where to stay The area is dotted with cute farmstays, forest cottages and lakeside retreats. For camping head to Honeymoon Pool or Potters Gorge.

Where to eat Locals refer to the Fergie Valley as a foodie's dream – it has a dozen boutique wineries, two craft breweries and many passionate chefs.

ARIANA SVENSON/LONELY PLANET ©

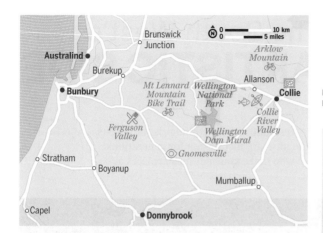

Left Wellington Dam
Below Honeymoon Pool

The world's biggest dam mural You literally can't miss the 8000-sq-metre mural along the **Wellington Dam** wall, just a short drive west of the small town of Collie. When artist Guido van Helten applied for the job, he didn't submit a design but instead proposed meeting with the people of the Collie River Valley. The final result, completed in 2021, is a mural that depicts their lives on the water. Follow the fantastic **Collie Mural Trail** to discover 40 murals in the area, including works by local Aboriginal peoples.

Ancient forest The massive expanse of the jarrah, marri and yarri forests of the **Wellington National Park** forms the lungs of this beautiful area and is heaven for hikers, bikers and birdwatchers. Year-round, the Collie River provides spots for swimming, canoeing and fishing – or simply a moment of meditation alongside the slow-moving river. While you can't miss the gloriously named **Honeymoon Pool**, make sure to do the full loop drive that meanders past swimming holes. Stop for a refreshing dip at **Long Pool**. From September to October the park comes alive with wildflowers.

Gnomesville This just might be the quirkiest spot you'll visit on your trip here. Some years ago a collection of garden gnomes congregated on a random roundabout 15km from Dardanup in the Ferguson Valley. Word got out and the community, well, grew and grew... At last count, there were over 10,000 gnomes. It's a lot of fun to take a look around. Be part of the story and bring your own gnome.

🚴 Mountain Biking in the Valley

Mt Lennard Mountain Bike Trail This trail at Pile Rd in Wellington National Park is considered one of WA's best. The organic nature of the trail means plenty of fresh air and trees, while the jump area at the bottom gives riders a place to go all out.

Arklow Mountain bike trails Nearby in Collie, these trails are a combination of old forestry tracks and railway formations for those with beginner and intermediate skills. Think multiple log rides, big jumps and fast roller-coast descents. These are part of the broader Wambenger Trails network, named for the threatened carnivorous marsupial that is native to these parts.

Hire bikes at the **Kiosk at the Dam**, or at **Crank'n Cycles'n Toys** in Collie, which gets great reviews.

26 The South West's
ARTISTIC SIDE

ART | GALLERIES | FESTIVALS

The dramatic South West landscape, with its pristine forests and rugged coastlines, is the ultimate inspiration for generations of artists, writers and those who make gourmet masterpieces and creations for the oenophile.

PHOTOGRAPHER PETER KOVACSY @ 2022
BLUE BIG SKY BY PETER KOVACSY

📖 Literary Festival

Held in May, the **Margaret River Readers & Writers Festival**, the biggest literary event in regional WA, brings together emerging and established storytellers from WA and further afield. This thought-provoking event provides artistic interaction with the incredible surrounding environment and is both inspiring and intriguing.

🗺 How to

When to go Immerse yourself in this creative, meandering itinerary at any time of the year.

Support local artists There's nothing better than meeting the maker of your chosen piece. Check if **Margaret River Region Open Studios** aligns with your visit, when over 100 artists open their studio doors.

Go even further Extend your road trip further south to Northcliffe where the 1.2km **Understory & Art Nature Trail** shows an incredible collection of artworks that grow symbiotically out of the forest.

03 One of Australia's most creative jewellers, **John Miller Design** in Yallingup creates meaningful pieces using the native flora, fauna and landscape for inspiration.

INDIAN OCEAN

Australind •

Bunbury

01 With over 40 murals around the port city, especially off Victoria St, Bunbury is a must stop for art lovers. Don't miss the **Bunbury Regional Art Gallery**.

Stratham ○

Cape Naturaliste

Geographe Bay

Dunsborough

Capel ○   **Donnybrook** •

Busselton ○

Yallingup

02 The **Bina Maya Gallery** in Quedjinup is the only Aboriginal fine art gallery in the Margaret River region. Drop in to see a fantastic range of works by Aboriginal peoples from across the country.

Wilyabrup

○ Cowaramup

Margaret River

Nannup ○

Leeuwin-Naturaliste National Park

Blackwood River

○ Karridale

Manjimup ○

○ Augusta

Flinders Bay

05 For those looking for a unique memory, make a visit to **Peter Kovacsy Studio** (pictured p130) in Pemberton. A well-known artist, he specialises in glass, timber and metal sculptures.

→ Pemberton

04 Margaret River is a wealth of artistic endeavour. Visit **Melting Pot Glass Studio** to learn more about glassmaking and **JahRoc Galleries** for handcrafted bespoke furniture.

D'Entrecasteaux National Park

Northcliffe •

N   0 ___ 20 km
    0 ___ 10 miles

27 Margaret River's
UNDERWORLD

CAVES | HISTORY | LIGHTHOUSES

Not all of Margaret River's treasures are visible at first glance. In fact, the entire Cape to Cape area, between the lighthouses of Cape Naturaliste and Cape Leeuwin, features caves eroded from the sandstone Leeuwin-Naturaliste Ridge. The result is a bejewelled network of 150 caves to explore along the aptly named Caves Rd and breathtaking lighthouses standing sentinel on a wilderness coast.

MATT DEAKIN/SHUTTERSTOCK ©

🗺 How to

Getting around It's around a 1½-hour drive from Cape to Cape on Caves Rd, along which is a wealth of caves, tranquil forest, and places to eat and drink. Reduce driving time by focusing on the northern or southern cape – don't try to do them all in one day.

When to go The caves all share the same slightly humid atmosphere, which makes them great to visit year-around.

Some fitness required Both lighthouses and all of the caves have a lot of steps; you'll need reasonable physical fitness.

🗼 The Cape Lighthouses

The **Cape Naturaliste** and **Cape Leeuwin Lighthouses**, both still operational, provide the perfect juxtaposition to the darkness of the caves with wild views, turbulent oceans and salty wind in your hair. Cape Leeuwin Lighthouse (pictured), the tallest mainland lighthouse in Australia, stands at the most south-westerly tip of the country.

Bunbury ●

Stratham ○

Cape Naturaliste Lighthouse

Geographe Bay

○ Capel

Bunker Bay

Dunsborough

Busselton

Yallingup ●

01 After a short guided tour through **Ngilgi Cave**, the most northerly of the caves, near Yallingup, take in the bright colours, stalagmites and stalactites in your own time.

Wilyabrup ○

Caves Rd

○ Cowaramup

Gracetown ○

02 The self-guided **Mammoth Cave**, near Margaret River town, provides universal access for the first section and is a good choice if you have little kids.

● **Margaret River**

04 For a more adventurous caving experience, head to the 86m-deep **Giants Cave**. Get in contact with Margaret River Climbing Co for caving and abseiling tours.

03 The remarkable **Lake Cave** is named for its beautiful lake and reflections, but it's just as memorable for its karri-framed entry (and lots of steps).

Leeuwin-Naturaliste National Park

Caves Rd

○ Karridale

05 The most southerly cave is considered by many to be the most beautiful: **Jewel Cave**, 8km northwest of Augusta, has three massive, crystal-encrusted chambers.

○ Augusta

Flinders Bay

Cape Leeuwin Lighthouse

0 — 20 km
0 — 10 miles

28

Up the Adrenaline
LEVEL

ADVENTURE | ZIPLINES | WATER SPORTS

▬▬ Seen it all before? Then up the ante with some fun-fuelled adventures on the land, on the water or up in the trees. From ziplining, ropes courses and horse riding to coasteering and kayaking, each adrenaline-filled activity will highlight the beauty of this region in a unique and unforgettable way.

TIM CAMPBELL ©

📱 **How to**

Get ready None of these activities are for the faint-hearted – but that's why the rewards are enormous. Always consider whether an activity is right for you, or have a chat with the operator first.

Hitting the surf
Margaret River isn't just for the experienced surfer. A number of surf schools operate in sheltered beaches and bays so that you can get a taste for this exhilarating sport.

LEAH PIRONE/SHUTTERSTOCK ©

CHAMELEONSEYE/GETTY IMAGES ©

Far left Ziplining with Forest Adventures Busselton
Below left Sugarloaf Rock
Left Kayaking, Margaret River

Ziplines and ropes course The area has two high rope adventure courses – it's an incredible way to challenge yourself while also getting close to the trees. You can zip through the towering tuart trees at **Forest Adventures Busselton** or head over to **Next Level Monkey Business** at Clancy's Fish Pub in Dunsborough.

On a SUP or kayak Options for stand-up paddleboarding (SUP) abound. For white-sand beaches and turquoise waters, try **Stand Up Surfing** at Gnarabup Beach. For kayakers and canoeists, sunset canoe tours on the Margaret River are offered by Margaret River Discovery Tours (p113), while a combination of wild food tastings and an exploration of this tranquil waterway are on the menu with **Bushtucker Tours**. For an unplugged kayaking experience, the pristine Blackwood River is South West Australia's largest river and offers unspoilt stretches of scenery – check out **Blackwood River Canoeing** or **Margaret River Stand Up Paddle** for tour options.

Thrilling boat rides If you want the buzz without exerting too much energy, then check out Dunsborough-based **Jet Adventures**. It's a guaranteed thrill as you jet across the water at 90km/h to gorgeous places along the coast, such as Castle Rock and Sugarloaf Rock, where people normally can't get to. Expect to see seals, dolphins, sea lions and birdlife, as well as an entirely new perspective of the coast.

What is Coasteering?

Coasteering is like mountaineering but on the ocean's edge – you surge through gaps in the canals, jump off rocks, zipline across channels and get to places no one else goes. When I first saw coasteering in Cornwall in the UK, I knew it would be awesome in Margaret River – we have warmer water, bigger waves and better fish.

Suited up in a wetsuit, lifejacket and helmet, people come to conquer their fear of the ocean or for an adrenaline rush. We do the coasteering at a spot that is great on all swells, and in fact it can be more exciting in winter. It's a totally immersive experience for everyone with jumping, splashing and even wave riding. Everyone agrees on one thing: it's a life-changing experience.

■ **Recommended by Cam O'Beirne**
Owner of Margaret River Adventure Co
@margaretriveradventure

Listings

BEST OF THE REST

 Epic Adventures

Bibbulmun Track

One of the world's great long-distance walking trails, this 1000km track goes from Kalamunda/Calamunnda outside Perth to Albany/Kinjarling on the South Coast. Hiking a short section can be just as rewarding.

Cape to Cape Track

Hike this wonderful 124km track that follows the Leeuwin-Naturaliste Ridge from Cape Naturaliste in the north to Cape Leeuwin in the south. The full trek takes about seven days.

Munda Biddi Trail

Supposedly the longest continuous bike trail in the world, the Munda Biddi Trail covers over 1000km, passing through Collie, Donnybrook, Manjimup and Northcliffe before heading down to the South Coast. Munda Biddi means 'path through the forest'.

 Community Connection

Ngalang Wongi Aboriginal Cultural Tours

Join a fun and informative walking tour with multi-talented Tony to learn about the culture and food of the Noongar peoples in and around Bunbury.

Donnybrook Artisan Hub

Support local artists at the Donnybrook Artisan Hub where a diverse range of arts and crafts are on show. Makers on Mount in Manjimup is another good option.

Origins Centre

A weekend retreat at the Origins Centre offers a tranquil setting alongside the charming Balingup Brook, with beautiful gardens and native bush.

 Start with Coffee

White Elephant Cafe $$

Top coffee, mouth-watering breakfasts and a choice beachside location overlooking the waves at Gnarabup Beach.

Drift $$

Enjoy a cosy breakfast or brunch made from excellent fresh produce at this Margaret River institution.

Egberts $

Loved by Margaret River locals for the sensational coffee, delicious pastries and smiling staff.

 Food for the Soul

Hidden River Estate $$

With stunning views across the vines, Hidden River Estate Pemberton offers tastings and delicious meals. Families love the converted tram carriage that adjoins a cubby house.

Hooked Up Fish n Chips $

Take your blanket and pull up a spot to watch the sunset over Surfers Point at Prevelly while munching on delicious fish and chips. During the day, watch the surf.

ARIANA SVENSON/LONELY PLANET ©

Olio Bello

Miki's Open Kitchen — $$$

Fresh local produce is used and adapted to create unique tastes for the tailor-made Japanese degustation menu in Margaret River.

Park Donnybrook — $

In the Goods Shed at Station Sq, Park Donnybrook serves wholesome, local and lovingly prepared cakes and savoury dishes. It makes a great road-trip stop.

Unique Flavours

Yallingup Cheese Company

Craft your own artisanal cheese using organic milk in an immersive workshop experience led by the head cheesemaker, and learn how to pair cheese and wine.

Tinderbox

Step into this whimsical store and let the incredible aroma of the divine handmade natural beauty products relax your senses.

Cape Lavender Teahouse

A sweet stop for tea, scones and lavender treats, Cape Lavender Teahouse in Yallingup is famous for its lavender ice cream.

Olio Bello

Be transported to the Mediterranean at this organic olive farm and tasting room in Cowaramup. The cafe-restaurant serves delicious pasta and there is a gift shop.

Craft Brews

Beerfarm

Innovative Beerfarm in Metricup offers many intriguing beers, including Calm Ya Farm and Milk Stout. It also caters for all the family, with great kids' activities.

Nannup Brewing Company

Head to this Nannup microbrewery, opened in 2021, for relaxed vibes, curated music events, pub food and, of course, great craft beer.

Truffle, Manjimup

The Cidery

With the deliciously tart Pink Lady apple being developed in Manjimup, it was the natural choice for the unique all-natural ciders and apple juices of The Cidery at Bridgetown.

Local Celebrations

Bridgetown Blues Festival

This blues festival in November attracts some of the best acts from around the world and is a wonderful springboard for Aussie talent – John Butler started on the streets here.

Nannup Garden Festival

Tulips are the centrepiece of the Nannup Garden Festival, with a record-breaking 20,000 bulbs planted in recent years. Held in the second half of August.

Manjimup Cherry Harmony Festival

Each December the town of Manjimup is painted red in celebration of the cherry harvest and the diversity of the horticultural industry that grows in this veritable food bowl.

Truffle Kerfuffle Festival

The Manjimup area is the southern hemisphere's largest producer of black Périgord truffles. Each June they are celebrated with the Truffle Kerfuffle Festival held at Fonty's Pool.

Scan to find more things to do in Margaret River & the South West online

SOUTH COAST

BEACHES | WINERIES | FOOD

SOUTH COAST
Trip Builder

There is no place that captures the breathtaking power of the ocean quite like the South Coast of Western Australia. From isolated windswept beaches through to massive ancient forests, rugged mountain climbs to remote islands, this is a destination for true wilderness lovers. Pair this with some of the freshest air you'll ever breathe, award-winning wineries and a surprisingly innovative food scene and you have paradise in the rough.

Take a selfie on the beach at Lucky Bay and explore the sublime beaches around **Esperance** (p145)
🚗 5hr from Albany

Explore the botanically significant, diverse **Fitzgerald River National Park** from Hopetoun (p143)
🚗 2hr from Esperance

Visit the only place in Australia where you can experience the might of the killer whale: Bremer Bay (p143)
🚗 2hr from Albany

Take in the wild and pristine land-scape of the **Walpole Wilderness Area**, with ancient forests and imposing granite peaks (p143)
🚗 30min from Denmark

Don't miss the sweepings views from the **Granite Skywalk** at Granite Rock in Porongurup National Park (p143)
🚗 45min from Albany

Learn about different aspects of Australia's history in the charming port of **Albany/Kinjarling** (p156)
🚗 5hr from Perth

Narrogin
Lake Grace
Lake King
Salmon Gums
Dundas Nature Reserve
Grass Patch
Dumbleyung
Wagin
Pingrup
Ravensthorpe
Munglinup
Lucky Bay
Katanning
Jerramungup
Ongerup
Hopetoun
Stokes National Park
Cape Le Grand National Park
Stirling Range National Park
Manjimup
Cranbrook
Wellstead
Pemberton
Mt Barker
Porongurup National Park
Denmark
Walpole

JOHANNA POOL/SHUTTERSTOCK ©

SOUTHERN OCEAN

0 100 km
0 50 miles

Practicalities

ARRIVING

✈ Esperance and Albany have daily flights arrive from Perth from where you can then hire a car.

CONNECT

Mobile is pretty good in the towns; between towns reception is spotty to non-existent. Visitor centres are staffed by volunteers but can offer on-the-spot advice and maps.

MONEY

Card payment is common in major towns; carry some cash for remote areas, farm-gate trails, farmers markets and inevitable internet outages.

WHERE TO STAY

Town	Pros/Cons
Albany	Something for everyone, with access to supplies and delicious food.
Denmark	Boutique and luxury accommodation right through to utilitarian stays by the sea.
Esperance	World-class off-grid camping in Cape Le Grande National Park; the town has options too.
Porongorup Area	Get away from it all in a variety of places to stays, many featuring views of the ranges.

EATING & DRINKING

The fresh produce of this region – oysters (pictured top left), seafood, marron, heirloom vegetables, cheeses, the list goes on – is as exceptional as the wine (pictured bottom left). Trust us, everything tastes sensational on the South Coast.

Must-try marron
Due South (p151)

Best winery
Any in the Great Southern wine region (p151)

GETTING AROUND

Car The best option, especially if you also plan to visit the South West. Many remote spots require a 4WD.

Bus Buses run between Perth, Esperance, Albany and along the South Coast. Schedules are infrequent (at best, daily).

City tours A fun way to explore Albany and surrounds is with Busy Blue Bus Tours.

SOUTH COAST FIND YOUR FEET

BIRAK	**BUNURU**	**DJERAN**	**MAKURU**	**DJILBA**	**KAMBARANG**
DEC–JAN	FEB–MAR	APR–MAY	JUN–JUL	AUG–SEP	OCT–NOV
Dry, sunny, long days – great for water sports.	Hot – go fishing.	Colours deepen and perfect mild weather.	Hardy folk won't mind the torrential downpours.	Warm weather arrives – it's time to get outdoors.	Wildflowers dot the coast.

29 The Power of **WILDERNESS**

NATIONAL PARKS | VIEWPOINTS | HIKING

Everything about the South Coast's magnificent national parks is grand and breathtaking, from the towering red tingle trees and canopy walkway views to the huge botanical diversity. Whether doing a gentle walk, hike or even kayaking, explore a world rich with Gondwanan relictual species – some are clearly dinosaur sized, and others are not.

PHILIP SCHUBERT/SHUTTERSTOCK ©

🏛 **How to**

Getting around You'll be best off with your own car here; some national parks roads are unsealed but you should manage with a 2WD.

When to visit Wildflower season starts in late September and runs through to November – try not to miss it.

Top tip Save money by investing in a National Parks Pass so you can visit all parks across the state; five-, 14- or 30-day options and annual passes are available online.

ADWO/SHUTTERSTOCK ©

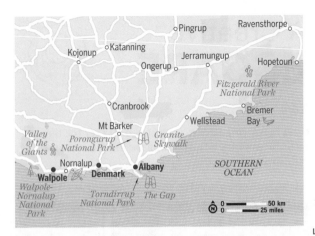

Left Granite Skywalk, Castle Rock
Below Valley of the Giants Tree Top Walk

Walk with giants The **Walpole-Nornalup National Park** is home to red tingle trees, which are among some of the largest living eucalyptus (reaching up to 45m tall with a girth of around 22m). These fascinating trees grow in a tiny patch of forest which has maintained a special microclimate – not dissimilar to the days of the dinosaurs. Take the 13km return kayaking or paddle trail from the Nornalup town jetty up the magnificent Frankland River to the **Monastery Landing**, named for its awe-inspiring solemnity. Or visit the 40m-high, 600m-long **Valley of the Giants Tree Top Walk** – a park highlight.

Stunning views The 670m-high suspended **Granite Skywalk** at Castle Rock takes you through the karri and marri forest of Porongurup National Park to scenic lookout points. In **Torndirrup National Park**, the impressive Gap falls 25m into the ocean, eroded away by the waves of the powerful Great Southern Ocean. The Natural Bridge and Blowholes are other inspiring natural features here.

A pristine wilderness Finally, don't miss the majesty of the **Fitzgerald River National Park**, one of the most diverse botanical regions on earth and a paradise for nature lovers and adventurers. On the edge of the Southern Ocean, the quartzite peak of **East Mt Barren** provides 360-degree views after a short but challenging climb to the summit (2.6km return), accessed from the Hopetoun side. You can also access the remote Fitzgerald from **Bremer Bay**, where over 150 killer whales come to feed from January to March each year.

🗺 WOW Wilderness

If you do one tour, then this should be it.

Meet passionate ecoguide Gary Muir on a **WOW Wilderness** (wowwilderness.com.au) cruise across the pristine Nornalup Inlet to Circus Beach.

Gary's passion for the environment – nay, the world – and its history are woven together with his in-depth knowledge of the Walpole Wilderness area. A gifted orator, comedian and scientist, Gary teaches about the incredible biodiversity in this beautiful part of the world, as well as the idea that we are all linked – even to Walpole.

30 A Creative ESCAPE

ART | MURALS | STORYTELLING

Discover the spirit and the talented artists – scattered all over the the South Coast – that use this fertile country as inspiration for unique artworks depicting this geographically diverse land.

How to

Getting around Having your own car is going to make an exploration of these beautiful artworks a lot easier.

Spring festivals Time your visit with the **Southern Art & Craft Trail** (September), a regional celebration of textiles, jewellery, printmaking and woodcraft; the **Bloom Festival** (mid-September to October), which celebrates the wildflower tapestries across the region; and the **Esperance Wildflower Festival** (September).

ⓘ Heartland Journeys

Immerse yourself in this landscape by visiting the **Heartland Journeys** (heartlandjourneys. com.au) website, a valuable project created by Gondwana Link (p149), for thoughtfully constructed self-guided tours, a wealth of information about local places, nature and responsible travel, plus many stories from Noongar people about how to maintain Boodja (Country).

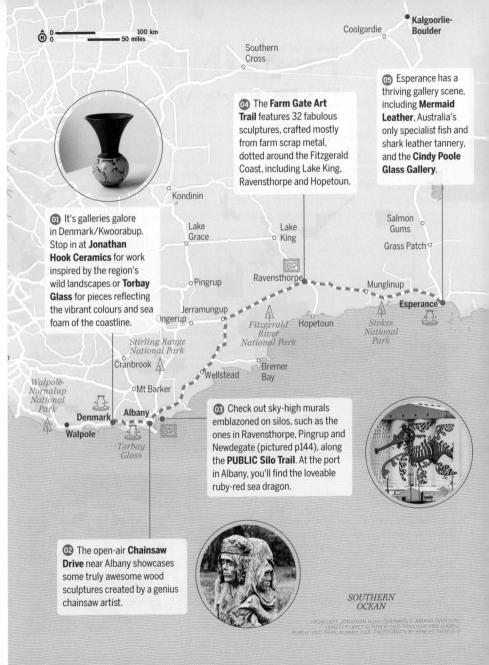

0 100 km
0 50 miles

Kalgoorlie-
Boulder

Coolgardie

Southern
Cross

04 The **Farm Gate Art Trail** features 32 fabulous sculptures, crafted mostly from farm scrap metal, dotted around the Fitzgerald Coast, including Lake King, Ravensthorpe and Hopetoun.

05 Esperance has a thriving gallery scene, including **Mermaid Leather**, Australia's only specialist fish and shark leather tannery, and the **Cindy Poole Glass Gallery**.

Kondinin

01 It's galleries galore in Denmark/Kwoorabup. Stop in at **Jonathan Hook Ceramics** for work inspired by the region's wild landscapes or **Torbay Glass** for pieces reflecting the vibrant colours and sea foam of the coastline.

Lake
Grace

Lake
King

Salmon
Gums

Grass Patch

Pingrup

Ravensthorpe

Munglinup

Esperance

Jerramungup

Ongerup

*Fitzgerald
River
National Park*

Hopetoun

*Stokes
National
Park*

*Stirling Range
National Park*

Cranbrook

Wellstead

Bremer
Bay

*Walpole-
Nornalup
National
Park*

Mt Barker

Denmark

Albany

Walpole

*Torbay
Glass*

03 Check out sky-high murals emblazoned on silos, such as the ones in Ravensthorpe, Pingrup and Newdegate (pictured p144), along the **PUBLIC Silo Trail**. At the port in Albany, you'll find the loveable ruby-red sea dragon.

02 The open-air **Chainsaw Drive** near Albany showcases some truly awesome wood sculptures created by a genius chainsaw artist.

*SOUTHERN
OCEAN*

FROM LEFT: JONATHAN HOOK CERAMICS & ARIANA SVENSON;
LONELY PLANET & PUBLIC SILO TRAIL YOK AND SHERYO,
PUBLIC SILO TRAIL ALBANY, 2018. PHOTOGRAPH BY BEWLEY SHAYLO ©

31 FEELING
Denmark's Vibe

ARTS | GOURMET FOOD | BEACHES

▬▬▬ Denmark/Kwoorabup charms with its tree-lined country drives, amazing food, wineries and breweries, and turquoise beaches just a stone's throw from town. But to really get to know this place, meet the folks that make Denmark tick. Not only do they embrace art and music, it's also home to one of WA's long-running intentional living communities and many other eco-living projects.

DENMARK YOGA CENTRE ©

🧘 How to

When to go Denmark is busiest from Christmas through all of January and then again at Easter. The rest of the year is more chilled.

Take it slow Allow time to wander along Strickland St and explore the boutiques, healing centres and health-food shops.

Family-friendly Denmark Good Food Factory produces tasty cider and toffee in William Bay and is home to the massive **Giant Cone** and a fun soccer golf course. Kids also love getting up close to the animals at **Denmark Animal Farm**.

DENMARK FARMHOUSE CHEESE & DUCKETTS MILL WINES ©

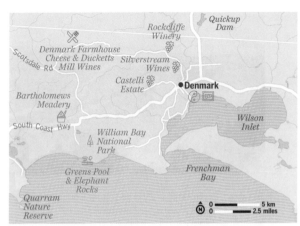

Rockcliffe Winery
Quickup Dam
Denmark Farmhouse Cheese & Ducketts Mill Wines
Scotsdale Rd
Silverstream Wines
Castelli Estate
●Denmark
Bartholomews Meadery
South Coast Hwy
Wilson Inlet
William Bay National Park
Greens Pool & Elephant Rocks
Frenchman Bay
Quarram Nature Reserve

0 — 5 km
0 — 2.5 miles

Left Denmark Yoga Centre
Below Platter, Denmark Farmhouse Cheese & Ducketts Mill Wines

SOUTH COAST EXPERIENCES

Empowering Artists

With its creative vibe, you immediately sense that Denmark is a crucible of artistic passion, and **Denmark Arts**, which organises a number of arts events and festivals, goes a long way to support this.

Now 40 years old, the **Denmark Arts Markets** showcase the talent of craftspeople, musicians and entertainers. 'I've travelled to markets through the state and nowhere is there a stage that provides such a springboard for artists to find their feet.

The **Festival of Voice** (denmarkfestivalofvoice. com.au), held in June, is more of your average music festival – it celebrates the power and beauty of voice in all its forms. The audience and performers leave deeply touched. In October, **Brave New Works** helps the community bring to life innovative performing projects.'

■ Recommended by Kira Schimmelpfennig *Denmark Arts Market Coordinator* @denmarkfestivalofvoice.com.au

Yoga and wellness The amount of natural therapies on offer in Denmark is astounding – options include massage therapy, sound healing, wellness retreats and, of course, yoga. Take a class with a true forest yogi at **Karuna Sanctuary** or explore the teachings at the **Denmark Yoga Centre**. Better yet, base yourself at the Aiyana Forest Retreat, the Cove or any one of the forest cottages on offer (there are many) and then DIY your very own wellness stay. Check out the noticeboards around town for up-to-date classes and therapies. Pure bliss!

Farm-gate trails The best way to introduce yourself to Denmark's diverse food offerings is by taking a drive through the magnificent surrounding countryside and stopping at some of the many wineries, boutique food providers or art galleries (p159). Do a tasting at **Silverstream Wines**, enjoy the magnificent views at **Castelli Estate** or visit **Rockcliffe Winery** for a glass of shiraz or cabernet sauvignon and live music. Still not satisfied? The unique honey ice cream from **Bartholomew's Meadery** or a cheese platter at **Denmark Farmhouse Cheese & Ducketts Mill Wines** might do the trick.

Turquoise water and granite elephants On the edge of William Bay National Park, a quick drive southwest of Denmark, **Greens Pool** is a perfect turquoise natural pool fringed by white sands. A short walk around the headland is **Elephant Rocks**, where towering granite boulders look like herds of elephants standing in the water. Both are top selfie spots but also a magnificent introduction to the South Coast. The sheltered water provides calm conditions for swimming and snorkelling; there are also some great short hikes.

Southwest Australia's Biodiversity Hotspot

SOME OF THE MOST BIOLOGICALLY DIVERSE ECOSYSTEMS ON EARTH

The Southwest Australia Biodiversity Hotspot extends over the whole southwestern tip of WA, from Exmouth in the north to Esperance in the south, loosely corresponding to the land of the Noongar peoples. This is an area of exceptional natural beauty and home to thousands of endemic plants and animals.

Left Fitzgerald River National Park
Centre Numbat (banded anteater)
Right WA Christmas tree (*Nuytsia floribunda*)

ALFOTOKUNST/SHUTTERSTOCK ©

Travel to this part of the world and you will find yourself in a place that has the highest concentration of rare and endangered species in Australia. Indeed, so significant are the plants and animals here that the area was recognised as the Southwest Australia Biodiversity Hotspot. It is one of 36 hotspots in the world, and for a long time was the only one in Australia.

The hotspot is home to 5570 plant species, half of which can't be found anywhere else in the world. These unique plants are, in turn, supported by a vast range of species including seven species of mammals (such as the quokka, numbat and 12 endemic species of birds). There are also 34 species of reptiles and 28 species of frogs endemic to this region.

With research continuing every day, groups of passionate scientists are unravelling mysteries of such fascinating creatures as jewel beetles and even moths that pollinate plants. While spiders and other invertebrates are not so well known, it is highly likely their level of endemism is also high.

Due to agriculture and the introduction of foreign species, only 30% of Southwest Australia's original vegetation remains in a pristine condition. But the hotspot designation means that conservation, restoration and protection are today at the forefront of work here.

The Fitzgerald Biosphere

At the heart of the hotspot are the Stirling Range and Fitzgerald River National Parks, where the diversity of landscapes means that, within just 5km, you might find a

KEN GRIFFITHS/SHUTTERSTOCK ©

ALFOTOKUNST/SHUTTERSTOCK ©

number of completely different suites of plant species. This is also where you can find the Fitzgerald Biosphere, one of the world's most botanically significant regions and a Unesco World Network of Biosphere Reserve. Not only is it special because of its pristine state, but for the zone of cooperation around

> The hotspot designation means that conservation, restoration and protection are at the forefront of work here.

it. This area has been embraced by community groups who have created opportunities for people to learn more. The Yongergnow Australian Malleefowl Centre in Ongerup, for example, provides the chance to see the endangered Malleefowl up close.

Gondwana Link

Another conservation project is Gondwana Link, which aims to establish a 1000km stretch of healthy, connected wildlife habitat from the wet forests of the southwest to the dry woodlands and mallee of inland Australia. The project is focused on such things as protecting bushland, restoring habitat health as well as connecting small individual projects to the bigger picture. The importance of having people on board with the scientific pursuits – especially visitors – is also key. For this reason, the Heartland Journeys website (p144) was created, through which stories about the important natural values of the area and Aboriginal peoples' management of the land are shared.

✍ Cryptic Bird Puzzles

While the quokka is the cute and slightly brash poster child of the Southwest Australia Biodiversity Hotspot, many of the threatened birds are really cryptic and that's what makes them so exciting.

We were at Cheynes Beach recently, not far from Albany, and we'd spent a bit of time getting our ears accustomed to the different calls. We heard the calls of a noisy scrub-bird, western whipbird, western bristle-bird and the Australasian bittern, and all three species of black cockatoo flew overhead.

The secret to immersing yourself in this wildly diverse landscape is simple – be observant. Stop, look and listen, and you'll uncover a world that is so special it almost brings tears to the eye. Being prepared and knowing what to look for is vital. An excellent guide is *Morcombe's Birds of Australia*.

■ **Tips by Sarah Comer**
Regional Ecologist, Department of Biodiversity, Parks & Attractions
@exploreparkswa

32 The South Coast
FOR FOODIES

AWARD-WINNING CUISINE | DISTILLERIES | REGIONAL SPECIALITIES

While the South Coast's big sister Margaret River/Wooditchup has all the fame, those in the know have a little secret – it's all happening down on the South Coast. The passionate food scene here includes award-winning wines, innovative chefs, cannabis-based gin and the region's answer to crayfish or lobster – the endemic marron.

ZOE VAN ZANTEN ©

🗺 How to

When to go For long relaxed lunches, avoid long weekends or public holidays; with fresh food available year-round, you'll discover something new whatever the season.

Food festival Held in May, *Taste Great Southern* is a celebration of regional food and wine, including long table lunches, markets and music and wine sessions.

Fresh markets The **Albany Farmers Markets** (Collie St) sells fresh seasonal produce direct to the community. Also check out the **Albany Boat Shed Markets**.

ARIANA SVENSON/LONELY PLANET ©

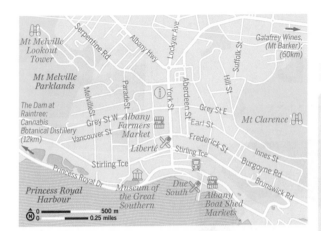

Left The Dam at Raintree
Below BBQ marron

SOUTH COAST EXPERIENCES

The Great Southern Wine Region

The picturesque Great Southern region – encompassing Denmark, Albany, Mt Barker, Franklin River and Porongurup – is a rising star in the Australian wine industry and is becoming increasingly well known for producing some high-quality wines. Winemaker Kim Tyrer of Galafrey Wines, located in Mt Barker, 60km northeast of Albany, says it's a region for those in the know. 'In the Great Southern our wines are underestimated but offer excellent quality.

'We have warm days but cool nights here, giving us slow ripening periods. We make some great shiraz and riesling. Each year our wines are well represented in the top 25 rieslings in Australia, including wines from Castle Rock, Dukes, Galafrey and Forest Hill.'

■ Recommended by Kim Tyrer
CEO & Winemaker at Galafrey Wines
@galafreywines

WA's new foodie capital Yep, we heard Albany described that way! And it all comes down to the growing group of forward-thinking chefs and producers getting together to have conversations about fresh produce and food. Start your foodie adventures here with an unlikely trip to bohemian Paris at award-winning **Liberté**, located within the historic London Hotel. Owner and chef Amy Hamilton has paired the decor perfectly to the French Vietnamese dishes.

Freshwater crayfish The shell of the marron, which is endemic to southwestern Australia, is normally black or brown but can also be a vibrant cobalt blue. All turn to red when cooked. Whatever you do, don't miss the opportunity to try it. Head to the cavernous **Due South** in Albany for seasonal specials like the Korean chilli crab and marron, or take a drive to the family-run **Marron Tale Cafe & Farm** near Bow Bridge for the marron fettuccine. If you're self-catering, farm-gate fresh marron is sold around the region.

Heady pours Ready for something a bit different? Head to **The Dam at Raintree** (thedam.raintree.com.au), a stunning property just out of Denmark, to sample hemp-distilled spirits in the seltzers and cocktails and an excellent seasonal menu featuring local produce (including marron). You can also tour the on-site **Cannabis Botanical Distillery**, one of the first distilleries in WA that uses cannabis sativa to make its spirit base. Behind this project is innovative farmer Steve Birkbeck.

Outta this
WORLD

01 Bubblegum pink
Take a flight from Esperance to see the hot-pink Lake Hillier, located on Middle Island.

02 Australia's best beach 2022
The incongruously named Misery Beach has crystal-white sand, azure waters and a spectacular granite backdrop.

03 Bluff Knoll
The state's third highest peak, a great hike (p158) and, famously, the only place it snows in WA.

04 Stonehenge
Yup, you read that right! Visit a full-size replica made of Esperance Pink Granite.

05 Bald Head
The huge granite headland at the end of a challenging 13km return walk on the Flinders Peninsula.

06 The tassel flower
This flower (Leuco-pogon verticillatus) was the design inspiration for the pylons at the Valley of the Giants Tree Top Walk (p143) near Walpole.

07 Chittic
The pretty orange, red or yellow flower of the *Lambertia inermis* pops out during spring and summer.

08 Royal hakea
Keep an eye out for the extraterrestrial-looking leaves of this endemic plant from June to August; its Noongar name is *Tallyongut*.

09 Monumental public art
The PUBLIC Silo mural (p145) by Amok Island in Ravensthorpe showcases the six stages of a flowering *Banksia baxteri*.

10 Resident kangaroos
Lucky Bay near Esperance is so beautiful that even the local kangaroos choose to hang out here.

33 For Beach **LOVERS**

WHITE SAND | SWIMMING | SOLITUDE

The South Coast juxtaposes a wild and powerful coastline with turquoise water, long expanses of white sand and, quite often, blissful seclusion. Whether you're tempted by the remote white swathes found in national parks or the gentle kid-friendly city beaches with waterfront cafes in sight, getting your toes in the sand should be a top priority.

ARIANA SVENSON/LONELY PLANET ©

🗺 **How to**

Swim safe Don't underestimate the water on the South Coast. Follow the signs and look out for rips, even on popular swimming beaches.

Avoid the crowds Most beaches see few people, except on school and public holidays. To explore off the beaten track, hire a 4WD.

Water sports SUP or snorkel at spots like Peaceful Bay, Twilight Beach in Esperance and Greens Pool. The water can be very cold year-round; consider wearing a wetsuit or shorty.

ARIANA SVENSON/LONELY PLANET ©

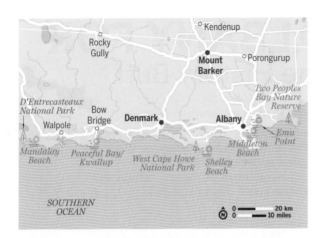

Left Middleton Beach, Albany
Below Mandalay Beach, Walpole

SOUTH COAST EXPERIENCES

Family-friendly Picturesque **Middleton Beach** and **Emu Point**, both within Albany city, offer the quintessential day at the seaside experience with safe swimming enclosures, playgrounds for the kiddies and excellent cafes such as Three Anchors at Middleton Beach and Emu Point Cafe. Both beaches get bonus points for the excellent walking trails and photo ops.

Easy access The only 2WD accessible spot in West Cape Howe National Park is **Shelley Beach** – and what a spot! This pristine beach is perfect for swimming, camping and fishing, and it's the best spot on the South Coast for paragliding – watch as these graceful crafts flip and float on the breeze from a cliff above you.

A peaceful option Between Walpole and Denmark, **Peaceful Bay/Kwallup** is a less popular option than nearby Greens Pool (p147) in William Bay National Park, but this pretty turquoise bay has a sheltered swimming area and a busy boat launch. Home to a small settlement and caravan park, families have been holidaying here for generations and there is a real 'step back in time' vibe. Don't miss the delish fish and chips.

True wilderness In the remote D'Entrecasteaux National Park, just 20km west of Walpole, the sublimely beautiful **Mandalay Beach** has views out to Chatham Island. The beach is named for the shipwrecked *Barque Mandalay,* which emerges every few years from the shifting sands and wild surf – you never know, you might just see it! This is a spot for contemplation, not swimming.

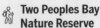

Two Peoples Bay Nature Reserve

Popular for its white sand, aquamarine waters and granite rock outcrops, **Two Peoples Bay** and **Little Beach**, both located within the Two Peoples Bay Nature Reserve around 35km east of Albany, have been ranked in the 'best beaches in Australia' – yet their real treasures lie deeper.

Regional ecologist Sarah Comer says, 'Take the 4.6km Heritage Trail from the Two Peoples Bay Visitor Centre to the beach, and you are in a truly extraordinary landscape of animal diversity. Both quendas and quokkas can be seen on the trail. Keep your ear attuned to the call of the noisy scrub-bird, which was rediscovered here after it was thought to be extinct. You might also see a seal basking on the rocks or whales in the bay.'

■ **Recommended by Sarah Comer**
Regional Ecologist, Department of Biodiversity, Parks & Attractions
@exploreparkswa

34 ALBANY FOR
the History Buff

HEARTBREAKING | THOUGHT-PROVOKING | FASCINATING

▬▬▬ If you love stepping back in time, Albany/Kinjarling should be a port of call. Learn about the local Menang culture, peel back the layers of the first European settlement in WA at King George Sound and walk in the footsteps of Australian diggers – Albany was many Anzacs' last sight of home before they headed off to the Great War.

WACATION IMAGES/ALAMY STOCK PHOTO ©

🗺 How to

Allow time Any one of these information-packed spots could be visited in an hour, but to really take it in and piece it all together, you need to go much slower and immerse yourself in the stories.

Go deeper To learn about Menang Noongar people and culture, book an insightful walking tour with Kurrah Mia (p159). Albany's Museum of the Great Southern and the informative **Kodja Place** (kodjaplace.com.au), in Kojonup on the highway to Perth, also have stories of the Noongar people.

EMMA JONES/SHUTTERSTOCK ©

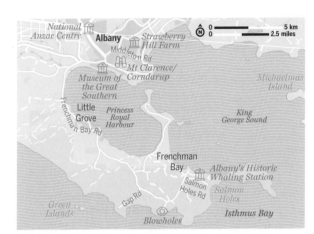

National Anzac Centre
Albany
Strawberry Hill Farm
Middleton Rd
Mt Clarence/ Corndarup
Museum of the Great Southern
Michaelmas Island
Frenchman Bay Rd
Little Grove
Princess Royal Harbour
King George Sound
Frenchman Bay
Albany's Historic Whaling Station
Salmon Holes Rd
Salmon Holes
Green Islands
Gap Rd
Isthmus Bay
Blowholes

0 — 5 km
0 — 2.5 miles

Left *Cheynes IV*, Historic Whaling Station
Below National Anzac Centre

Step back in time Board the 19th-century **Brig Amity** replica at the Museum of the Great Southern, overlooking the Princess Royal Harbour, and experience the journey from Sydney to King George Sound as this tiny ship battled perilous winds while carrying its small crew, convicts and animals to their new home. They anchored not far from the replica, where they established the first European settlement on the west coast of Australia in 1826.

The first European farm Established in 1827, **Strawberry Hill Farm at Barmup** is the oldest farm in WA. You can visit the original buildings as well as the visitor centre, completed in 2020, which aims to acknowledge that, for thousands of years before, Barmup (meaning 'place of tall trees' in Noongar) was a significant area for Menang people.

Australia's whaling past A visit to **Albany's Historic Whaling Station** at Discovery Bay provides an illuminating – and confronting – interactive experience as you board the whale chaser *Cheynes IV* and see the whale processing factory. While here you can also visit the Australian Wildlife Park to see a range of wildlife, including bandicoots and wombats, and the Regional Wildflower Garden.

Coastal hikes and views Near the top of **Mt Clarence/ Corndarup** is the Desert Mounted Corps Memorial. Take the 3.2km heritage walk for spectacular views out across the town of Albany and the surrounding bays. The 4km Ellen Cove Board walk to Albany Port is a longer option, with the ruins of the Port King Lighthouse and the Mustafa Kemal Atatürk monument potential stops along the way.

A Place of Pilgrimage

The **National Anzac Centre** (nationalanzac centre.com.au), on Mt Clarence (Corndarup), is a state-of-the-art interpretation experience where visitors assume the identity of one of 32 Anzacs who left Albany in 1914 for the Great War. Through audio and multimedia presentations, you are drawn into the Gallipoli campaign and onto the mud of the Western Front. The centre is adjacent to the **Princess Royal Fortress**, another treasure trove of military history.

Many believe that the the first dawn service on ANZAC Day was held in Albany in 1930, with a procession up a bush track to the top of Mt Clarence.

Listings

BEST OF THE REST

Outdoor Adventures

HMAS Perth Wreck

The HMAS *Perth* wreck near Albany is a good spot for recreational divers, with a 133m-long artificial reef and interpretative trail. Snorkellers and swimmers can also see the wreck from the surface.

Woody Island

Take a day trip to Woody Island from Esperance or stay a while and glamp or stop in a safari hut. Either way, don't miss snorkelling the pristine waters of Shearwater Bay.

King George Sound

From late May to October whales often rest within King George Sound, making whale watching from Albany an excellent opportunity to see these creatures up close.

Wilson Inlet

For a serene and calming experience, enjoy a beautiful paddle from the Wilson Inlet to the centre of Denmark. Hire a kayak or a paddleboat at the Rivermouth Caravan Park.

Kalgan Queen

Entertaining and very knowledgeable Captain Jack of the *Kalgan Queen* will take you on a leisurely cruise around Oyster Bay and up the Kalgan River. Morning tea includes damper and local tastings.

Esperance Island Cruises

Visit some of the 105 islands that make up the Recherche Archipelago on a half-day scenic wildlife cruise out of Esperance. Each island has unique species and snorkelling equipment is provided.

Barna Mia Nocturnal Wildlife Experience

Take a guided tour through this wildlife sanctuary in Williams for a chance to see a numbat (WA's animal emblem) or even a bilby, woylie or quenda.

South Coast Surfing

If you want to try riding the waves, take a lesson with an experienced instructor at Ocean Beach in Denmark, where the conditions are ideal with small surf and a sheltered bay. In the most part, however, surfing in this region isn't for beginners or the inexperienced.

Denmark Thrills Adventure Park

Smile, laugh and scream with excitement at this adventure park, home to the world's longest globe-riding track.

Unmissable Hikes

Bluff Knoll

Hike the highest (1099m), and most well-known, peak in the Stirling Ranges, a paradise for hikers and photographers: incredible biodiversity, stark jagged peaks and wildflowers galore.

ADWO/SHUTTERSTOCK ©

Esperance Island Cruises

Nancy Peak

This 5.5km loop walk offers sweeping views out to the Stirling Ranges. Reward yourself after your hike with a pizza and a local craft beer at Karri On Bar at historic Karribank.

 Art Galleries

Kurrah Mia

This Aboriginal-owned art and craft gallery in Albany provides an insight into Noongar culture through its authentic art. Take an insightful walking tour to learn even more.

The Surf Gallery

The Evolution of Surfboard exhibition at this gallery in Youngs Siding, is possibly Australia's largest publicly displayed private collection of boards and surf memorabilia.

Petrichor Gallery

Lovely natural light illuminates the art at this gallery in Walpole. Exhibitions showcase the beauty of the natural environment across a range of mediums.

Makers Collective & Magic Marron Shop

An innovative cooperative in Walpole with a fabulous range of artworks, textiles and jewellery from talented locals, plus pond-to-plate marron.

 Unique Flavours

Boston Brewing Co $$

For an all-round great family day out you can't go past Boston Brewing at Willoughby Park near Denmark. The brewpub food is consistently tasty, the craft beer flows and the wines from Willoughby Park are respected.

Garrison $$$

Sitting atop Mt Clarence/Corndarup, Garrison has lovely views of Albany's waterways, a menu with plenty of local influences and a carefully selected wine list.

Bilby

Maleeya's Thai Café $$

This place is described as the best Thai in WA. Asian herbs from their organic veggie garden are used to absolute perfection. Located in the idyllic Porongurup ranges.

Lucky Bay Brewing $$

Claiming to be the most genuinely local craft beer in Australia, Lucky Bay Brewing is on everyone's list when in Esperance. Serves up huge pizza portions, too.

The Telegraph on Bremer $$

With expansive gardens and views to the inlet, The Telegraph at Bremer Bay is housed in the lovingly restored original Telegraph building. Breakfast on the verandah gets stellar reviews.

The Nornabar $$

This fabulous little restaurant in the tiny village of Nornalup serves tasty Sri Lankan and Asian-inspired dishes (including grilled marron); the lemon posset is raved about.

Limeburners

With a spot overlooking Frenchman Bay, award-winning Limeburners is famed for its single-malt whiskies. While you're here, tour the distillery or try the tasting flight.

MONKEY MIA & THE CENTRAL WEST

NATURE | CULTURE | ADVENTURE

Ancient Stories of the West

NARAYAN MUKAVILLI/SHUTTERSTOCK

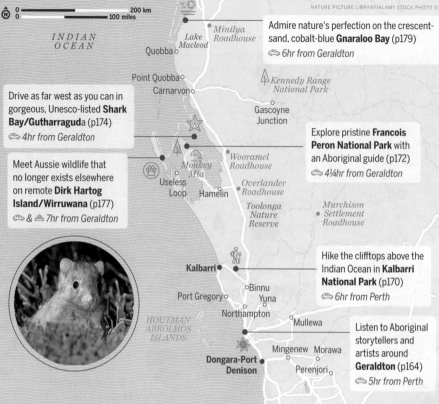

N

0 ——————— 200 km
0 ——————— 100 miles

*INDIAN
OCEAN*

Quobba ○

Point Quobba ○

Carnarvon ○

Lake *Macleod*

*Minilya
Roadhouse*

Admire nature's perfection on the crescent-
sand, cobalt-blue **Gnaraloo Bay** (p179)
🚗 *6hr from Geraldton*

*Kennedy Range
National Park*

*Gascoyne
Junction*

Drive as far west as you can in
gorgeous, Unesco-listed **Shark
Bay/Gutharraguda** (p174)
🚗 *4hr from Geraldton*

Meet Aussie wildlife that
no longer exists elsewhere
on remote **Dirk Hartog
Island/Wirruwana** (p177)
🚗 & ⛴ *7hr from Geraldton*

*Monkey
Mia*

Useless
Loop   Hamelin

*Wooramel
Roadhouse*

*Overlander
Roadhouse*

Explore pristine **Francois
Peron National Park** with
an Aboriginal guide (p172)
🚗 *4¼hr from Geraldton*

*Toolonga
Nature
Reserve*

*Murchison
Settlement
Roadhouse*

Kalbarri ●

Hike the clifftops above the
Indian Ocean in **Kalbarri
National Park** (p170)
🚗 *6hr from Perth*

Port Gregory ○

○ Binnu
Yuna

*HOUTMAN
ABROLHOS
ISLANDS*

Northampton

Mullewa

Listen to Aboriginal
storytellers and
artists around
Geraldton (p164)
🚗 *5hr from Perth*

**Dongara-Port
Denison** ●

Mingenew Morawa

Perenjori ○

MONKEY MIA &
THE CENTRAL WEST
Trip Builder

▬▬▬ This is a land where outback deserts collide to miraculous effect
with the cerulean waters of the Indian Ocean. Here you can listen to
Aboriginal storytellers, experience incredible wildlife on land and sea,
and, often, simply stand open-mouthed and admire the view.

Practicalities

ARRIVING

✈ Flights connect Carnarvon, Geraldton and Shark Bay with Perth. Buses between Perth, Port Hedland and Broome stop at Dongara, Geraldton and Carnarvon, with connections to Kalbarri and Shark Bay.

FIND YOUR WAY

Telstra's mobile (cell) phone coverage extends across the region; other providers are more patchy. There's wi-fi in cafes, information centres and most accommodation.

MONEY

Most towns have ATMs and credit cards are widely accepted; some out-of-the-way places only accept cash.

WHERE TO STAY

Town	Pros/Cons
Geraldton	Lots of motels and caravan parks, but not much variety.
Carnarvon	Caters primarily to nomad retirees. Caravan parks rule.
Shark Bay	Wonderfully quiet options along the coast road to Denham. Motels, caravan parks, a resort and even an outback station stay.

EATING & DRINKING

Dongara-Port Denison, Geraldton and Carnarvon all have a good mix of cafes, bistros and seafood. Even smaller towns have at least one supermarket.

Don't miss
The coast's best steak sandwich at Southerlys p183)

Must-try drink
Locally distilled spiced rum at Illegal Tender Rum Co (pictured bottom left; p183)

GETTING AROUND

Car By far the most convenient way to get around. Car hire is best arranged as part of a trip from Broome or Perth; local car-rental options are limited.

Bus You wouldn't want to rely on local bus services to get around; some only operate three times a week.

MONKEY MIA & THE CENTRAL WEST FIND YOUR FEET

JAN–MAR	APR–JUN	JUL–SEP	OCT–DEC
Hot, humid and possible rain, but it's quiet.	Late rains possible, but May and June usually fine and less busy.	Fine weather but advance reservations of everything necessary.	Temperatures and humidity rising, but spring wildflowers in the south.

35 Ancient Stories of
THE WEST

CULTURE | HISTORY | INDIGENOUS ART

The story of the Western Australian coast here connects modern Geraldton with the region's ancient past. These are the traditional lands of the Southern Yamaji people; they tell an Indigenous story stretching back tens of thousands of years, tales of epic shipwrecks, and so much more besides. Listening to that story as told by Geraldton's Aboriginal and European storytellers is a fascinating window on the soul of Australia's west.

TRABANTOS/SHUTTERSTOCK ©

🗺 How to

Getting here & around
Reaching Geraldton by air, bus or car is easy. Having a vehicle while here makes things easier.

When to go The best weather is in the busy May-to-September months; wildflowers bloom from September until November.

More information
Geraldton Visitor Centre sells a number of books on the region's history, including Stan Gratte's *The Aboriginal History of Geraldton (Jambinu) and Surrounding Areas*, a fascinating companion for the road.

POSNOV/GETTY IMAGES ©

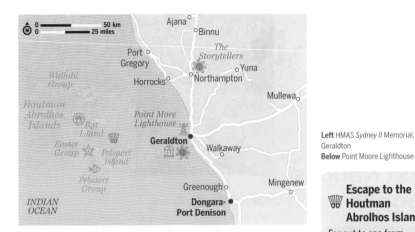

Left HMAS *Sydney II* Memorial, Geraldton
Below Point Moore Lighthouse

Looking out to sea The candy-bright **Point Moore Lighthouse** is where Geraldton meets the Indian Ocean and many stories intersect. This is more than just a lookout. The ships that brought the first Europeans to Australia passed by just out to sea, and it was here that the land's Indigenous peoples would have watched and wondered what it all meant. The views haven't changed in the 400 years since.

Local history At the **Museum of Geraldton**, one of the west's best museums, multimedia displays tell of ancient Aboriginal history. Here the Shipwreck Gallery brings to life the horror story of the *Batavia* (1616; p181) and, on a hill overlooking the town, the soulful **HMAS *Sydney II* Memorial** tells the wartime tale of the 1941 sinking of the vessel that killed 645 men.

Indigenous stories In town, **Yamaji Art** is an Aboriginal-owned art gallery where you can discover paintings, sculptures and craftwork from the local Wajarri, Noongar, Badimaya and Wilunyu peoples. Next, stop by the tourist office and pick up a map for the self-guided **Yamaji Drive Trail**, which covers 14 Indigenous sites around town. About 50km north of Geraldton, in Northampton, **The Storytellers – Keepers of the Dreaming** (www.facebook.com/TheStorytellersKeepers) is a special experience, at once art gallery and an opportunity to spend time with local artists.

Escape to the Houtman Abrolhos Islands

Far out to sea from Geraldton, 'the Abrolhos' is a lost-world archipelago of 122 islands and coral reefs. It's just 60km, yet a world, away from the mainland and is one of the west's most memorable wildlife experiences that only a fraction of visitors to the west ever see: look for sea lions, green turtles, carpet pythons, ospreys and the Tammar wallaby.

The reefs here promise fantastic diving and snorkelling with the world's southernmost Acropora (staghorn) coral. Visit the Abrolhos either on a live-aboard boat as a diver (p182) or on a scenic flight/island landing and snorkelling day tour.

Australia's First Nations People

CUSTODIANS OF THE EARTH'S OLDEST CONTINUOUS CULTURE

Indigenous Australian culture dates back at least 60,000 years. Prior to European invasion in 1788, there were approximately 300 distinct language groups and 500 dialects. Now, Indigenous peoples make up only 3% of the population. Most Indigenous people live in urban areas, though some communities maintain traditional lifestyles in remote regions.

Left Invasion Day protesters
Centre Dried quandong fruit
Right Ice cream made with indigenous ingredients

Walking the Dreaming

Aboriginal culture and spirituality revolve around Dreaming and Dreamtime. The Dreamtime tells us about how things came to be. It details the creation of the natural world – rivers, mountains, plants, animals, and everything in between.

The Dreaming explains why things are the way they are, such as the birth of the first platypus, how the echidna got her spines, or the meanings of certain constellations. The Dreaming is always occurring, without a defined beginning or end. It tells us about how we should behave, about our culture and families, and about living from and respecting the land.

Dreamtime and Dreaming stories differ across nations, though some nations share the same or similar stories. These stories have been passed down through oral storytelling, dance and art, and now many stories have also been written down.

An important part of the Dreaming is that Aboriginal people are the custodians, not the owners, of the land they live on. Instead, the relationship between the land and the people is a reciprocal one, where we care for the land because it cares for us.

Many of these Dreaming stories are connected to songlines, which are paths walked by the spirits in the Dreamtime. Songlines serve many purposes, such as preserving history, detailing agricultural practices and mapping the land.

Living off the Land

For many years it was assumed that Indigenous peoples were hunter-gatherer societies prior to invasion. However, Aboriginal testimonies and recent historical research indicate that Indigenous societies employed complex aquaculture and agriculture practices.

> The Dreaming tells us about how we should behave, about our culture and families, and about living from and respecting the land.

Structures such as weirs and dams still exist, and agricultural techniques and knowledges are being revived and passed on.

Many Aboriginal communities recognise different seasons from the ones in the Western calendar. These seasons usually align with the area's weather patterns or relate to the local flora and fauna.

The Noongar people of south west WA recognise six seasons – Birak, Bunuru, Djeran, Makuru, Djilba and Kambarang –which are indicated by changes in local plants and animals. Traditionally, Noongar people hunted and gathered food according to the seasons, being guided by the signs in nature as to which animal and plant resources were plentiful at those times. Understanding the Indigenous calendar in the area you are visiting may help you better prepare for the specific weather of the region. Knowing when to dress for the hot and windy, the wet and windy, or the cool and dry can make a big difference to your enjoyment of your travels.

Bush tucker (food) and bush medicine are still used today. Some bush tucker, such as pepperberries, quandongs and Davidson plums, is used in fusion cooking and can be found in restaurants.

ⓘ The Difficult Date

The date 26 January, when the First Fleet of settlers arrived at Sydney Cove in 1788, officially become Australia Day in 1948.

For Aboriginal peoples, 26 January is a more sombre occasion, marking the beginning of invasion, seizure of the land and erosion of our culture. It is referred to as the Day of Mourning, Survival Day or Invasion Day.

For many Indigenous people and their supporters, Invasion Day is a day of remembrance and resistance rather than celebration. The issue is contentious in Australia, and calls to keep or change the date occur every year.

Countries, Clans & Cousins

Individual clans exist within Aboriginal nations. Clans within the same language group usually speak dialects that are mutually intelligible. Within these clans are individual families, though Aboriginal families integrate the extended family more than most Western societies do. In some communities it is common to refer to your mother's sister as Mum rather than Aunty, and to call your first cousins your brother- or sister-cousins. Some people may use 'cousin' to refer to anyone within their clan, skin group or language group. 'Cuz' is also a term of affection among Aboriginal people even if they are from completely different nations.

Family and community ties are vital to Aboriginal culture. Your family tells you who you are and where you come from. Many nations identify family ties by plant and animal totems. It is common to have your personal totem plus three further totems indicating your nation, your clan and your family ties. Sadly, much of this information has been lost, and it is a difficult journey for some people to find their family totems.

> Family and community ties are vital to Aboriginal culture. Your family tells you who you are and where you come from.

Aboriginal People Today

Across Australia, it is estimated that only 75 Indigenous languages are still spoken, but there are continuing efforts to revive languages among Indigenous communities. It is now possible to listen to music, watch TV shows or take classes in a number of Aboriginal languages. Aboriginal words are also present in the Australian vernacular. Animals such as koalas, dingoes, barramundi and galahs derive their names from Aboriginal languages, as do billabongs and boogie boards.

Similarly, Aboriginal words from different communities have spread through Australian Aboriginal English, the dialect of English spoken by many Aboriginal people across the country.

Around 60% of Aboriginal people in Australia live on the East Coast. This will sometimes surprise visitors to Australia, who think that they do not see many Aboriginal people in the region. Others are confused when a light-skinned person identifies as Aboriginal. It is widely accepted among Aboriginal communities that your percentage of Aboriginality has little bearing

on your identity and involvement in the community. People with light skin and blonde hair will proudly call themselves Blak or identify as Blackfullas. A common metaphor is that of a cup of tea: no matter how much milk you put in the cup, no matter how pale it becomes, it's still tea.

This also means that a lot of Aboriginal people live off-Country, meaning that they live on the land of another nation.

Since 1975 the first Sunday of July has marked the beginning of Naidoc Week, which is dedicated to celebrating Aboriginal culture, history and perseverance. Communities, cities, schools and other institutions hold events that celebrate and build awareness about the rich and diverse Aboriginal cultures in Australia today.

Sorry Day (8 February) commemorates the day the Australian government formally apologised for its role in the Stolen Generations. From 1910 to the 1970s, Aboriginal children were forcibly removed from their families to integrate them into white society. Aboriginal people today still feel the effects of this policy through loss of culture, family ties and language. The apology was given in 2008.

■ by Caoimhe Hanrahan-Lawrence
Wiradjuri writer, currently living in Sydney on Wangal-Eora land

Far left Boomerang carving lesson
Left Aboriginal tools and weapons
Above left Traditional smoking ceremony performed at the openeing ceremony for Naidoc Week
Above right Painted banners to celebrate Naidoc Week

Signs of Respect

An Acknowledgement of Country and a Welcome to Country are important statements that identify and thank the custodians of the land on which an event takes place. Anyone, Aboriginal or not, can give an Acknowledgement. Welcomes can only be given by Elders from that country, or a member of the community who has been given permission by their Elders.

Elders and cultural teachers are usually referred to with 'Aunty' or 'Uncle' before their first name, in the same way that respect is conferred by the use of 'Sir' or 'Ma'am'. This recognises the knowledge and experience that our Elders hold.

36 The Kalbarri COAST

NATURE | ADVENTURE | WILDLIFE

■ West Coast Australia's promise to be the place where the outback meets the sea gets real at Kalbarri. This quiet, small seaside town is the launchpad for adventures on a grand scale, both out on the water and amid the epic cliffs, gorges and beaches of Kalbarri National Park. And wherever you go, the wildlife is as memorable as the scenery.

ELIZABETH GIVEN/ALAMY STOCK PHOTO ©

🗺 How to

Getting here & around
Having your own vehicle makes it easier to explore, but many companies include transport in their activities.

When to go May to September has the best weather but can be busy. Wildflowers bloom September to November; whales pass by June to November.

Top tip Microbrews and seafood in a junkyard with shark sculptures at **Finlay's Kalbarri** (finlayskalbarri.com.au).

SUEBEDOOR88/SHUTTERSTOCK ©

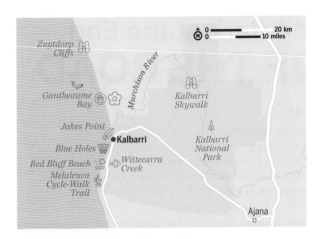

Left Kalbarri coast
Below Red Bluff Beach

Secret beaches Ease yourself into the grandeur of this soul-stirring stretch of coast by enjoying one of the glorious beaches south of Kalbarri. **Red Bluff Beach** and **Chinaman's Beach** are good for swimming, **Wittecarra Creek** is beloved by fishing folk, and **Blue Holes** is all about the snorkelling. Surfers love the big left-hand at **Jacques (Jakes) Point**. The sunsets in these parts are simply superb. While most visitors drive past, the beaches here are linked by the 8km-long **Melaleuca Cycle-Walk Trail**.

National park hikes Two other trails nearby – the coastal **Bigurda Trail** (8km one way), between Natural Bridge and Eagle Gorge, and **Red Bluff Trail** (5.5km one way) – are popular with locals and take you along the tops of stunning sandstone cliffs. Inland, short trails lead to lookouts over the river gorges of Kalbarri National Park: the best are Ross Graham Lookout, Hawks Head and Z-Bend. And everyone should visit the impressive **Kalbarri Skywalk**, opened in 2020, which hangs out over Murchison Gorge.

Gantheaume Bay The full drama of this magnificent coast is on show where the beautiful Murchison River snakes through steep gorges before reaching the sea. Wildflowers line paths frequented by kangaroos, emus and thorny devils, whales breach offshore and orchids struggle in the rocky ground. Away to the north, the towering line of the limestone **Zuytdorp Cliffs** remains aloof, pristine and remote.

Kalbarri Wildlife

Kalbarri Adventure Tours (kalbarritours.com.au) Paddle a canoe through the gorges of the national park.

Reefwalker Adventure Tours (reefwalker.com.au) Whale-watching and sunset cruises along the coast, plus fishing charters.

Big River Ranch (bigriverranch.net) Ride a horse across the beautiful Murchison River floodplain.

Feed the pelicans along the foreshore at 8.45am every morning.

37 The Park at the End
OF THE ROAD

CULTURE | NATURE | BEACHES

Venture beyond Francois Peron National Park and you'll fall off the map. This little-visited park occupies a long, narrow peninsula in the Shark Bay World Heritage Area and is one dramatic natural formation after another. It has been the homeland of the Malgana Aboriginal people, who call Shark Bay Gutharraguda (meaning 'two bays'), for tens of thousands of years.

NARAYAN MUKKAVILLI/SHUTTERSTOCK ©

🗺 How to

Getting here & around
Get to Denham by car (the quickest way to get here and around), then let the locals show you around.

When to go May to September or October are the best months. The rest of the year, you'll feel like you're wrapped in a wet glove.

Where to eat There are no services in the national park; head to Denham to sit with salty types at **Shark Bay Hotel** or eat seafood at **Old Pearler Restaurant** (built of shells).

MATT DEAKIN/SHUTTERSTOCK ©

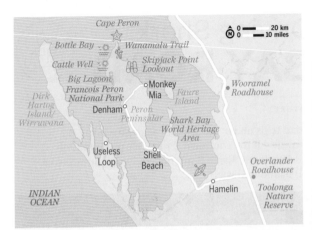

Left Skipjack Point Lookout, Shark Bay
Below Emus, Shark Bay

🖋 Feeling Nature

The Shark Bay World Heritage Area is the traditional lands of the Nhanda and Malgana peoples. Local Aboriginal man Darren 'Capes' Capewell runs kayaking and SUP tours past the red cliffs of Cape Peron, looking for bush tucker on land and teaching you how to let the Country talk to you. 'It's about *feeling* nature,' he says, 'more than it is just seeing it.'

The experience with Capes is a mix of history, storytelling and pure fun, and his campfire-at-sunset 'Didgeridoo Dreaming' tours are magical.

His favourite spot along this coast is Big Lagoon; he believes Shark Bay is the next big thing in kite-surfing; and he says the best sunsets are from aptly named Sunset Beach at Nicholson Point.

■ Darren 'Capes' Capewell
Wula Gura Nyinda Eco Adventures, Denham, Shark Bay
@wulagura.com.au

Pristine beaches Some of WA's loveliest and most deserted stretches of sand wrap around the Peron Peninsula (known to the local Malgana people as Wulyibidi). If you're lucky you might be the only one here. **Bottle Bay** and **Cattle Well** are simply gorgeous. But the most special experience awaits at **Cape Peron**, a pristine sweep of sand backed by red cliffs; watch for the bottlenose dolphins made famous by *National Geographic* in 2013 for driving their prey into the shallows. At first glance it looks like a tumultuous rush of waters, but stick around and what's happening soon becomes clear. Keep an eye out for a mother teaching its baby to fish.

The best views From Cape Peron, the fabulous **Wanamalu Trail** (3.6km return) follows the clifftop south along the peninsula to Skipjack Point. The views are magnificent here, so plan to spend longer than the one hour it takes. If you start out just after sunrise, you'll be rewarded with empty trails and incredible pink ocean views; sunsets are busier but equally memorable. The **Skipjack Point Lookout** platform provides expansive views of the coastline and, below, water so clear and blue it has to be seen to be believed. Here you might see dugongs, eagle rays, cownose rays, manta rays, stingrays, plus occasional pods of dolphins and even whales.

38 Driving Shark
BAY ROAD

DRIVING | NATURE | ADVENTURE

▬▬▬ When it comes to road trips under the tourist radar, Shark Bay Rd takes you to the very extremities of the continent. From Telegraph Station and Hamelin Pools to Shell Beach and Eagle Bluff, the landscape unfurls like some desert (and deserted) island fantasy.

ANDREA IZZOTTI/SHUTTERSTOCK ©

🗺 How to

Getting around A 2WD vehicle is enough on the main road but a 4WD is good for detours; check that your rental contract allows you to go off-road.

When to go May to September has near-perfect weather. Shark Bay's big horizons mean you'll barely notice that this is when most travellers visit.

Sleep like a shearer Stay in comfort in the converted shearers' quarters at **Hamelin Station Stay** and learn the story of this historic property.

◎ Rise Above It All

Everything out here has an epic scale, but the kilometres fall away when you take a scenic flight. **Shark Bay Aviation** operates out of Shark Bay Airport, flying out over the Zuytdorp Cliffs and Steep Point; the latter is the westernmost point on the map of Australia.

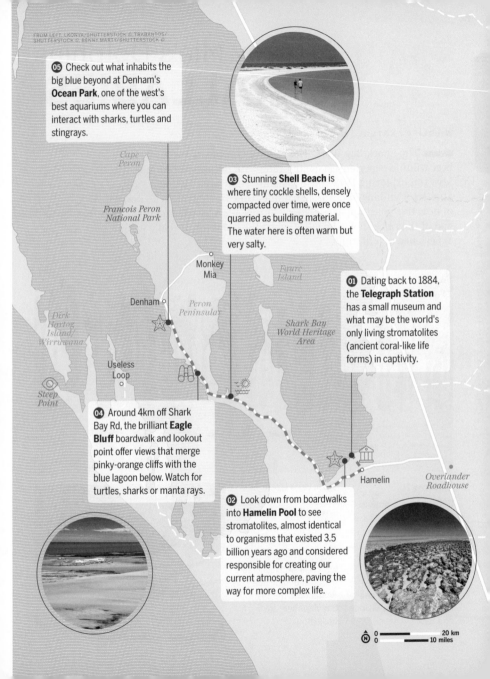

05 Check out what inhabits the big blue beyond at Denham's **Ocean Park**, one of the west's best aquariums where you can interact with sharks, turtles and stingrays.

03 Stunning **Shell Beach** is where tiny cockle shells, densely compacted over time, were once quarried as building material. The water here is often warm but very salty.

01 Dating back to 1884, the **Telegraph Station** has a small museum and what may be the world's only living stromatolites (ancient coral-like life forms) in captivity.

04 Around 4km off Shark Bay Rd, the brilliant **Eagle Bluff** boardwalk and lookout point offer views that merge pinky-orange cliffs with the blue lagoon below. Watch for turtles, sharks or manta rays.

02 Look down from boardwalks into **Hamelin Pool** to see stromatolites, almost identical to organisms that existed 3.5 billion years ago and considered responsible for creating our current atmosphere, paving the way for more complex life.

Cape Peron

Francois Peron National Park

Monkey Mia

Faure Island

Denham

Peron Peninsular

Dirk Hartog Island/ Wirruwana

Shark Bay World Heritage Area

Useless Loop

Steep Point

Hamelin

Overlander Roadhouse

0 — 20 km
N
0 — 10 miles

39 Monkey Mia's Dolphins
& WALLABIES

WILDLIFE | NATURE | NATIONAL PARKS

The Shark Bay World Heritage Area protects two of WA's best wildlife experiences: communing with dolphins at Monkey Mia and exploring Dirk Hartog Island/Wirruwana National Park, an ark for endangered Aussie wildlife. Dirk Hartog offers a glimpse of how this coast appeared before Europeans arrived. And if you're one of the select few who gets to feed the dolphins, it really is the experience of a lifetime.

BENNY MARTY/SHUTTERSTOCK ©

🗺 How to

Getting here & around Denham is the main base for visiting here. You'll need your own vehicle; a high-clearance 4WD is required for Wirruwana and only 20 are allowed on the island at any one time. Alternatively, visit on a tour.

When to go May to September has the best weather but can be busy. It's very hot and humid the rest of the year.

Top tip Linger over the local blue swimmer crab risotto at **Boughshed Restaurant**: the Shark Bay views here are brilliant.

AUSCAPE INTERNATIONAL PTY LTD/ALAMY STOCK PHOTO ©

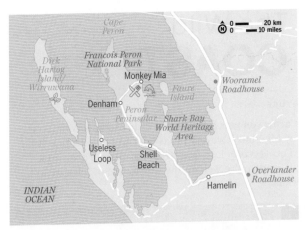

Left Watching wild dolphins, Monkey Mia
Below Banded hare-wallaby, Dirk Hartog Island/Wirruwana

Dolphins' morning ritual Everyone who comes to Monkey Mia to feed the wild Indo-Pacific bottlenose dolphins leaves with a big smile on their face. This morning ritual involves a select few wading into the shallow water to help the experts feed the dolphins while everyone else watches from the pier. The first feed begins around 7.45am, although dolphins don't turn up like clockwork; it gets a little less crowded and your chances of being chosen to get in the water increase when they return (as they often do) a second or third time until around noon. The dolphins may also pass the day close to the beachfront, so stick around after the buses leave.

Dirk Hartog Island/Wirruwana This slim, wind-raked island, which runs parallel to the Peron Peninsula (p173), once attracted Dutch, British and French explorers. WA's largest island is now a national park with a blissful lost-world feeling. With feral goats, sheep and cats removed, the island's biodiversity is becoming the talk of the nation: native plants have been replanted and endemic animals such as the boodie, banded hare-wallaby and rufous hare-wallaby have been reintroduced to restore the island to its 1616 splendour. Many of the species found here no longer survive on the Aussie mainland; you might also see dugongs and loggerhead turtles. Aboriginal-owned Wula Gura Nyinda Eco Adventures (p173) runs wildlife and cultural tours to Wirruwana.

Dolphin Volunteering

Dolphins have gravitas, and for many visitors, an all-too-brief encounter at feeding time leaves them wanting more. If you think this may apply to you, and if you can set aside anywhere between four and 14 days, consider volunteering (08-9948 1366; monkeymiavolunteers@westnet.com.au) to work with the dolphins.

It's amazing how much you'll learn in even this short space of time, and, no matter how long you stay, you'll leave thoroughly enchanted. It's the kind of deep-immersion wildlife encounter that will have you wondering what it takes to retrain and become a marine biologist.

40 The Wild COAST

NATURE | CULTURE | ADVENTURE

■■■ The coast north of Carnarvon gets a fraction of visitors when compared with Shark Bay and Monkey Mia, but it's every bit as wild and beautiful as its better-known neighbours. Locals *really* love this stretch of coast. Throw in a foray inland to Mt Augustus, and you're well on the way to one of the west's best under-the-radar experiences.

PHOTO VOLCANO/SHUTTERSTOCK ©

📍 How to

Getting around Rent a car in Perth or Broome – it will come in handy for getting here and you'll need it for exploring while you're here.

When to go May to September has the best weather but can be busy.

The rest of the year can be hot and very humid.

More info Carnarvon Visitor Centre has lots of information, including the coast's best surf spots.

Top tip Head to **Pickles Point Seafood** for the freshest possible seafood plus divine crab cakes.

JACK KINNY/SHUTTERSTOCK ©

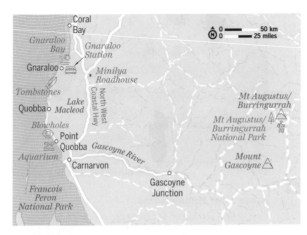

Left Gnaraloo Bay
Below Blowholes, Point Quobba

Quobba Coast Heading north from Carnarvon, the North West Coastal Hwy turns inland and takes with it most of the traffic. If you stay on the coast, known as the Quobba Coast, which runs from **Point Quobba** to Red Bluff, you'll traverse an increasingly wild and desolate shore that's the domain of surfers and fishing folk, breathtaking scenery and fire-in-the-sky sunsets. Stop at Point Quobba to snorkel the gorgeous sheltered lagoon known as the **Aquarium** and to see the impressive **Blowholes**, where big swells force sprays of water through sea caves and up, howling, out of narrow chimneys in the rocks. At high tide, high water levels often cover the blowholes; an incoming tide is the best time to visit.

Gnaraloo Bay Further north from Point Quobba is Gnaraloo Bay, a perfect crescent of white sand and as gorgeous as beaches come. Here you can snorkel, hike and kite-surf. Nearby, **Gnaraloo Station** is a legendary place to stay, catering to a select few adventurous travellers.

Tombstones Southwest of Gnaraloo Station, Tombstones has near-mythic status among surfers who come here from mid-April to October. Promising one of the longest, roundest tubes in the world, Tombstones is a heavy, scary, left-hander reef break. Even if you don't surf it's fun to watch the experts. Other spots for experienced surfers include Gnaraloo Bay, Midgies, Turtles and Fenceline.

🏛 Bigger than Uluru

In Wajarri country, 469km west then northwest of Carnarvon, **Mt Augustus/ Burringurrah** is, like so much along this coast, an incredibly well-kept secret.

Known as Burringurrah in the local Aboriginal language, it's twice as large (715m high, 8km long) as Uluru and just as beautiful.

The 49km loop drive around the rock offers fantastic views, and gives you access to walking trails and Aboriginal rock-art sites, including the superb summit trail (12km return, five to eight hours, requiring a high level of fitness). The best sunset views are from Emu Lookout. You'll need your own vehicle (2WD vehicles are fine).

A Long & Complicated History

INDIGENOUS AND COLONIAL HISTORIES COLLIDE

The human story of Monkey Mia and the Central West is a saga worthy of this most drama-filled of landscapes. It begins with one of the oldest stories of continuous human habitation on the planet, and ends with a story that challenges the whole premise of European arrival in Australia.

Since Time Immemorial

People first arrived on the northern shores of Australia at least 40,000 years ago, but it may be as long ago as 60,000 years. Finding out more is an archaeologist detective story, pieced together using traces left behind by these ancient lives – layers of carbon (the residue of their ancient fires) deep in the soil; piles of shells and fish bones marking the places where they hunted and ate; and paintings and engravings on remote rock walls.

These artworks tell stories of the Dreaming, the spiritual dimension where the earth and its people were created and the law was laid down. The descendants of these ancient artists and fire-makers don't need carbon-dating or university-trained archaeologists to know that their people have been here for a *very* long time – since the time of the Dreaming, in fact, and the stories from this time go to the heart of the spiritual and cultural life of contemporary Aboriginal people.

Before the first European ships arrived along this stretch of coast in the 17th century, Aboriginal groups lived remarkably sophisticated lives for their time, surviving in one of the most hostile landscapes on earth. This was the land of the Yinggarda, Bayungu, Malgana, Thadgari, Thalanyji, Wajarri, Badimaya and Wilunyu people. Each group lived in their own territories and maintained their own distinctive languages and traditions. In places like Mt Augustus/Burringurrah, they left behind finely rendered artworks that tell the story of their time.

Left Rock art, Mt Augustus/Burringurrah
Centre Captain Cook landing at Botany Bay
Right Replica of the *Duyfken*

European Settlement

For decades in modern Australia, it was an article of faith that Captain Cook 'discovered' Australia for Great Britain when he sailed into Botany Bay in 1770. The truth is rather different, and it all centres on the west.

Some historians claim the Aboriginal peoples' first contact with Europeans occurred when a Chinese admiral visited Australia in the 15th century. Others say that Portuguese navigators mapped the continent in the 16th century. Whatever the truth of these stories, there is no doubt that Dutch ships began arriving along the Western Australian coast in the 17th century, more than 150 years before Captain Cook first stepped ashore.

> The artworks tell stories of the Dreaming, the spiritual dimension where the earth and its people were created and the law was laid down.

In 1606 Dutchman Willem Janszoon sailed the speedy little ship *Duyfken* out of the Dutch settlement at Batavia (modern Jakarta) and found Cape York (the pointy bit at the top of Australia). Ten years later, another Dutch ship, the *Eendracht,* rode the trade winds, bound for the 'spice islands' of modern Indonesia. But the captain, Dirk Hartog, misjudged his position, and stumbled onto the island that now bears his name. Hartog inscribed the details of his visit onto a pewter plate and nailed it to a post.

But the Dutch had no interest in Australia. Their colonies were commercial interests, and nothing they saw convinced them to stick around. Nevertheless, their arrival was the precursor to later arrivals that would devastate local Aboriginal communities.

The Batavia

The story of the Dutch ship *Batavia* is one of the more infamous in maritime history.

After the ship sank off modern Geraldton in 1629, the captain, Francisco Pelsaert, sailed off to find a rescue vessel. While he was away, crewmen raped and murdered the men, women and children who had been on the ship.

When Pelsaert returned, he executed the murderers. Only two youths survived, exiled to a local beach.

Listings

BEST OF THE REST

Wildlife, Wildflowers & Lakes

Coalseam Conservation Park

In spring, visit this park on the Irwin River in Holmwood for carpets of everlastings (paper daisies) and ancient fossil shells embedded in its cliffs.

Greenough Wildlife & Bird Park

The animals you don't see out in the wild are easy to see here at this excellent sanctuary. There are grey and red kangaroos, dingoes and emus, as well as lots of birds and reptiles.

Hutt Lagoon

Visit this Insta-famous pink lake near Kalbarri National Park in the middle of the day to see it at its most vivid.

Galleries & Museums

Geraldton Regional Art Gallery

The air-conditioned salons of this small gallery hold landmark works such as those by Aussie greats like Norman Lindsay and Elizabeth Durack.

Gwoonwardu Mia

This Carnarvon icon has a gallery and shop featuring works from local Aboriginal artists and an ethnobotanical garden.

Central Greenough Historic Settlement

Greenough was quite a town in its 1860s heyday, and some of its traditional stone buildings, including two churches, police station and gaol, have been preserved.

Carnarvon Space & Technology Museum

This centre was established with NASA in 1966. It has fascinating, family-friendly space paraphernalia and a full-size, interactive mock-up of an *Apollo* command module.

Shark Bay World Heritage Discovery Centre

This has a gallery with stunning aerial photos, a world-class museum, and exhibits on marine and animal life, Aboriginal culture, early explorers and shipwrecks.

Adventures on the Water

Midwest Surf School

This Geraldton surf school has year-round lessons (and a choice of suitable beaches) to suit every level.

Northshore Beach

Off Dongara, this beach is one of the best-loved surfing areas along the coast. Surfers here can get a little territorial with newcomers, but that's true almost anywhere.

Batavia Coast Dive

Based in Geraldton, this place offers diving courses, and day trips to the Houtman Abrolhos Islands.

Eco Abrolhos

Eco Abrolhos offers live-aboard tours cruising, diving and snorkelling the islands from March to October.

Coalseam Conservation Park

Kalbarri Outback Action

This fun-loving Kalbarri outfit gets the whole desert-meets-the-sea thing: begin on the sand dunes overlooking the ocean, then snorkel out in the shallows.

Ocean Park Tours

This fantastic aquarium south of Denham runs boat tours and diving excursions to Steep Point and Dirk Hartog Island/Wirruwana. Watch out for whales from August to October.

KiteWest

From October to May, KiteWest offers kite-surfing, surfing and SUP lessons and yoga.

Food & Coffee Trucks

Green Beanie

Green Beanie is a campervan that pulls up at Granny's Beach in Dongara every morning to serve barista-brewed cups of coffee, cheese-and-ham toasties and blueberry muffins.

Bean Drifting Coffee Van

A coffee-and-snacks van by the beach in Kalbarri, on Red Bluff Rd. It's a local rite of passage to watch the waves roll in with one of their coffees.

Wild Ocean

With the best Jakarta street food in Kalbarri. Margaret sets up her van opposite the main wharf.

Eating

Salt Dish $$

Geraldton's coolest cafe has fine brekkies, good coffee and home-baked treats. We dream of the Exmouth prawn and spring-pea risotto.

Oceans Restaurant $$

Overlooking the waters at Ocean Park, Oceans combines the freshest wild-caught seafood with craft beers and award-winning wines.

Hutt Lagoon

Southerlys $$

The best place to watch the sunset in Port Denison, Southerlys does what may be the west's best steak sandwich.

Burnt Barrel $$$

In the Chapman Valley, this self-styled 'Outback brewBQ' does glorious smoked meats that Texans would love, as well as home-brew craft beers.

Cold Beers & Drinks

Cutler & Smith

A hipster sensibility meets down-to-earth Geraldton with comfy booths, craft beers and excellent food.

The Freemasons Hotel

This heritage-listed, self-proclaimed 'pub with personality' has been pulling beers in Geraldton since 1895. These days, there's live music, DJs and open-mic nights.

Geraldton Hotel

Around since 1860, this Geraldton institution has a glorious palm-shaded beer garden and weekend live music.

Illegal Tender Rum Co

Just inland from Port Denison, this distillery is a real find. Head here for a tour and tasting of its award-winning 1808 Barely Legal and Spiced rums.

NINGALOO COAST
& THE PILBARA

CULTURE | NATURE | WILDLIFE

0 100 km
0 50 miles

Soak up the drama of outback-meets-the-sea at **Cape Range National Park** on a dramatic coastal drive (p192)
🚗 1hr from Exmouth

Immerse yourself in the world of Indigenous art at **Murujuga National Park** and beyond (p199)
🚗 1hr from Karratha

Follow ancient Dreaming paths through the outback along the **Warlu Way** (p200)
🚗 3hr from Exmouth

Learn about the west's complicated mining miracle in rambunctious **Port Hedland** (p203)
🚗 8hr from Exmouth

INDIAN OCEAN

Montebello Islands Conservation Park

Barrow Island

Port Hedland

Dampier
Roebourne
Karratha
Whim Creek
Marble Bar

Fortescue Roadhouse
Millstream-Chichester National Park
Yandeyarra Aboriginal Land
Hillside

Muiron Islands
Onslow
Pannawonica

Swim with humpback whales and whale sharks on World Heritage–listed **Ningaloo Reef** (p188)
🚗 1 hr from Exmouth

Exmouth
Cane River
The Pilbara
Hamersley Gorge
Wittenoom

Nanutarra Roadhouse
Tom Price

Coral Bay
Paraburdoo
Karijini National Park

Newman

NINGALOO COAST & THE PILBARA
Trip Builder

Two of the grand natural landscapes of Australia's west – world-class Ningaloo Reef, close to Australia's westernmost point, and then northeast to the extraordinary geological formations of the Pilbara – combine with Indigenous rock art and astonishing marine life. The result is one of Australia's most underrated destinations.

Practicalities

ARRIVING

 Port Hedland has the region's busiest airport, with further Perth connections through Learmonth (36km south of Exmouth) and Karratha. Buses between Perth and Broome stop in most coastal towns.

FIND YOUR WAY

With one major road linking most towns, it's very difficult to get lost. Local tourist offices have town maps.

MONEY

Most towns have ATMs; credit cards are widely accepted. Mining towns like Karratha and Port Hedland can be expensive.

WHERE TO STAY

Town	Pros/Cons
Exmouth	Pretty town, handy for Ningaloo, and everything from motels and caravan parks to apartments and a resort.
Karratha	Convenient for exploring the Pilbara coast, with apartments, motels and a caravan park.
Shark Bay	Fascinating town, if rough around the edges; motels and a caravan park.

EATING & DRINKING

Most towns have plenty of cafes and restaurants, but the focus is more quantity than quality or variety and at times you might be better off self-catering (or be forced to in remote areas). Always order a bucket of local prawns when they're on the menu (pictured bottom left).

Best boutique beer
Froth Craft Brewery (pictured top left, p205)

Must-try seafood
A bucket of Exmouth prawns at Learmonth's Bundegi Beach Shack (p205)

GETTING AROUND

Car Having your own vehicle gives you maximum flexibility; a 2WD is usually sufficient. For car rental, try a town with an airport.

Bus Buses run daily at most between the coastal towns, limiting your options.

Air Flights between Karratha and Port Hedland.

JAN–MAR	**APR–JUN**	**JUL–SEP**	**OCT–DEC**
Uncomfortably humid but relatively few visitors.	May and June often fine and rarely crowded; rains possible.	Fine, clear weather and perfect conditions; book everything early.	Getting warmer and more humid, but usually not too busy.

41

More than Whale
SHARKS

WILDLIFE | NATURE | ADVENTURE

Most people come to Unesco World Heritage-listed Ningaloo to swim with the whale sharks – and you should too. What few people realise is that these waters have some of the southern hemisphere's richest marine life and, as they're really close to shore, the 260km reef, is one of the most accessible in the world. In addition to whale sharks, there are humpback whales and turtles.

How to

Getting here & around
Exmouth is the main base for Ningaloo. It's connected by air to Perth, and just about anywhere by road. Coral Bay is also good.

When to go Whale sharks are here from mid-March to mid-August. For humpbacks it's July to October.

Tours Try **Kings Ningaloo Reef Tours**, **Ningaloo Whale Shark-N-Dive** or **Three Islands Whale Shark Dive** for whale shark and interactive whale tours.

Swimming with Whale Sharks

Ningaloo is one of the few places in the world where solitary speckled whale sharks (*Rhiniodon typus*) arrive like clockwork each year to feed on plankton and small fish. The largest fish in the world, whale sharks can reach up to 18m long (yes, that long!) and are believed to live 70 to 100 years. Whale sharks encountered at Ningaloo are mostly between 3m and 12m (a 12m whale shark may weigh as much as 11 tonnes and have a mouth more than 1m wide).

From mid-March to mid-August, you can go out on a tour boat, jump over the side, and snorkel and swim alongside these extraordinary creatures.

Conservation Efforts

When you're back on dry land, upload your amazing whale-shark pics to **Wildbook for Sharks** (sharkbook.ai), which will identify and track your whale shark. Or add new meaning to your snorkelling or diving adventures by collecting marine data; visit reefcheckaustralia.org for information.

Above left Snorkelling with whale sharks
Above Baby green sea turtle
Left Vlamingh Head Lighthouse

Humpback Whales

You thought whale sharks were big? You may think again when you get in the water, usually from July to October, with the humpback whales that make their migration down the WA coastline to their Antarctic feeding grounds; whale sharks often reach 8m long, while humpbacks are usually double that and can weigh 30,000kg. Go with an operator to be in the water right next to the whales, or simply head up to **Vlamingh Head Lighthouse** to do some land-based whale-spotting.

Nesting Marine Turtles

Between December and March, you can join a two-hour guided tour run by the **Jurabi Turtle Centre** (www.ningalooturtles.org. au/jurabi.html) to see nesting green and loggerhead turtles on the beach; tours depart a few evenings each week and advance bookings are essential. You can help with their conservation by volunteering on the **Ningaloo Turtle Program**, a five-week commitment that helps with turtle monitoring; but book ahead.

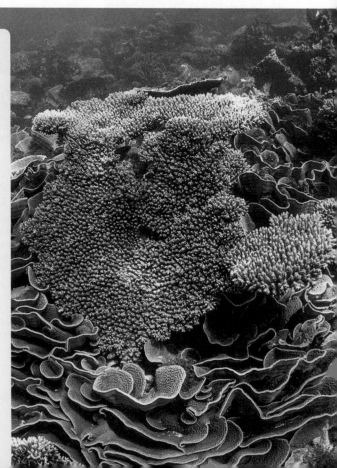

Drift Snorkelling at Turquoise Beach

There's nothing quite like drift snorkelling at utterly gorgeous Turquoise Beach, which is off the Yardie Creek road on the western shore of Cape Range National Park.

Drift snorkelling is only for strong swimmers. The current carries you over coral bommies, where you can watch for everything from bulbous brain corals to delicate branching staghorns. Avoid swimming when currents are strong and don't miss the exit point or you'll be carried out to sea.

Most people try to head out from the Drift car park. Instead, head 300m south along the beach, then wade 40m out to sea.

Underwater Explorations

Over 220 species of hard coral have been recorded in Ningaloo. While less colourful than soft corals (which are normally found in deeper water on the outer reef), hard corals are all about incredible formations. Spawning, where branches of hermaphroditic coral simultaneously eject eggs and sperm into the water, occurs after full and new moons between February and May. It is this spawning that attracts the whale sharks and makes possible one of the greatest natural wonders under the Australian sea. There's also an astonishing diversity of fish, rays, sharks and other marine life.

Snorkelling and diving Ningaloo rivals the much-better-known Great Barrier Reef, but sees a fraction of the visitors. To get an easy look at the hard corals, try **Oyster Stacks**, 69km south of Exmouth, where the bommies (submerged offshore reefs) are just metres offshore. Alternatively, kayak to a specially constructed mooring out on the reef, then jump overboard to snorkel with only fellow kayakers for company. Tether your craft and snorkel at Bundegi Beach (p204), **Tantabiddi Beach** and Osprey in the north, and **Maud** in the south (close to Coral Bay).

Left Ningaloo Reef
Above Swimming with a sea turtle

42 The Gorges of **CAPE RANGE**

DRIVING | HIKING | OUTDOORS

While most people head out on the water, you'll get a whole new perspective on the remarkable Ningaloo Coast by exploring on land. Cape Range National Park, southwest of Exmouth and extending along the west coast of the North West Cape, is dominated by jagged limestone peaks and cut through with heavily incised gorges. Visiting involves a spectacular combination of scenic drives and beautiful hikes.

ROB BAYER/SHUTTERSTOCK ©

How to

Getting here & around
Cape Range is best visited on a day trip from Exmouth. You'll need your own car to get around.

When to go
Temperatures can soar to over 50°C in summer. If you plan on hiking,

attempt longer trails only between April and October.

Wonderful wildlife
Watch out for the rare black-flanked rock wallaby, as well as dingoes, kangaroos and some of the park's 160 recorded bird species.

FROZYGRAPHIE/SHUTTERSTOCK ©

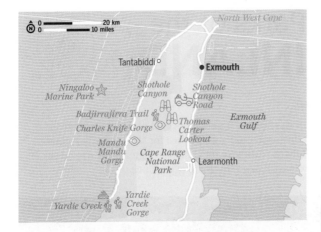

Left Yardie Creek Gorge
Below Shothole Canyon Road

Dramatic drives Around 14km south of Exmouth, the 12km-long, unsealed **Shothole Canyon Road** runs deep into the heart of the canyon, meandering along a dry creek bed and passing some colourful, dramatic rock formations before reaching a picnic area and a short trail. Officially this road is 4WD only, but it's suitable for 2WDs with decent clearance during the dry months. Over on the east coast, starting 22km south of Exmouth, a very scenic, partially sealed, and at times extremely narrow, 11km-long road ascends a knife-edge ridge via rickety corners; again, a 4WD is recommended. A rough track (passable by 2WD) continues to **Thomas Carter Lookout** (311m), with great views over **Charles Knife Gorge**.

Gorge hiking From near the Thomas Carter Lookout, you can walk the 6.8km **Badjirrajirra Trail**. This scenic loop (two to three hours) wanders gently through spinifex and several steep rocky gullies. If you don't want to do the whole loop, walk to the **Shothole Viewpoint** (around 4km return), which is the trail's scenic highlight. Other hiking possibilities include the pleasant, occasionally steep 3km return walk onto the picturesque rim of **Mandu Mandu Gorge** or the two walking trails at water-filled **Yardie Creek Gorge**: the gentle Nature Walk is 1.2km return, or the longer, steeper trail is 2km return and takes you high above the creek.

Yardie Creek Boat Tour

A relaxing one-hour cruise up the short, sheer Yardie Creek Gorge is a fine alternative (or addition) to a more strenuous hike.

The steep rock walls are good places to see rare black-flanked rock wallabies. These cute little marsupials live in tiny, isolated populations across northwestern Australia, and this is one of the best places to see them anywhere in the country.

Departure times (and days) vary with the seasons; there are no cruises from early January to late March. See yardiecreekboat tours.com.au for more information.

43 Parks of the **INLAND**

DRIVING | CULTURE | NATURE

The outback south of Karratha is a magical world of red-rock gorges, desert massifs and sites of deep spiritual significance for the local Aboriginal people. Two parks in the Pilbara – Millstream Chichester and Karijini – rank among Australia's best, yet least-known, outback experiences.

BECAUZ GAO/SHUTTERSTOCK ©

📷 **How to**

Getting here & around
If travelling on your own, take a 4WD. Millstream Chichester is around 150km southeast of Karratha, while Karijini is equidistant (around 350km) from Karratha and Port Hedland.

When to go The best months are May to October. Don't even think about heading out in the hot months (November to April).

KEN GRIFFITHS/SHUTTERSTOCK ©

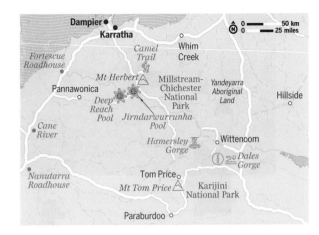

Dampier •
Karratha o

Camel
Trail
Fortescue
Roadhouse

Whim
Creek

Mt Herbert △
Pannawonica o
Deep
Reach
Pool

Millstream-
Chichester
National
Park

Yandeyarra
Aboriginal
Land

Hillside
o

Jirndarwurrunha
Pool

Cane
River •

Hamersley
Gorge

o Wittenoom

Dales
Gorge

Nanutarra
Roadhouse •

Tom Price o
Mt Tom Price △

Karijini
National Park

Paraburdoo o

0 — 50 km
0 — 25 miles

N

Millstream Chichester National Park This national park is a superb, rarely visited mix of rugged, rocky terrain and tranquil, oasis-like waterholes. Wildlife here includes 120 bird species, and signature mammal species such as the euro (sometimes known as the hills kangaroo) and the endangered northern quoll. Our favourite section of the park is in the north, which sees very few visitors. East off the Manuwarra Red Dog Hwy (formerly known as Karratha-Tom Price Rd), you'll encounter rolling hills, rocky peaks and escarpments; the Roebourne-Wittenoom Rd section is especially scenic with stunning breakaways and eroded mesas. **Mt Herbert** is a quick hike to the summit for glorious views, while the **Chichester Range Camel Trail** is a challenging six-hour hike across the sandstone from Mt Herbert to lush Python Pool and back.

Karijini National Park Were Karijini anywhere less remote, it would be one of Australia's premier attractions. The traditional lands of the Banyjima, Kurrama and Innawonga peoples, Karijini has at least 15 narrow, breathtaking gorges which shelter hidden pools and spectacular waterfalls, and in spring, kaleidoscopic wildflower displays. Watch out for red kangaroos, echidnas, rock wallabies and more. Anchor your visit around **Dales Gorge** (including Fern Pool), **Hamersley Gorge**, Hancock Gorge and Oxer Lookout. Swimming in one of these rockholes with no one else around is a classic, unforgettable outback experience.

Left Dales Gorge, Karijini National Park
Below Euro

🜄 Sacred Waters

Millstream Chichester National Park is the traditional lands of the Yindjibarndi people and they fought a long, brave battle for control over it.

Two remote pools in particular carry deep significance. **Deep Reach Pool** is the resting place of the Warlu (creation serpent). The water is deep and the banks can be steep, so use the steps. Be respectful here (no shouting or splashing). There's no swimming at beautiful lily- and palm-fringed **Jirndarwurrunha Pool**, which is surrounded by wetlands and carries profound significance for locals.

To really get the most out of your visit, come here with Ngurrangga Tours (p198).

Pilbara's Great Mining Debate

MINING, THE ENVIRONMENT AND INDIGENOUS LANDS

The Pilbara's epic story has three major characters: Aboriginal Australians, the mining industry and an often-pristine natural environment. In this, the Pilbara is at once a story for our times. When these three characters meet, and very often collide, it's a fascinating tale. Understanding it will greatly enhance your visit.

Left The red earth of the Pilbara
Centre Miners, the Pilbara
Right Geologists taking rock samples

ELECTRA/SHUTTERSTOCK ©

If you fly into many towns along the Western Australian coast, whether in Port Hedland or Tom Price, you'll notice one thing straight away: signs of the fly-in, fly-out (FIFO) lifestyle remain ubiquitous. Large clutches of workers nonchalantly board their flights to remote mines and oil and gas plants. Some will be wearing their fluorescent orange or yellow 'high-vis' vests, required attire on-site, and an understated badge of honour at city airports. It's a reminder that even as mining activity slows from the boom years a decade ago, mining remains the biggest game in town out west.

Environmental & Cultural Concerns

Perhaps because it is such a beautiful place, with so many sites of profound significance for Aboriginal Australians, the WA coast has seen many flashpoints. In the Pilbara, one controversial mining site is the Burrup Peninsula (p198) in the Dampier Archipelago, which is the location of many petroglyphs (rock art) believed to date from the last ice age. In 2007 Woodside Petroleum Ltd had several petroglyphs gingerly removed and fenced off in a separate area to better facilitate development. Some argue that the works are not discrete: that the disruption of one petroglyph compromises the entire site.

More recently, mining giant Rio Tinto showed that very little has changed when it comes to mining companies and their dealings with Aboriginal groups. In 2020 Rio Tinto destroyed two caves in Juukan Gorge in the Hammersley Ranges in the Pilbara to make way for an expansion of its iron-ore mine. The cave was a sacred

Several petroglyphs were gingerly removed and fenced off in a separate area to better facilitate development.

site for the Puutu Kunti Kurrama and Pinikura (PKKP) traditional owners, providing as it did a 4000-year-old genetic link to the modern PKKP community and evidence of continuous Indigenous occupation of the area for 46,000 years. Rio Tinto was fined and it apologised, but the sense of spiritual and cultural loss for the PKKP is a wound that may never heal.

The Yindjibarndi & Fortescue

Employment of Aboriginal Australians within the mining industry is very low. In 2008 mining magnate Andrew 'Twiggy' Forrest boldly promised support for 50,000 jobs for Aboriginal Australians. But even as Forrest's Fortescue Metals Group (FMG) was trying to increase Aboriginal employment in the mining industry, FMG's legal battles over mining leases on Yindjibarndi land (around Millstream Chichester National Park) told a different story.

Detailed in fascinating detail by Paul Cleary in his book *Title Fight: How the Yindjibarndi Battled and Defeated a Mining Giant* (2021), the case pitted Indigenous Elders against the legal might of one of Australia's richest companies. Finally, in 2020, after more than a decade, the Yindjibarndi won their case in the High Court of Australia. The effect was to recognise the Yindjibarndi's native title over many of the lands that FMG was seeking to mine. The ruling also effectively forces mining companies to more closely negotiate in good faith with native title holders.

🌿 Saving Ningaloo

You'll still see 'Save Ningaloo' stickers around from one of WA's most fiercely contested environmental campaigns.

'Save Ningaloo', with its thousands of protesters, successfully blocked the development of a massive marina resort (slated for 2003) on a loggerhead-turtle nesting ground.

In late 2012 BHP Billiton submitted a proposal to the state government to explore for liquefied natural gas 5km from Ningaloo's perimeter. This proposal was also rejected.

Apart from mining threats to Ningaloo, coral bleaching (which occurred in 2022) is an increasing danger. According to park authorities, bleaching events could take place at least every five years by 2041.

44

Indigenous Art in
THE PILBARA

ABORIGINAL CULTURE | NATURE | ART

Aboriginal peoples having been living on this land for more than 40,000 years and their remarkable stories are told across the region through art, both ancient and modern. It begins with rock art on the Burrup Peninsula north of Karratha and takes on an altogether more contemporary cast with the local artists still at work just up the road in Roebourne.

SUZANNE LONG/ALAMY STOCK PHOTO ©

📷 How to

Guided tours By far the best way to see the Murujuga rock art is on a guided tour. **Ngurrangga Tours** runs insightful tours led by traditional owners of the land. Aboriginal-owned and -operated **Experience Murujuga** is also excellent.

When to go The best months are May to October.

Tasmanian tigers? Rock art tells an extraordinary story; see if you can find the thylacine, a species not seen on mainland Australia in 3000 years.

MATT DEAKIN/SHUTTERSTOCK ©

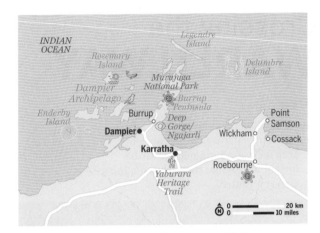

Left Rock art, Ngajarli/Deep Gorge
Below Dampier Archipelago

Dampier Archipelago

The 42-island Dampier Archipelago has piercing blue sea and sky and islands littered with rocky outcrops, white-sand beaches and mangrove forests.

The islands shelter rock-wallabies, northern quolls and countless shorebirds, the same animals that appear in millennia-old rock art on the islands. Offshore, coral reefs, sponge gardens and underwater seagrass plains provide habitat for green, hawksbill, flatback and loggerhead turtles, dugongs, dolphins, humpback whales and over 650 fish species. Most of the islands are uninhabited.

Helispirit (p234) runs scenic flights over the islands, while Ngurrangga Tours (p198) combines flights with rock art tours. Some local operators also offer boat tours which include diving and/or snorkelling.

Murujuga National Park Tucked away in the gorges of the Burrup Peninsula, Unesco World Heritage-listed Murujuga National Park is home to what may be the world's largest concentration of rock art: there are an estimated 1 million rock engravings or petroglyphs in the park. Some date back 30,000 years, and at **Ngajarli/Deep Gorge** alone, a veritable menagerie adorns the walls: fish, goannas, turtles, ospreys, kangaroos, the thylacine (once popularly known as the Tasmanian tiger) and more can all be seen from the boardwalk. If you're on the half-day tour with Ngurrangga Tours, your guide, Clinton Walker, is a Ngarluma man and gifted storyteller. The traditional owners of the park come from five different groups (Ngarluma, Yindjibarndi, Yaburara, Mardudhunera and Wong-Goo-Tt-Oo), collectively known as the Ngarda-Ngarli.

Yaburara Heritage Trail In Karratha, these three trail loops (2.25km to 3.75km long), nicely complement the rock art of Murujuga with Yaburara rock art, stone quarries and shell middens, plus excellent lookout points. Bring plenty of water and start your walks early.

Yinjaa-Barni Art In Roebourne, just 39km up the road from Karratha, this Aboriginal-run gallery showcases the best in Pilbara art with a particular focus on works by Yindjibarndi artists. Pilbara painting styles are renowned for their bold, bright colours; styles vary from traditional to abstract. Don't rush a visit here: stay long enough to sit, watch the artists at work and have a chat.

Crossing the
WARLU WAY

DRIVING | ADVENTURE | NATURE

▬▬▬ The Warlu Way crosses the Pilbara and is a barely known, fascinating link between modern traveller routes and ancient Dreaming stories from the deep well of Aboriginal knowledge. Hiking in red rock gorges, ancient Aboriginal rock art and mining towns are among the attractions en route.

TRAVELLLIGHT/SHUTTERSTOCK ©

🗺 **How to**

Getting here & around You can join at many places along the route, from near Exmouth in the south to Cape Keraudren in the north.

When to go May to September has the best weather. It's fiercely hot and humid the rest of the year.

Take the inland route There are four different route variations that form part of the **Warlu Way** (warluway.com.au). The inland route is the least travelled.

🗺 **The Dreaming Serpent**

This scenic drive follows the path of the Warlu, the Dreaming serpent who travelled the Pilbara, creating waterways as he went.

The entire route, which is dotted with interpretive signage, covers over 2500km, but you can pick and choose which sections to drive.

INDIAN OCEAN

05 The coastal reserve of **Cape Keraudren** marks the starting point of epic Eighty Mile Beach, a little-trammelled stretch of sand and wilder alternative to Broome's better-known Cable Beach.

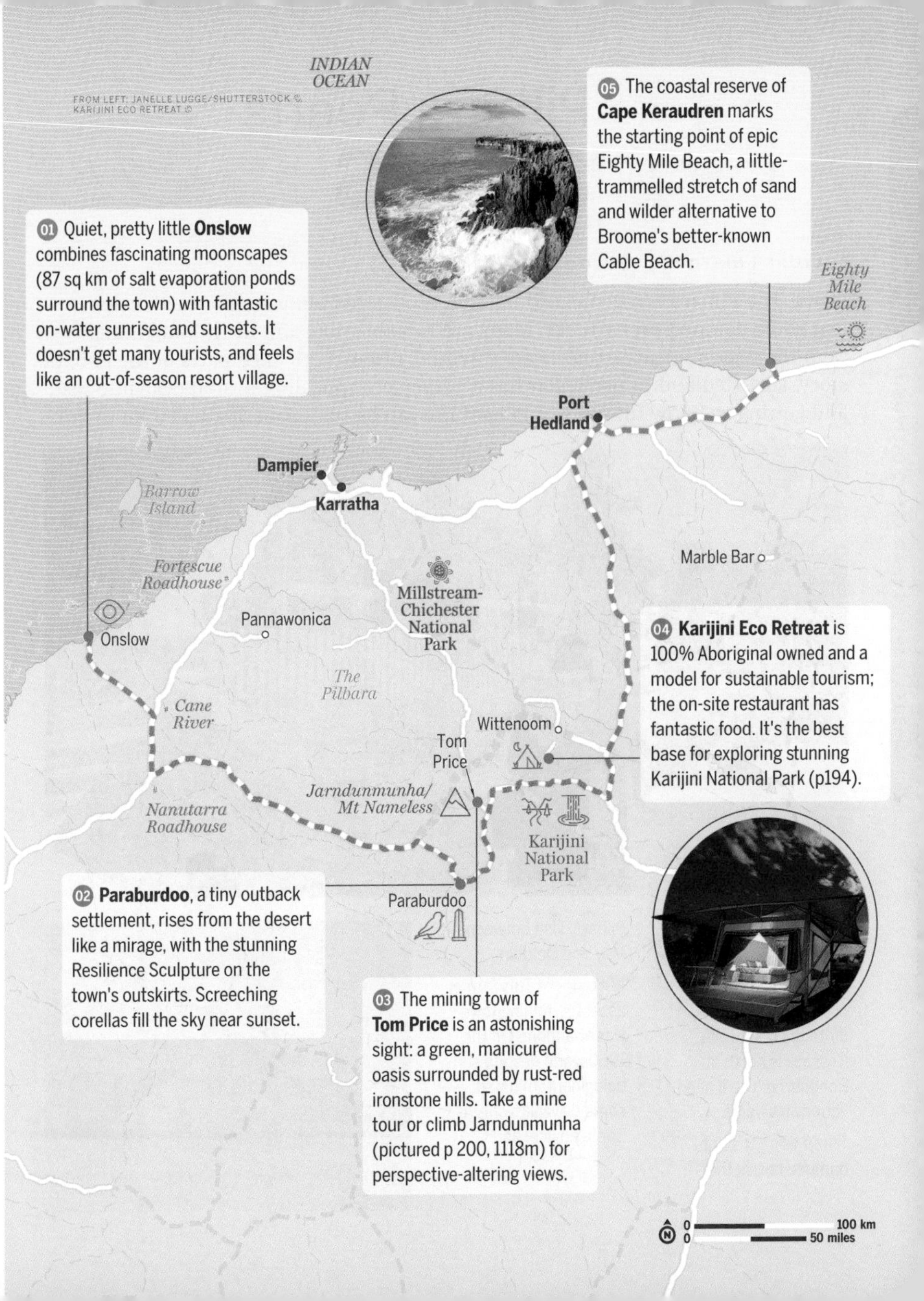

01 Quiet, pretty little **Onslow** combines fascinating moonscapes (87 sq km of salt evaporation ponds surround the town) with fantastic on-water sunrises and sunsets. It doesn't get many tourists, and feels like an out-of-season resort village.

Eighty Mile Beach

Port Hedland

Dampier

Barrow Island

Karratha

Marble Bar

Fortescue Roadhouse

Pannawonica

Millstream-Chichester National Park

04 **Karijini Eco Retreat** is 100% Aboriginal owned and a model for sustainable tourism; the on-site restaurant has fantastic food. It's the best base for exploring stunning Karijini National Park (p194).

Onslow

The Pilbara

Cane River

Wittenoom

Tom Price

Nanutarra Roadhouse

Jarndunmunha/ Mt Nameless

Karijini National Park

02 **Paraburdoo**, a tiny outback settlement, rises from the desert like a mirage, with the stunning Resilience Sculpture on the town's outskirts. Screeching corellas fill the sky near sunset.

Paraburdoo

03 The mining town of **Tom Price** is an astonishing sight: a green, manicured oasis surrounded by rust-red ironstone hills. Take a mine tour or climb Jarndunmunha (pictured p 200, 1118m) for perspective-altering views.

N 0   100 km
  0   50 miles

46 Pilbara Pearls & PITS

CULTURE | HISTORY | GEOLOGY

The Pilbara is a geological miracle, a blistered landscape of earth colours and some damned pretty rocks. Many are valuable, too, and the mining industry (and the region's pearling past) are essential, often-overlooked parts of the Pilbara story. Port Hedland in particular has a perversely appealing post-apocalyptic cast, and getting to know this side of Pilbara life can be both sobering and a lot of fun.

Post Office & Telegraph Office

COSSACK

GENEVIEVE VALLEE/ALAMY STOCK PHOTO ©

🗺 How to

Getting here & around
Port Hedland is well connected by road and air to the rest of WA. Cossack is north of Roebourne; you'll need your own vehicle.

When to go It's hot, damned hot, in the Pilbara; visit between May and October.

Wittenoom This former asbestos-mining town was abandoned in the 1960s, and despite still being contaminated, some travellers still visit. Some advice: don't.

SIMON PHELPS PHOTOGRAPHY/GETTY IMAGES ©

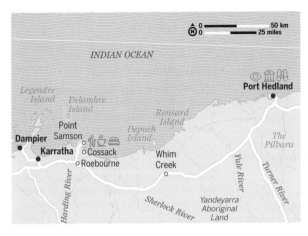

Left Post Office & Telegraph Office, Cossack
Below Salt pile, Port Hedland

Mining Tours

Mt Whaleback Mine Tour Descend into Newman's BHP Billiton's Mt Whaleback, the world's largest open-cut iron-ore mine. Tours are run by Newton Visitor Centre.

Lestok Tours From Tom Price visitor centre runs 1½-hour mine tours into the massive bowels of Rio Tinto's huge, open-cut Hamersley iron-ore mine.

Salt Eco Tour Head down the road to Dampier for a journey through the world of salt production. The tour includes a visit to wildlife-rich wetlands, and stories from the Ngarla traditional owners.

Twilight Industry Tour Get up close with the world's largest bulk loading port and learn about the mining companies that make Port Hedland tick.

Cossack The former pearling port of Cossack is the right kind of ghost town: eerily quiet, scenic and filled with ghosts. Even though it was abandoned in the 1950s, it still feels like Cossack's last people just left. Many of the bluestone buildings date from the late 1800s, and there's a pretty beach to boot. The local Aboriginal Corporation has restored some of the buildings to open a cafe, a museum, a gallery and a small B&B. There's a 5km-long **Cossack Heritage Trail**, and the **Pioneer Cemetery** has a Japanese section that bears poignant witness to Cossack's pearling past; many Aboriginal people were also kidnapped and enslaved in the industry. To get the best of a visit, leave Roebourne before dawn: you'll be one of few living souls in Cossack for a few hours.

Port Hedland This quintessential mining town is bright lights, rowdy pubs and FIFO miners spending their earnings. There's more to Port Hedland if you dig a little deeper, but it remains one of Australia's best places to glimpse the boom-bust cycle of Australia's ongoing mining and resources boom. Start with open-air **Don Rhodes Mining Museum**, with rusted trains, engines and mining machinery, then head for **Marapikurrinya Park** to watch ridiculously large iron-ore carriers and salt ships pass by; from the visitor centre, grab a list of the times the largest ships are arriving and departing. At sunset visit **Redbank Bridge Salt and Train Lookout** to admire pink-tinted mountains of salt and cargo trains going past.

Listings

BEST OF THE REST

Beautiful Beaches

Bill's Bay

Bill's Bay is Coral Bay's perfectly positioned town beach. Easy access and sheltered waters make this a favourite with everyone; snorkellers should keep to the southern end.

Bundegi Beach

Located 13km north of Exmouth, the calm, sheltered waters of Bundegi Beach (and reef) provide pleasant swimming, snorkelling, diving, kayaking and fishing.

Hearson's Cove

A fine pebble beach with calm waters for swimming and a picnic area. There's also great mudflat exploring at low tide and, from March to November, Staircase to the Moon viewing.

Diving & Snorkelling

Exmouth Navy Pier

Point Murat has one of the world's very best shore dives, under the Navy Pier. There's fantastic marine life, including nudibranchs, scorpion fish, moray eels and reef sharks. Go with **Dive Ningaloo** (diveningaloo.com.au).

Coral Bay Ecotours

Carbon-neutral tours include glass-bottom-boat cruises with snorkelling, wildlife-spotting trips to see manta ray and humpback whales, and snorkelling with whale sharks.

Ningaloo Marine Interactions

Sustainably run excursions to the outer reef include two-hour whale watching (seasonal), half-day manta ray interaction (year-round) and six-hour wildlife-spotting cruises with snorkelling.

Ningaloo Reef Dive & Snorkel

This PADI and eco-certified crew offers snorkelling with whale sharks (March to July) and manta rays (all year), reef dives, courses and 'humpback whale in-water interaction' tours.

Ocean Eco Adventures

A well-set-up operator with a luxurious vessel and its own wildlife-spotting microlight. Swim with whale sharks and humpback interaction and whale-watching tours are on offer.

Lighthouse Bay

There's great diving at Lighthouse Bay at sites such as the Labyrinth, Blizzard Reef and Helga's Tunnels. Dive operators in Exmouth can take you out.

Art Centres & Galleries

Spinifex Hill Studios

At this South Hedland studio and gallery, you'll find a considerable range of styles including those from Noongar, Banjima, Innawongka, Martu, Kariyarra, Nyiyaparli and Yamatji Pilbara cultural groups, plus works from the Torres Strait Islands.

Ningaloo Reef

East Pilbara Arts Centre

One of the state's most successful art collectives, Martumili Artists, has a beautiful gallery and workspace in Newman, in which to admire the acclaimed, vibrant art of the Martu people.

Courthouse Gallery

More than a gallery, this leafy arts HQ is the centre of all goodness in Port Hedland. Inside are stunning local contemporary and Aboriginal art exhibitions.

Seafood & More

Bill's Bar $$

The courtyard at Bill's in Coral Bay is a fine spot to enjoy fish tacos, the catch of the day, the fabulous fish curry or a bucket of prawns – washed down with a boutique ale.

Fin's Cafe $$

Fin's is a super-casual outdoor place in Coral Bay with an ever-changing menu that focuses on breakfasts, local seafood and an irresistible king snapper burger.

The Social Society $

Everything is vegan or vegetarian and made from locally sourced organic ingredients at this Exmouth cafe.

Bundegi Beach Shack $

As popular with surfers just in out of the ocean as with suits, Bundegi offers good coffee, ample brekkies, homemade burgers and buckets of Exmouth prawns.

Karijini Eco Retreat Restaurant $$

Chefs serve up fantastic dishes often accented by bush tucker ingredients.

Craft Beers

Froth Craft Brewery

This cracking Exmouth microbrewery has great ales as well as burgers. Rock out to live music with a beer in hand or sip an excellent coffee.

Prawns on ice

Whalebone Brewing Co

Drop by this Exmouth microbrewery for a hoppy Big Bone IPA or a refreshing pale ale under the stars, with pizza and occasional live music events to keep things going.

North West Brewing Co

Order a paddle of six beers to taste this Karratha microbrewery's IPAs, lager and draughts. It also has a full menu of meals and bar snacks.

Station Stays

Bullara Station

At this friendly, 2WD-accessible set-up 65km north of Coral Bay, accommodation includes stylishly renovated shearers' quarters, self-contained cottages and camp sites.

Ningaloo Station

The original station here, 50km north of Coral Bay, offers five self-sufficient wilderness camp sites on pristine coastline. Shearing-shed and other station accommodation is available.

Pardoo Station

With kilometres of tidal tracks, great angling, birding and secluded beaches, this working station is an antithesis to cookie-cutter beach vacations. Try to be here during the annual cattle muster.

BROOME &
THE KIMBERLEY

NATURE I ADVENTURE I CULTURE

**Experience
Broome & the
Kimberley
online**

BROOME & THE KIMBERLEY
Trip Builder

Mention the Kimberley to most Australians and their eyes glaze over: its remote red rock escarpments are a beloved canvas for adventures. Wildly spectacular landscapes, timeless rock art and rich Aboriginal heritage: it's all front and centre here. Most adventures begin in Broome.

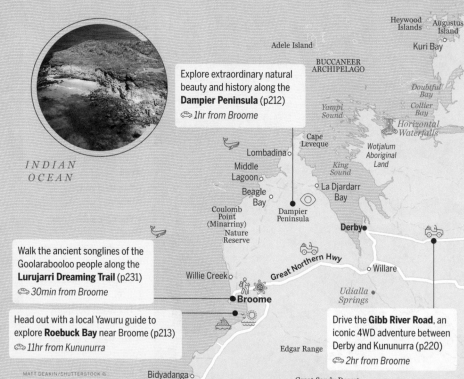

TIMOR SEA

BONAPARTE ARCHIPELAGO

Heywood Islands   Augustus Island

Adele Island   Kuri Bay

BUCCANEER ARCHIPELAGO

Explore extraordinary natural beauty and history along the **Dampier Peninsula** (p212)
🚗 *1hr from Broome*

Doubtful Bay

Yampi Sound   *Collier Bay*

Horizontal Waterfalls

Cape Leveque

Lombadina   Wotjalum Aboriginal Land

Middle Lagoon   *King Sound*

Beagle Bay   La Djardarr Bay

Coulomb Point (Minarriny) Nature Reserve   Dampier Peninsula

Derby

INDIAN OCEAN

Walk the ancient songlines of the Goolarabooloo people along the **Lurujarri Dreaming Trail** (p231)
🚗 *30min from Broome*

Willie Creek   Great Northern Hwy   Willare

Broome

Udialla Springs

Head out with a local Yawuru guide to explore **Roebuck Bay** near Broome (p213)
🚗 *11hr from Kununurra*

Drive the **Gibb River Road**, an iconic 4WD adventure between Derby and Kununurra (p220)
🚗 *2hr from Broome*

Edgar Range

MATT DEAKIN/SHUTTERSTOCK ©

Bidyadanga   Great Sandy Desert

Great Sandy Desert

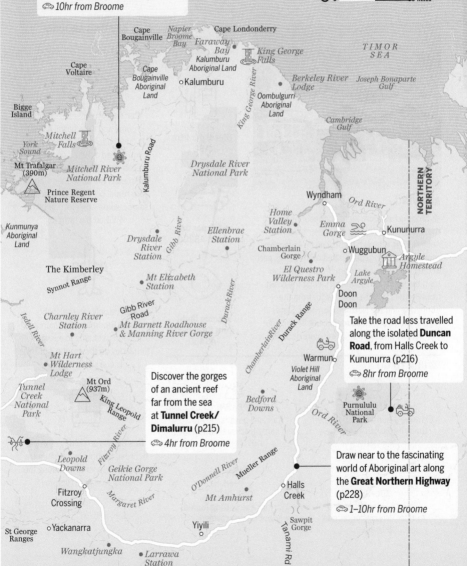

Read the Kimberley's story through the ancient rock art on an escape to the remote and beautiful **Mitchell Plateau/Ngauwudu** (p226)
🚗 10hr from Broome

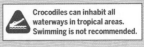

Crocodiles can inhabit all waterways in tropical areas. Swimming is not recommended.

Take the road less travelled along the isolated **Duncan Road**, from Halls Creek to Kununurra (p216)
🚗 8hr from Broome

Discover the gorges of an ancient reef far from the sea at **Tunnel Creek/Dimalurru** (p215)
🚗 4hr from Broome

Draw near to the fascinating world of Aboriginal art along the **Great Northern Highway** (p228)
🚗 1–10hr from Broome

Practicalities

INFINITY/ALAMY STOCK PHOTO ©

ARRIVING

✈ Broome has more flight connections to the rest of Australia than any other town in Australia's northwest; flights can be expensive, especially in high season. Most roads in this part of the country lead to/from Broome, whether from the south and southwest along the coast from Perth (2000km away) or to/from the Kimberley and the Northern Territory. Semi-regular buses ply these routes, but having your own vehicle gives you so many more options.

WHEN TO GO

JAN–MAR
Extremely humid and unsealed roads impassable; relatively few visitors.

APR–JUN
Rain still possible in April and some tracks still uncertain, but often fine.

JUL–SEP
Fine, clear weather and perfect driving conditions; book ahead.

OCT–DEC
Warmer and getting humid, but rarely crowded.

HOW MUCH FOR A

Diesel per litre A$2

4WD per day from A$200

Scenic flight from Kununurra A$450

GETTING AROUND

Car You can rent cars in both Broome and Kununurra. A 2WD is enough for sealed roads, but you'll need a 4WD if doing the Gibb River Road or anywhere off-road in the Kimberley. Check your rental contract: bizarre as it seems, some won't let you take a 4WD off the tarmac.

Air The only internal flights connect Broome with Kununurra, it seems a shame to miss the Kimberley on the ground, but this is one scenic flight.

Bus Buses run six days a week between Broome and Kununurra stopping in most towns along the Great Northern Highway.

EATING & DRINKING

Seafood tops the menu in Broome, Kununurra and some places in between. If you're ordering barramundi (pictured top right), make sure it's wild-caught, not from a fish farm – trust us, you'll taste the difference. Further away from civilisation, expect plenty of fried food at remote roadhouses, with each trying to outdo the other in the size of their beef burgers (with all the usual ingredients, including egg and beetroot).

Best barramundi burger
Cable Beach General Store & Cafe (p234)

Best beer
Chango (chilli/mango) at Matso's Broome Brewery (pictured bottom right; p235)

CONNECT & FIND YOUR WAY

Wi-fi is available at many cafes, hotels and businesses in larger towns, although connections may be slower than you're used to. Along most rural roads and remote roadhouses, any wi-fi you come across is a bonus, and mobile phone coverage can be patchy at best. A GPS unit and sat phone are essential if you're heading off-road.

WHERE TO STAY

Broome has far and away the biggest selection, with hostels, camping, caravan parks, motels, B&Bs and resorts. Elsewhere, choice is more limited. Some cattle stations in the Kimberley offer accommodation in converted shearers' quarters and homesteads.

Town	Pros/Cons
Broome	Lots of choice, but prices can be extortionate during the Dry.
Derby	Station stays, B&Bs, caravan parks and more; book ahead in high season.
Kununurra	Lots of choice with big price swings between the Wet and the Dry; watch for mosquitoes if camping.
Wyndham	A few choice options, including a B&B and a farmstay.

WAITOC

The **Western Australian Indigenous Tourism Operators Council** (WAITOC; waitoc.com) website is a fabulous resource that connects you to Aboriginal-owned and -operated tours, art centres and more.

MONEY

Broome and the Kimberley are expensive. Try travelling in the shoulder season (April to mid-May, or October) to keep prices down, but the weather's a risk. Carry cash for out-of-the-way expenses where there may be no ATM.

47 Beyond
BROOME

BEACHES | NATURE | CULTURE

■■■ Broome *can* be a destination in its own right, but we love it especially as a starting point for magical explorations of the Dampier Peninsula. Once out experiencing the peninsula, the world and its noise very quickly fade from view. It's all rather splendid, with Aboriginal communities, beautiful Cape Leveque and James Price Point, and beaches, headlands and red pindan cliffs that rank among Broome's best-kept secrets.

🗺 How to

Getting around Join a tour, or travel in your own car; a 2WD vehicle should be sufficient.

When to go Visit from October to April and you could get very wet.

Expect fine weather May to September.

Top tip Explore the Dampier Peninsula and learn its traditional stories with Bardi-Jawi man Bolo Angus and his family of **Lullumb Tours**.

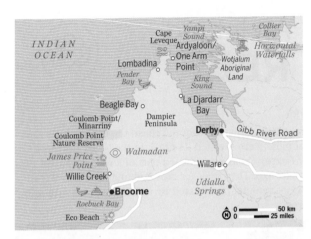

BROOME & THE KIMBERLEY EXPERIENCES

Roebuck Bay & Mangrove Tours

Local Yawuru man Bart Pigram describes Roebuck Bay, just south of Broome, as one of the northwest's hidden corners and says it's very often deserted.

He recommends exploring the bay on the Snubfin Dolphin Eco Tour run by the eco-friendly **Broome Whale Watching** (broome whalewatching.com.au); snubfin dolphins are one of Australia's rarest dolphin species and the tours are among the best wildlife experiences along the northwest coast. Then take one of the mangrove or other tours (such as a Broome city tour) by Bart's own **Narlijia Experiences** (toursbroome.com.au).

Both tours offer a holistic experience that connects the beauty and health of the bay ecosystem with its Indigenous stories from the past.

■ **Recommended by Bart Pigram**
Vice Chair of the WAITOC and owner of Narlijia Experiences, Broome
@narlijia

Broome's northern beaches Frequented mainly by anglers, locals and adventurous travellers, unsealed, sandy and sometimes corrugated Manari Rd runs roughly northwest of Broome through Goolarabooloo Country. Along the way you'll pass beaches that will feel like they're yours alone. **James Price Point** is our favourite. Here you can walk beneath or along the striking red pindan cliffs of **Walmadan** (named for the proud warrior who once lived here) and feel as if you're standing on the outer precipices of an entire continent; they're 35km from Cape Leveque Rd. It's right in the middle of the **Lurujarri Songline**.

Cape Leveque As far as you can go on the Dampier Peninsula without falling into the sea, spectacular Cape Leveque has stunning red cliffs and gorgeous white beaches perfect for swimming and snorkelling. A short drive south, between Middle Lagoon and Cape Leveque, **Lombadina** is a beautiful tree-fringed Aboriginal community that offers fishing, whale-watching, 4WD, mud-crabbing, kayaking and walking tours. Don't miss the paperbark church.

Pender Bay Exquisitely remote, this pristine bay is an important calving ground for humpback whales and many can be seen offshore from May to November. The easiest access is from either Whale Song Cafe, if open, or via the small Pender Bay campground, between Mercedes Cove and Whale Song. Few travellers make it out this way, meaning there is a very special power about this place.

48 An Inland **REEF**

NATURE | HIKING | WILDLIFE

As difficult as it is to imagine this far from the coast, the three gorges that make up the three national parks here – which lie north of the Great Northern Highway and northwest of Fitzroy Crossing – formed part of a western 'Great Barrier Reef' 350 million years ago. They're never crowded and they're pretty in a very Kimberley kind of way – remote, punctuated by waterholes, and with red, rocky outcrops as a backdrop.

RYAN HOI/SHUTTERSTOCK ©

🗺 **How to**

Getting here & around
Windjana Gorge and Tunnel Creek National Parks are accessed via the unsealed Fairfield-Leopold Downs Rd (linking the Great Northern Highway with the Gibb River Road). Geikie Gorge National Park is 22km northeast of Fitzroy Crossing along a sealed road. You'll need a 4WD or to come on a tour.

When to go The best weather and road conditions are from May to September.

Top tip Freshwater crocodiles inhabit the parks' waterholes. Always ask your guide or seek local advice before venturing close to the water's edge.

PHILIP SCHUBERT/SHUTTERSTOCK ©

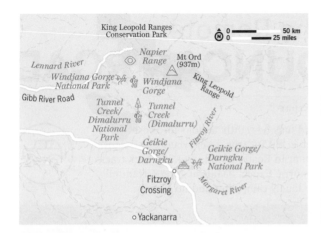

Left Boat tour, Geikie Gorge/Darngku
Below Tunnel Creek/Dimalurru

Geikie Gorge/Darngku The easiest of the three gorges to reach (and hence the busiest), 8km-long Gelkie Gorge is best appreciated from the water. **Darngku Heritage Tours** runs informative cruises through the gorge led by local Bunuba guides. You'll learn about Aboriginal culture and bush tucker as you admire the technicolour 30m-high cliffs and grapple with their difficult-to-imagine oceanic origins.

Tunnel Creek/Dimalurru Tunnel Creek cuts through the **Napier Range** for almost 1km. It was formed over millions of years by waters eroding the limestone, and was famously the hideout of Jandamarra, a Bunuba man who waged a guerrilla campaign against the police and European settlers for three years in the 19th century before he was killed. In the Dry, you can walk the full length by wading partly through knee-deep water. There's rock art around the far entrance. For the best experience, **Bungoolee Tours** (bungoolee.com.au), run by Bunuba lawman Dillon Andrews, operates two-hour Tunnel Creek tours explaining the story of Jandamarra.

Windjana Gorge The sheer walls soar 100m above the Lennard River in this gorge sacred to the Bunuba people. The waters contract in the Dry to a series of pools; scores of freshwater crocodiles often line the riverbank (swimming is not recommended). The gorge is a sandy 7km-return walk from the campground. Bungoolee Tours organises a tour that combines Windjana Gorge with Tunnel Creek.

📖 Jandamarra's Story

Bunuba land stretches across the southern reaches of the Kimberley, from Fitzroy Crossing to the Wunaamin Miliwundi (formerly King Leopold) Ranges.

Jandamarra was a respected Aboriginal stockman on a local cattle station, and became friends with an English stockman named Bill Richardson. When Richardson became a police officer, Jandamarra became his tracker.

The late 19th century was a lawless time on the frontier, and Bunuba Elders asked Jandamarra to show his loyalty to his people. He shot Richardson, then waged a three-year guerrilla campaign against the police and European settlers.

A police tracker shot and killed Jandamarra on 1 April 1897.

49 The Remote
DUNCAN ROAD

DRIVING | ADVENTURE | NATURE

■■■■ The Gibb River Road may be rightly famous for those seeking a Kimberley traverse, but for true desert silence and lightly trammelled tracks, take Duncan Road instead, a 445km back track from Halls Creek to Kununurra. Expect beautiful gorges, tranquil billabongs, breathtakingly lonely camp sites and no crowds.

JACK KINNY/SHUTTERSTOCK ©

🗺 How to

Getting here & around You must have a 4WD; check if your rental company allows you to take the vehicle along this road.

When to go Duncan Road is open from May or June until September.

Fuel & track conditions There are no services on the entire Duncan – carry enough food, water and fuel for at least 500km. Enquire at Halls Creek or Kununurra visitor centres about road conditions.

ⓘ Freshie or Saltie?

Crocodiles are a constant throughout the Kimberley, but not all crocodiles were created equal. You might get a nasty bite from a freshwater croc (freshie to the locals) if you step on one, but they're otherwise harmless. Saltwater crocs (salties), on the other hand, can grow up to 6m and they're *always* dangerous.

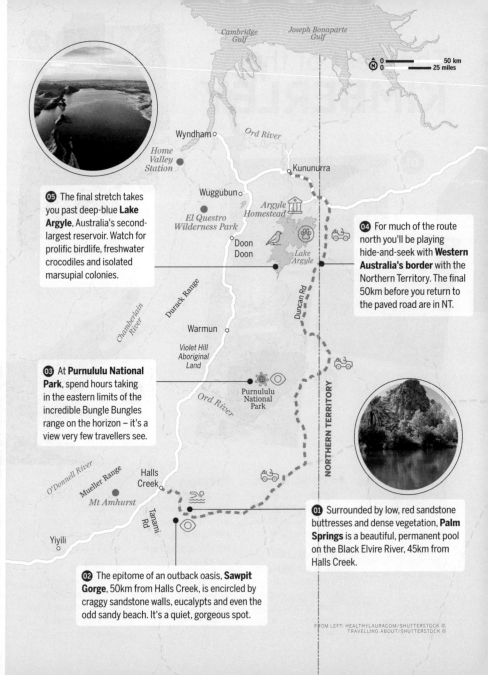

Cambridge Gulf

Joseph Bonaparte Gulf

N 0 ___ 50 km
0 ___ 25 miles

Wyndham

Ord River

Home Valley Station

Kununurra

Wuggubun

Argyle Homestead

05 The final stretch takes you past deep-blue **Lake Argyle**, Australia's second-largest reservoir. Watch for prolific birdlife, freshwater crocodiles and isolated marsupial colonies.

El Questro Wilderness Park

Doon Doon

Lake Argyle

04 For much of the route north you'll be playing hide-and-seek with **Western Australia's border** with the Northern Territory. The final 50km before you return to the paved road are in NT.

Durack Range

Chamberlain River

Duncan Rd

Warmun

Violet Hill Aboriginal Land

03 At **Purnululu National Park**, spend hours taking in the eastern limits of the incredible Bungle Bungles range on the horizon – it's a view very few travellers see.

Ord River

Purnululu National Park

NORTHERN TERRITORY

O'Donnell River

Mueller Range

Halls Creek

Mt Amhurst

Tanami Rd

Yiyili

01 Surrounded by low, red sandstone buttresses and dense vegetation, **Palm Springs** is a beautiful, permanent pool on the Black Elvire River, 45km from Halls Creek.

02 The epitome of an outback oasis, **Sawpit Gorge**, 50km from Halls Creek, is encircled by craggy sandstone walls, eucalypts and even the odd sandy beach. It's a quiet, gorgeous spot.

FROM LEFT: HEALTHYLAURACOM/SHUTTERSTOCK ©; TRAVELLING ABOUT/SHUTTERSTOCK ©

The Best of the
KIMBERLEY

01 Horizontal Falls
These extraordinary tides gush through narrow coastal gorges in the Buccaneer Archipelago. To the Dambimangari people, they're the Wongudd (creator snake).

02 4WDs
Don't leave home without one. The sealed Great Northern Highway aside, most Kimberley tracks are rugged without rain and impassable with it.

03 Rock art
The Kimberley region is one of the oldest continuously inhabited lands on earth, and it's incredible rock art tells the stories of the ages.

04 Gorges
Nothing screams 'Kimberley!' quite like a rich-red sandstone cliff-face set against the blue of a northern Australian sky.

05 Saltwater crocodiles
Lurking in many a Kimberley body of water, these ancient, fascinating creatures (p216) deserve your respect – never enter the water unless you're sure it's croc-free.

06 Brolgas
Graceful and ungainly in equal measure, the brolga is a classic Aussie bird and re-assuring presence in the

06

07

08

09

10

wetlands and rivers of the Kimberley's interior.

07 Dingoes
The Kimberley's apex predator lopes through undergrowth and across floodplains. It's best seen close to sunrise and sunset.

08 Cattle stations
Cattle stations the size of small European countries stretch across the Kimberley with farmstay accommodation and cattle musters central to outback lore.

09 Boab trees
Bulging at the base and with branches that make it look like it was planted upside down, the boab stands sentinel by many a Kimberley roadside.

10 Waterholes & waterfalls
A cooling oasis in a world of rock and sand: the waterholes and waterfalls here are classics of the Kimberley's escarpment country.

50
The Epic Gibb
RIVER ROAD

DRIVING | NATURE | CULTURE

On this 660km 4WD journey along Gibb River Road, a former cattle route between Derby and the Kununurra, you will cross rivers, pass beneath fabulous red sandstone outcrops and see rock art stretching back millennia, while traversing the Kimberley in all its glory.

🗺 How to

The route Most travellers start in Derby, but you could also begin in Kununurra. Along the main track (which takes at least three days), you'll share the Gibb with lots of other vehicles, but there are many quiet, worthwhile detours. Bring supplies for at least a week.

Driving You'll require a high-clearance 4WD and need to know how to drive it. If renting, check the rental company allows you to drive the Gibb. For road conditions see travelmap. mainroads.wa.gov.au.

When to go Gibb River Road is usually open from May until November, but late/early rains can change this.

Western Gibb

The Western Gibb is a relatively gentle precursor to what lies ahead. You will hardly hit full speed before, 4km out of Derby, you can pull over at **Mowanjum Art & Culture Centre** where Mowanjum artists recreate Wandjina and Gwion Gwion images in an incredible gallery. At the 119km mark, the first of the Gibb's enticing detours, to **Windjana Gorge**, branches away to the south. The gorge is a stunning, if popular spot, with a waterhole surrounded by a sandy beach, boulders and sandstone cliffs.

One detour that is far less frequented is the rough 29km track to **Bell Gorge**; you'd be surprised how many travellers turn around at the first corrugations. Your reward is magnificent with a picturesque

✅ Carson River Track

Aboriginal-owned Just Over the Hills (p233) is one of few operators currently permitted to run tag-along 4WD tours along the legendary Carson River Track between Kalumburu and Wyndham via one of Australia's remotest communities, Oombulgurri. This is as remote as it gets, and you may drive for days without seeing another vehicle.

Above left Bell Gorge
Above Freshwater crocodiles, Windjana Gorge National Park
Left Windjana Gorge

waterfall and plunge pool. Another fabulous road-less-travelled detour is the 50km side track to **Mount Hart Wilderness Lodge**, which lies deep in the Wunaamin Miliwundi Ranges (formerly King Leopold Ranges) Conservation Park. It's a glorious road in, and a stay here is a fascinating insight into station life.

Central Gibb

Most travellers continue along the main Gibb track. But if you have the time, it's worth detouring off along some quieter trails.

The superb **Mornington Wilderness Camp** is one of the most rewarding excursions off the Gibb. Reached via a turn-off 247km from Derby, it has a 95km driveway across the wild, lonely savannah. Run by the Australian Wildlife Conservancy (AWC) and devoted to conserving the Kimberley's endangered fauna, it offers excellent canoeing, swimming, birdwatching and bushwalking. Don't miss the sunsets at sublime Sir John Gorge.

Reached via another detour 44km off the Gibb is another AWC property, the historic **Charnley River Station**. It offers shaded,

♨ Kalumburu

Isolated Kalumburu, Western Australia's most northerly settlement nearly 380km north of the Gibb River Road, is a picturesque Aboriginal community nestled beneath giant mango trees and coconut palms on the King Edward River.

The Wunambal and Kwini are the traditional owners. There's rock art and a WWII bomber wreck nearby, and stunning hourglass **Wongalala Falls**, which only opened to non-Aboriginal tourists in 2018, empties into a large, perfectly circular plunge pool. Most of all, it's a chance to spend time in an Aboriginal community (two-thirds of which runs on solar power) while it goes quietly about its daily business.

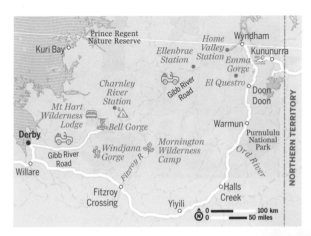

Left Rock art, Kalumburu
Below El Questro Wilderness Park

grassy camp sites, excellent birdwatching and the stunning, multitiered Grevillea Gorge and adjacent Lily Pools.

And if you're really keen to have it all to yourself, **Munja Track** is desperately remote and one of the most challenging 4WD tracks in the country. It leads from the Mt Elizabeth Station turn-off (338km from Derby) through the Kimberley's heart and soul to the Indian Ocean coastline at Walcott Inlet.

Eastern Gibb

The eastern Gibb River Road is gorgeous, although it's more difficult to escape the crowds. One exception comes at the Kalumburu turn-off. Follow it for an adventure very few undertake.

Highlights along the main track include the scones at **Ellenbrae Station**, crossing the mighty **Durack River** then climbing through the **Pentecost Ranges** with panoramic views of the Cockburn Ranges, Cambridge Gulf and Pentecost River. Close to the **Pentecost River crossing** – the most photographed river crossing in the Kimberley, with wonderful escarpments in the background – the cliff-lined **El Questro Wilderness Park** looms on the right. While it may be busy and the road sealed, **Emma Gorge** is one last piece of magic before you return to civilisation: this sublime plunge pool and waterfall is one of the prettiest in the whole Kimberley.

Paradise Almost Lost

THE BATTLE FOR JAMES PRICE POINT

Western Australia is a hotly contested frontier when it comes to the environment and mining. This is Australia's richest state for underground resources, but it also has few peers when it comes to natural beauty. When the battle lines are drawn between the two, it's always a fascinating story.

Left Protest signs, Jame Price Point
Centre Dinosaur footprints
Right Largetooth sawfish

PHILIP SCHUBERT/SHUTTERSTOCK ©

The Battle Begins

In 2005, a multinational consortium involving Woodside Petroleum, BP, Royal Dutch Shell and others partnered with the WA government to announce plans for the world's biggest liquefied natural gas (LNG) station at James Price Point. It would have been a lucrative project for the state, providing jobs and tax revenues for many years to come. But there was more than money at stake.

James Price Point is an expanse of wilderness along the Kimberley coast 60km north of Broome and is a place of staggering natural beauty. Aside from its dinosaur fossils dating back 135 million years, the proposed site for the plant was a playground for dolphins, dugongs and breeding bilbies. Humpback whales breed and calve along the coastline, and the rainforest backing the coast harbours a multitude of plant species. And, importantly, this is the traditional Aboriginal land of the local Goolarabooloo people.

Paradise Saved

The battle over James Price Point became one of Australia's defining environmental battlegrounds in the first decade of the 21st century. On one side was the powerful mining sector backed by a government eager to show it was open for business. Arrayed against them were environmental groups and the local Goolarabooloo people. It was a public relations disaster for the government, with images of local Indigenous peoples and others being forcibly removed by police as the bulldozers moved in being beamed around the country.

In 2013 the Supreme Court of Western Australia overruled the WA Environment Minister and the WA

Environmental Protection Authority to block the proposed Browse LNG plant at James Price Point. In response, eight years after first proposing the development, Woodside Petroleum Ltd and its coalition partners announced that the refineries were not economically viable.

When it comes to the region's heritage, their withdrawal was just as well. A 2016 University of Queensland study of the region's cretaceous footprints concluded that they are the world's largest dinosaur footprint collection, with 21 species represented. The site may also contain the world's largest single dinosaur footprint. Further sauropod footprints were found here in 2017, measuring a massive 1.7m across, breaking the record for 'world's biggest' again. A 2019 Federal Court ruling also confirmed that 93.5% of the Kimberley is now under some form of native title protection.

> The battle over James Price Point became one of Australia's defining environmental battlegrounds.

Despite this, and despite the state government's policy to transition to net-zero carbon emissions by 2050, the powerful mining lobby retains a strong hold over government policy in the west. These interests can still trump the rights of traditional land owners and environmental concerns. In late 2021, close to Fitzroy Crossing, the Nyikina Warrwa traditional custodians stepped up their campaign to protect the sacred Martuwarra river, which is a habitat for the endangered freshwater sawfish.

At around the same time, it emerged in late 2021 – nine years after Woodside and its partners announced their withdrawal – that the WA government has not given up on the idea of an LNG plant, possibly even at James Price Point. The battle, it seems, may not be over yet.

Emu-Man

For many Australians, the very public struggle for the future of James Price Point introduced them for the first time to the remarkable natural heritage of the Dampier Peninsula.

Of course, local Aboriginal Jabirr Jabirr and Goolarabooloo people have always known about these footprints on the beach: to them, the footprints represent the steps of Emu-man, their Dreaming ancestor who lives today in the land, the people and their stories.

For the moment at least, it's this kind of deep liquid time, rather than liquid natural gas, that has won the day.

51 Deep in the KIMBERLEY

NATURE | HIKING | ROCK ART

Even in a region where everywhere is remote and paved roads are hundreds of kilometres distant, the Mitchell Plateau/Ngauwudu is what lies beyond. Very few travellers make it out here, to a land that is very much the essence of the Kimberley's wild and captivating charm: stunning landscapes, lots of wildlife, ancient rock art and a generally soul-stirring experience.

AUSCAPE/UNIVERSAL IMAGES GROUP VIA GETTY IMAGES ©

🗺 How to

Getting here & around
You'll need a well-equipped, high-clearance 4WD to get here. Fill up at Drysdale River Station and check the road conditions before setting off. You can fly here from Kununurra on a tour.

When to go Roads here depend on the rains.

They're usually passable from May or June until September.

Wunambal Gaambera Country This is the only place in mainland Australia to have experienced no mammal extinctions since Europeans arrived.

JANELLE LUGGE/SHUTTERSTOCK ©

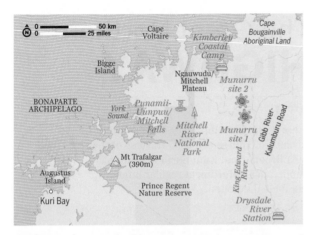

Left Gwion Gwion images
Below Mitchell Falls/Punamii-Uunpuu

Munurru rock art There's rock art across the Kimberley, but the two Munurru sites are two of the best. The first Munurru site has incredible Wandjina and kangaroo rock art on the rear of a clump of sandstone boulders; Wandjina is an arresting and culturally significant rain-maker spirit found across the Kimberley. The second site features Gwion Gwion images, a style of painting unique to the Kimberley and dominated by elegant, stylised human figures. Much debate surrounds the dating of the Gwion Gwion paintings, with estimates ranging from 12,000 to 45,000 years old. Both sites are accessible from the **Munurru Campground** on the banks of the King Edward River.

National Heritage–listed waterfall Mitchell River National Park contains the stunning, multi-tiered **Mitchell Falls/Punamii-Uunpuu**. The easy 8.6km-return trail from the dusty Mertens Campground meanders through spinifex, woodlands and gorge country, dotted with Wandjina and Gwion Gwion rock-art sites, secluded waterholes, lizards, wallabies and brolga. The falls are stunning, whether trickling in the Dry, or raging in the Wet (when only visible from the air). You can swim in the long pool above the falls, but swimming in the lower pools is strictly forbidden because of their cultural importance to the Wunambal people. Set out to explore it all early enough in the morning and it will feel like your own personal paradise, especially early or late in the season.

ⓘ **Ununguu Visitor Pass**

The far north region of the Kimberley is Wunambal Gaambera Country.

To visit approved locations here, you must purchase the Ununguu Visitor Pass (adult/family five-day pass $45/110), which covers the Ngauwudu Road Zone (ie Mitchell Plateau, Mitchell Falls and Munurru Campground).

Passes can be bought online from **Wunambal Gaambera Aboriginal Corporation** (wunambalgaambera. org.au).

52 The Great Northern
HIGHWAY

DRIVING | NATURE | ADVENTURE

Just because you're not doing the Gibb River Road doesn't mean you can't have an adventure. This sealed-road traverse of the southern Kimberley between Broome and Kununurra is stunning, with red-rock Kimberley landscapes unfurling at regular intervals. There are even some drama-fuelled detours.

DAVID PETIT/SHUTTERSTOCK ©

🗺 How to

Getting here & around You can drive the road in either direction; car-rental companies offer one-way packages. You'll need a 4WD for the detours.

When to go May to September is best. Roads to Mimbi and Purnululu may be impassable at other times, and high humidity and rainfall can spoil your fun.

Doon Doon Roadhouse Truckers dream of the Doon Doon burger or an egg-and-bacon roll at this classic outback roadhouse, 105km south of Kununurra.

🗺 Wolfe Creek

Rarely visited **Wolfe Creek meteorite crater** (pictured) is a fantastic excursion from Halls Creek. According to the local Jaru people, Kandimalal is where a huge rainbow serpent emerged from the ground. The impressive crater (880m across and 60m deep) is remote (137km south along Tanami Rd) and eerie. Take a scenic flight over the site from Halls Creek.

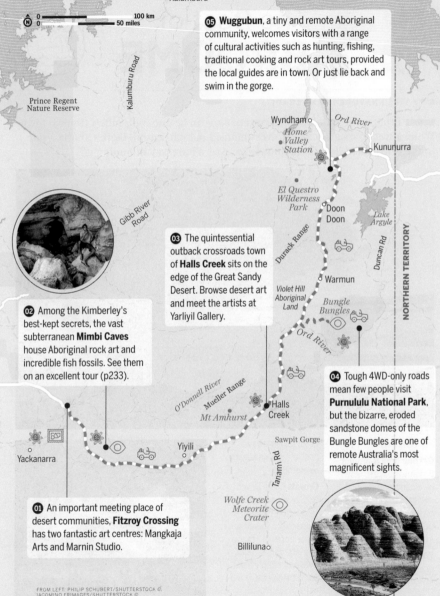

○ Kalumburu

0 ———— 100 km
0 ———— 50 miles

N

Prince Regent
Nature Reserve

Kalumburu Road

Gibb River Road

05 **Wuggubun**, a tiny and remote Aboriginal community, welcomes visitors with a range of cultural activities such as hunting, fishing, traditional cooking and rock art tours, provided the local guides are in town. Or just lie back and swim in the gorge.

Wyndham ○
Home
Valley
Station

Ord River

○ Kununurra

El Questro
Wilderness
Park

Doon
Doon

Lake
Argyle

Durack Range

Duncan Rd

NORTHERN TERRITORY

03 The quintessential outback crossroads town of **Halls Creek** sits on the edge of the Great Sandy Desert. Browse desert art and meet the artists at Yarliyil Gallery.

Violet Hill
Aboriginal
Land

○ Warmun

*Bungle
Bungles*

Ord River

02 Among the Kimberley's best-kept secrets, the vast subterranean **Mimbi Caves** house Aboriginal rock art and incredible fish fossils. See them on an excellent tour (p233).

O'Donnell River

Mueller Range

Mt Amhurst

Halls
Creek

Sawpit Gorge

04 Tough 4WD-only roads mean few people visit **Purnululu National Park**, but the bizarre, eroded sandstone domes of the Bungle Bungles are one of remote Australia's most magnificent sights.

○ Yiyili

Tanami Rd

○ Yackanarra

01 An important meeting place of desert communities, **Fitzroy Crossing** has two fantastic art centres: Mangkaja Arts and Marnin Studio.

*Wolfe Creek
Meteorite
Crater*

Billiluna ○

FROM LEFT: PHILIP SCHUBERT/SHUTTERSTOCK ©;
IACOMINO FRIMAGES/SHUTTERSTOCK ©

53 The Best of
BROOME

CITY LIFE | NATURE | LANDSCAPE

Broome (or Rubibi, its Yawuru name) can be one cool, sultry, tropical town. While attractions here can get overwhelmed in high season, there's another side to the town and a little local knowledge goes a long way in finding it.

METRIOGNOME/SHUTTERSTOCK ©

📷 How to

Getting here & around
Broome is easy to reach by air and long road, and easy to get around on foot. Having a car or joining a tour makes everything easier.

When to go Broome is uncomfortably humid from October to April when rain is always possible. Come May to September.

Crowds Cable Beach (p232) sunsets are wonderful – but be prepared to share the experience with many tourists, camels and 4WDs, or simply head some place else.

IMAGE PROFESSIONALS GMBH/ ALAMY STOCK PHOTO ©

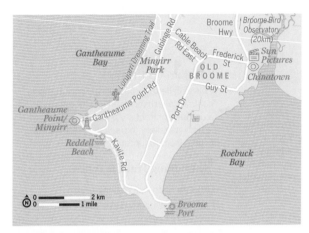

Left Sunset, Gantheaume Pt/Minyirr
Below Sun Pictures

Sunsets beyond Cable For a glorious sunset, watch the pindan cliffs turn scarlet along **Reddell Beach**. Nearby, the lookout at **Gantheaume Point/Minyirr** is beautiful at dawn or sunset. Not far away, and only visible at very low tide, is a 135-million-year-old secret: one of the world's most varied collections of **dinosaur footprints**. Grab a map from the visitor centre. Walking trails also lead through the red dunes of **Minyirr Park**, a spiritual place for the Yawuru people.

Nature's show The RAMSAR-recognised tidal mudflats of **Broome Bird Observatory** at Roebuck Bay are where thousands of migratory birds, coming from as far away as Siberia, stop to rest and feed. It's a spectacular sight in a peaceful coastal setting. Just as impressive but, after dark, are the brilliant two-hour stargazing tours run by Greg Quicke of **Astro Tours**. Greg's commentary brings the night sky alive.

Broome's story Yawuru local Johani Mamid of **Mabu Buru Broome Aboriginal Tours** (broomeaboriginaltours.com.au) runs excellent cultural tours in and around Broome, covering everything from the history of Broome and the lands here prior to white colonisation to local indigenous bush foods.

The big screen Broome has a wonderfully retro feel at times, nowhere more so than at **Sun Pictures**, the world's oldest operating picture gardens, having opened in 1916. If only these walls could talk: the Sun building has witnessed war, floods, low-flying aircraft and racial segregation.

✅ Lurujarri Dreaming Trail

This incredible 82km walk follows a section of ancient songline north along the coast from Gantheaume Point/ Minyirr to Coulomb Point/Minarriny. The local Goolarabooloo people organise several nine-day guided walking trips each dry season, staying at traditional camp sites. There is a strong emphasis on sharing Aboriginal culture with activities like spear-making, bush-tucker hunting, fishing, mud-crabbing and native jewellery making.

The songline (an oral memory map of stories, song and dance describing the landscape, handed down from generation to generation) stretches from Cape Leveque to the deserts south of Broome.

Listings

BEST OF THE REST

 Beaches

Cable Beach

WA's most famous landmark offers turquoise waters and beautiful white sand curving away to the sunset. Two or three times a month between March and October, watch for the Staircase to the Moon phenomenon out over the tidal flats.

 Art Centres

Bungalow

This outpost of Broome's well-known Short Street Gallery holds a stunning collection of canvases from across the Kimberley and beyond. If you're not heading out into remote communities, and even if you are, stop by for a primer.

Nagula Jarndu Women's Resource Centre

Another excellent Broome gallery, this studio gallery, run by Yawuru women, showcases and sells beautiful screen- and block-printed textiles and other crafts.

Bidyadanga Community Art Centre

Bringing together inspiration from the desert to the coast, five different language groups create brilliant acrylic artworks in WA's largest Aboriginal community. It's just down the coast from Broome and easy to reach.

Norval Gallery

Kimberley art legends Mark and Mary Norval have set up an exciting gallery in an old tin shed on the edge of Derby. There's always a chance to see visiting Aboriginal artists in action at one of the many workshops.

Waringarri Aboriginal Arts

This excellent Kununurra gallery-studio hosts local artists working with ochres in a unique abstract style and runs 1½-hour, artist-led gallery tours. It also represents artists from Kalumburu.

Walking Trails & Tours

Broome Historical Walking Tours

Fabulous 1½-hour walking tour examining Broome's history – from WWII back to the pearling days – through site visits and photographs with raconteur Wil telling some fabulous stories.

Joonjoo Botanical Trail

This 2.3km trail through Derby begins opposite the Gibb River Road turn-off and has neat interpretive displays from the local Nyikina people. It's a fascinating introduction to local ethno-botanical traditions.

Bushwalking Corridors

Three bushwalking corridors have been established across Wunambel Gaambera Country. The corridors are all arduous, remote and trackless undertakings and groups need to be totally self-sufficient.

PORTADOWN/SHUTTERSTOCK ©

Cable Beach

Jetty to Jetty Trail

This self-guided, 3.4km heritage trail created by local Yawuru people takes you along Broome's Roebuck Bay foreshore with 13 stops at historical and cultural sites of significance. Download the Jetty to Jetty app to hear stories told by local Elders.

Kayaking & Diving

Broome Adventure Company

Glide past turtles, hidden beaches and sea caves on these eco-certified coastal kayaking trips. It's a wonderful way to explore the superb coastline near Broome, free of crowds and all engine noise.

Odyssey Expeditions

Runs several eight-day, live-aboard diving tours each spring to the Rowley Shoals Marine Park, three coral atolls 300km from Broome on Australia's continental shelf. You must be an experienced diver.

Aboriginal-led Tours

Mimbi Caves

Aboriginal-owned and -operated Mimbi Caves Tours runs trips to Mimbi Caves, a subterranean labyrinth housing Aboriginal rock art and fish fossils. The tours include an introduction to local Dreaming stories, bush tucker and traditional medicines.

Uptuyu Adventures

Down in Nyikina Country on the Fitzroy River, 50km from the Great Northern Highway, Neville runs 'designer' cultural tours taking in wetlands, rock art, fishing and Aboriginal communities.

Lullumb Tours

Take an inspiring journey through Bardi Jawi culture and the mangroves, paperbark forests, salt plains, creeks and springs of the Dampier Peninsula.

Kayakers, Gantheaume Pt/Minyirr, Broome

Kimberley Dreamtime Adventure Tours

Aboriginal-owned-and-operated cultural tours based in Nyikina Mangala Country on Mt Anderson Station, 126km southeast of Derby. Camp under the stars, ride camels, fish, hunt, walk and learn about Aboriginal culture.

Luridgii Tours

Be personally guided through the gorges, thermal pools and Dreaming stories of Miriuwung Country by the traditional owners on these 4WD cultural tag-alongs, starting from Doon Doon Roadhouse. Cultural Awareness tours are also offered.

Waringarri Art & Culture Tours

The Waringarri mob in Kununurra run informative 2½-hour art and culture tours around Mirima National Park (including a stunning Sunset Tour) and longer 'On Country' tours at local sites with traditional custodians.

Just Over the Hills

These Aboriginal-run 4WD tag-along tours showcase local culture and rock art in the remote East Kimberley. It also runs all-inclusive women-only tours on demand, sharing experiences with local Aboriginal women.

Scenic Flights

Broome Aviation

Half-day flights to Cape Leveque and the Horizontal Falls from Broome. Full-day tours add on the Devonian Reef National Parks, Bell Gorge and Mt Hart, Mitchell Falls or even the Bungle Bungles. Wow.

Fly Broome

Flies a loop from Broome out over the Dampier Peninsula and Buccaneer Falls to the Horizontal Falls, then lands at Cape Leveque for an inclusive meal and swim at the resort.

Horizontal Falls Seaplane Adventures

Operating out of Derby, this mob runs flights to Horizontal Falls land on Talbot Bay before transferring to high-powered speedboats for an adrenaline-packed ride through both sets of falls.

HeliSpirit

The Kimberley's largest chopper outfit offers scenic flights over the Bungle Bungles, Mitchell Falls, Kununurra, King George Falls, Lake Argyle and anywhere else in the Kimberley.

Bungle Bungle Guided Tours

Aboriginal-run half-day walking tours to Cathedral Gorge and Echidna Chasm and a full-day helicopter ride/hike to Piccaninny Gorge inside Purnululu National Park. Tours can be linked up with scenic flights from Kununurra, Warmun and Halls Creek.

✕ Broome Dining & Beyond

Sydney Cove Oyster Bar $$$

In quite a coup for Broome, this Sydney classic relocated to Broome in 2021, bringing with it an expert's touch and marrying it to fresh, local and sustainably sourced produce.

The Aarli $$

Ask any Broome local where they love eating and most will say the Aarli, with its wonderful outdoor relaxed dining and the shared plates that Broome does so well.

Cable Beach General Store & Cafe $

We dream about the general store's barramundi burger and order it at every available opportunity when we're here.

Sampey Meats $

Carnivores can stock up for the Gibb and any other wild Kimberley trails with homemade jerkies, biltong and succulent vacuum-sealed steaks at this butcher shop in Derby.

Wild Mango $

Hip and healthy offerings here in Kununurra include breakfast burritos, pancakes, chai smoothies, real coffee and homemade gelato.

Croc Cafe & Bakery $

Billed as WA's 'most northern bakery', the quirky selection of pies at this Wyndham bakery include crocodile and barramundi. Enjoy under the mango trees in the courtyard.

The Wharf Restaurant $$

Watch for whales and enjoy chilli crab or barramundi wings in Broome. Don't order the oysters before 2pm.

Bungle Bungles, Purnululu National Park

Best Brews

Matso's Broome Brewery

There's only one order to kick things off here: a Chango (50/50 chilli/mango beer) and a half-kilo bucket of prawns. Enjoy live music on the verandah most afternoons.

Crossing Inn

For a true outback beer experience, sink a cold one at the Kimberley's oldest pub at Fitzroy Crossing. Friday nights can be rowdy and there's not a pretension in sight.

Moontide Distillery

Opened in Broome in 2020, Moontide uses Kimberley monsoonal rainwater and native botanicals in its gins.

Coffee & Cold Drinks

Good Cartel

The hippest place in Broome to grab a great coffee, healthy juice and Mexican-themed brekkies. Locals queue for its lunchtime burgers.

Bay Club

The Mangrove Hotel's casual outdoor bar is perfect for a few early bevvies while contemplating Roebuck Bay. Sophisticated, healthy bistro meals and live music complement excellent Staircase to the Moon viewing.

Little Local

This appealing little cafe and provedore is fast becoming a Broome favourite thanks to its artful cooking and commitment to local produce.

Mabu Mayi Café

Aboriginal owned and run in Broome, this cafe uses traditional Yawuru ingredients in its dishes and fun native sodas (eg lemon myrtle, or mango and rosella). It also supports local Aboriginal employment.

Matro's Broome Brewery

Station Stays

Home Valley Station

Leave the privations of the Gibb behind at Home Valley Station, a hospitality training resort for local Aboriginal men and women.

Ellenbrae Station

Famous for its fresh scones, atmospheric Ellenbrae Station is located 70km east of the Kalumburu turn-off. The stockmen cabins evoke the storied past of cattle musters and remote homesteads in their nostalgic decor.

Drysdale River Station

Fifty-nine kilometres from the Gibb, Drysdale River is a Kimberley icon and an oasis of fuel, meals and accommodation. Staying here is a window on the world of working cattle stations.

Parry Creek Farm

Surrounded by Parry Lagoons Nature Reserve, 25km from Wyndham, this tranquil farm with grassy camp sites attracts hordes of wildlife. It's all about the location and surroundings here, with, among other highlights, a raised boardwalk overlooking a billabong.

 Scan to find more things to do in Broome & the Kimberley online

Practicalities

ARRIVING

238

GETTING AROUND

240

SAFE TRAVEL

242

MONEY

243

RESPONSIBLE TRAVEL

244

ACCOMMODATION

246

ESSENTIALS

248

Right Bungle Bungles, Purnululu National Park (p217)

EASY STEPS FROM THE AIRPORT TO THE CITY CENTRE

Most domestic and all international travellers arrive through Perth. You can fly into, or out from, a number of other regional airports from interstate airports. Otherwise, it's a long drive from South Australia or the Northern Territory.

AT THE AIRPORT

EQROY/SHUTTERSTOCK ©

SIM CARDS
You'll have more choice if you wait to buy a SIM Card in the city centre. **Telstra** (telstra.com.au) has much wider mobile-phone coverage across WA than **Optus** (optus.com.au) and **Vodafone** (vodafone.com.au), both of which have shops in Perth's international arrivals hall.

CURRENCY EXCHANGE
There are a number of Travelex foreign currency exchange counters in Perth Airport. Exchange rates are generally comparable to the banks and forex bureaux in the city centre, and you may even be able to negotiate for a slightly better rate for large amounts and major currencies.

 WI-FI Fast, free wi-fi at Perth Airport; coverage reaches bus stops and Uber/taxi pick-up points.

 ATMS All major banks have ATMs at Perth Airport and foreign cards are accepted. Find them located on both sides of the security checks.

 CHARGING STATIONS Most dining areas have a small number of charging stations; bring an international adaptor.

 ESSENTIALS
Perth Airport has most of the facilities you'll need, but choice is limited when it comes to shops and restaurants after you've passed through international departure screening. The domestic terminal is well served by shops and restaurants. If seeking a GST customs refund, turn right after passing through security but before completing passport control.

GETTING TO THE CITY CENTRE

Bus Transperth bus 40 travels between T3 and T4 and Elizabeth Quay Bus Station. Bus 380 connects T1 and T2 with the same station.

Shuttle bus Private shuttle buses depart every 20 minutes.

EARDLEY235/SHUTTERSTOCK ©

HOW MUCH FOR A

Bus
A$4.90
40min

Shuttle bus
A$18–24
20–30min

Taxi
from A$45
15–20min

The terminals
T1 handles most international flights, plus Virgin Australia interstate flights. T2 handles most regional WA flights. T3 is for Jetstar flights; T4 handles all Qantas flights.

Between terminals
It's a short walk or free shuttle bus between terminals at Perth Airport.

Restrictions With Western Australia's borders closed to international flights, and restrictions in place for domestic flights for almost two years, Perth Airport was almost deserted. As things get back to normal, expect things to change – shop and restaurant closures, but possibly also other new businesses moving in to fill the gaps.

WEST COAST AUSTRALIA ARRIVING

OTHER POINTS OF ENTRY

Broome Airport Perth may be far and away Western Australia's busiest airport, but that's not to say there aren't others. The busiest of the other airports is Broome, although its activity is seasonal: flights come and go regularly from May or June to September or October, then taper off to much quieter arrival/departure boards the rest of the year; there's also a peak around Christmas and New Year.

Regional airports Geraldton, Port Hedland and Kununurra all have single-terminal airports that come to life whenever a flight arrives from interstate or from elsewhere in WA. Some airports only handle intra-WA flights to/from Perth. These include Albany, Esperance and Exmouth (Learmonth). There's also a convenient, direct Melbourne–Margaret River (Busselton) service three times a week.

Interstate by road Although many desert land trails cross into Western Australia from the Northern Territory and South Australia, there are only two paved roads. In the south, the epic Eyre Hwy runs across the barren Nullabor Plain from SA's Port Augusta to Perth (around 2400km). Up north, the road from Katherine in the NT to Kununurra is a more-beautiful 515km stretch of tarmac.

TRANSPORT TIPS TO HELP YOU GET AROUND

Having your own vehicle is the best way to explore West Coast Australia. Remember, however, that distances are vast and, unless you have unlimited time, it might be worth taking some internal flights if you plan on covering much of the coast. If you plan on going off-road, you'll need a 4WD (and experience driving one).

THE COASTAL ROAD

The main coast road is well maintained and good for driving, although it's single-lane in either direction most of the way; be mindful of large trucks. You're never far from the coast, although the road does veer inland for long stretches in some areas.

THE INLAND ROUTE

The main alternative to the coastal highway is the inland route which connects Perth with Port Hedland. It leaves the coast north of Perth and crosses 1628 desert kilometres. It's a long way between fuel stops, so fill up when and where you can.

CAR RENTAL PER DAY

4WD vehicle from A$250

Petrol (Perth) A$1.88 per litre

Perth parking A$5 per hour

BUS Buses run along the main coast road between Perth and Broome, and between Perth and Kununurra or Wyndham. They're comfortable and reliable, but long-distance intercity services rarely run more often than once a day, thereby limiting their usefulness.

CAR RENTALS One option is to drive along the coast in one direction and then fly back. Remember, though, that many car-rental companies have one-way drop-off fees which can be exorbitant. This sometimes doesn't apply between Broome and Kununurra.

DRIVING ESSENTIALS

Drive on the left, steering wheels are on the right.

.05
Blood alcohol limit is 0.05%.

The speed limit is 50km/h in built-up areas, to 110 km/h in rural areas.

18
Legal driving age is 18.

Take notice of 'Next petrol ... km' signs.

4WD RENTAL If renting a 4WD, make sure you understand where you can and can't go. Some car-rental companies rent 4WD vehicles, but won't allow you to take them off road. Those that do may have restrictions on which tracks are allowed. If renting in Broome or Kununurra, the Gibb River Road (p220) is probably fine, but always read the rental contract's small print. If you ignore restrictions and travel on an unsealed road, you won't be covered by insurance.

NIGHT DRIVING Be careful when driving at night. Most roads between towns are poorly lit, and oncoming large trucks with strong headlights can be disorienting. If you do have to travel between sunset to sunrise, you should lower your speed and watch out for wildlife: after dark is when all manner of Australian animals are out and about and they often cross the road without warning. Be particularly careful at dusk and dawn.

SLOW TRAVEL In the spirit of 'slow travel' trends in the post-pandemic age, it's sometimes better to spend more time in a small number of places than trying to cover too much territory. This works along this coast, where it's often a long way between pit stops.

WEATHER Keep an eye on weather reports. It doesn't rain often along this coast, but it can be pretty torrential when it does. After rains, unsealed roads can become impassable, and even paved roads can become slippery and subject to flash flooding.

KNOW YOUR CARBON FOOTPRINT
A domestic flight from Perth to Broome would emit about 629kg of carbon dioxide per passenger. A bus would emit 60kg for the same distance, per passenger, while a normal car would emit 420kg (that's for the whole car, not per passenger).

WEST COAST AUSTRALIA GETTING AROUND

ROAD DISTANCE CHART (KMS)

	Perth	Margaret River	Albany	Geraldton	Denham	Exmouth	Port Hedland	Broome	Halls Creek
Margaret River	275								
Albany	418	343							
Geraldton	419	683	821						
Denham	823	1092	1229	408					
Exmouth	1249	1517	1654	834	683				
Port Hedland	1630	1904	1985	1337	1187	778			
Broome	2224	2498	2578	1931	1781	1372	610		
Halls Creek	2840	3113	3194	2547	2396	1987	1225	686	
Kununurra	3197	3472	3552	2905	2755	2346	1583	1044	358

SAFE TRAVEL

West Coast Australia is a safe destination, with low crime rates and excellent road safety. As with any travel, always keep an eye on your belongings and drive carefully in unfamiliar road conditions. Wild weather is the greatest threat.

 SWIMMING SAFETY Swimming deaths occur here every year, even at seemingly tranquil spots. Rips and strong currents can be especially dangerous; always get advice on local conditions before swimming.

 ROAD CONDITIONS If you're driving on an unsealed road, drive much more slowly than you would on tarmac. If you have to brake or turn suddenly, it's easy to lose control of your vehicle if you're travelling at speed. Always make sure that you have plenty of fuel and supplies when travelling off-road and/or in remote areas.

 CYCLONES From November to April, cyclones are possible in the northwest and few years pass without a cyclone wreaking havoc in tropical far northern Australia. If you're travelling anywhere along the coast between Exmouth and Wyndham during cyclone season, check local weather forecasts regularly and always follow local advice on evacuating in advance of an approaching storm.

Wildlife Western Australia has its share of fearsome native creatures. But your chances of encountering a venomous snake or any other dangerous animal is quite small. Always be aware of your surroundings when walking in bush or rocky areas.

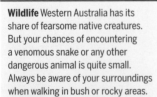

Jellyfish Stinging jellyfish are relatively rare in Western Australian waters, but always check local beach conditions and signage before swimming.

ROAD CLOSURES Rains can wash away unsealed roads in northern Western Australia, and many such roads and tracks will be closed for up to six months every year. If a road is closed, don't try and continue. Apart from the dangers of doing so, you may void your insurance cover.

WET SEASON Northern Western Australia's wet season runs from December to April and can seriously impact upon your travel plans.

QUICK TIPS TO HELP YOU MANAGE YOUR MONEY

CREDIT CARDS Credit cards are widely accepted, and are essential for hiring a car. They can also be used to get cash advances over the counter at banks and from many ATMs, though you'll incur immediate interest. Diners Club and American Express are not widely accepted in Australia. If travelling into the outback, carry enough cash for emergencies in case cards aren't accepted.

BANKING FEES
Withdrawing cash via ATMs or Eftpos with a card from an overseas or different bank may attract significant fees. Before travelling, check costs with your bank and ask about fee-free options.

BARGAINING
Gentle haggling is OK at some weekend markets, but it's generally not done in Australia. It's acceptable to ask for a small discount on expensive items when paying cash or buying more than one item.

CURRENCY

Australian dollar

HOW MUCH FOR A

Coffee (Perth)
A$4.50

Pint of beer (Perth)
from A$9

Fish & chips for 2 (Perth)
A$25–40

CHANGING MONEY Changing foreign currency is rarely a problem at banks and licensed moneychangers such as Travelex in Perth or Broome. Otherwise, change money at a bank.

ATMS & EFTPOS
Australian banks have ATMs in most medium-sized towns all over Western Australia. You'll even find them in some outback roadhouses. Many businesses also allow you to take out cash at the point of sale.

CONTACTLESS
In most larger towns and, to a lesser extent, Broome, contactless payment and services such as Apple Pay are commonly used. In smaller and more remote towns, you should always have cash in case cashless payments are not available or connections are down.

DEBIT CARDS

A debit card enables you to draw money from your home bank account. Any card connected to the international banking network (Cirrus, Maestro and Eurocard) should work with your PIN, but expect substantial fees. Companies such as Travelex offer debit cards with set withdrawal fees and a balance you can top up from your personal bank account while on the road.

Always carry extra cash for when your card (or local ATM) doesn't work or when only cash is accepted.

TIPPING
It's common, especially in Perth and the South West, but by no means obligatory, to tip in restaurants and upmarket cafes if the service warrants it. Taxi drivers in Perth and other large towns also appreciate you rounding up the fare. Tipping is not expected at hotels. In outback roadhouses, they'll chase you out the door, thinking you've forgotten your change.

RESPONSIBLE TRAVEL

Tips to leave a lighter footprint, support local and have a positive impact on local communities.

ON THE ROAD

Aboriginal-owned tours
Wherever possible, go on a tour guided by an Indigenous guide. If the company is Aboriginal-owned, all the better.

Electric vehicles Car-rental companies are increasingly offering electric vehicles for hire. Charging stations are still a little thin on the ground north of Perth, but it's certainly an option in and around Perth and the South West.

Buy from the artist When purchasing Aboriginal art, always make sure that proceeds from the sale will go direct to the artist. Aboriginal-owned and -run art centres work on this basis.

Car pooling If you plan on driving, consider getting together with other travellers to share a vehicle. It's a fun way to meet other people, to get to go further, as well as reducing each person's individual carbon footprint from the excursion.

GIVE BACK

Broome opportunities Volunteer conservation postings are offered by Roebuck Bay Working Group, Broome Bird Observatory and Environs Kimberley.

Department of Parks & Wildlife (dpaw.wa.gov.au) Offers opportunities at national parks all over WA, from turtle tagging at Ningaloo Marine Park to feral-animal control at Shark Bay. Online, click on the 'Get Involved' tab and then 'Volunteering Opportunities'.

Gabyon Station (gabyon.com.au) This working sheep station accepts volunteers as part of the WWOOF program. Participants do a few hours of work each day in return for bed and board.

Monkey Mia Marine Reserve (monkeymiavolunteers@westnet. com.au) Volunteer to work full time with dolphins for between four and 14 days – it's popular, so apply several months in advance.

DOS & DON'TS

Don't discuss controversial Indigenous or mining issues in public unless invited to do so by someone you trust; tempers run high on these complicated issues.

Do keep a respectful distance from wildlife, including while out diving or snorkelling. Encourage your tour operator to do the same.

Don't take photos in Indigenous communities without permission.

LEAVE A SMALL FOOTPRINT

Engine-free activities Wherever possible, hike, kayak or cycle when it comes to exploring your natural surroundings. Take tours that aim for low or zero carbon emissions through their activities.

Plastic bags Use your own reusable bags when shopping.

Carry out the trash Always carry out any rubbish or packaging you carry into natural areas.

Clean your shoes If hiking anywhere in southwestern WA (especially Stirling Range National Park), clean your shoes and all other equipment to prevent the spread of an introduced fungus known as Phytophthora dieback; the fungus can be devastating for vegetation elsewhere.

DOMONABIKE/ALAMY STOCK PHOTO ©

SUPPORT LOCAL

Buy locally made products and souvenirs, and buy direct from local producers where possible.

Indigenous art should only be bought buy from stores displaying or otherwise adhering to the Indigenous Art Code (indigenousartcode.org).

Western Australian Indigenous Tourism Operators Council (waitoc.com) is a fabulous resource for finding Aboriginal-owned and Indigenous-run tour operators in Western Australia.

WEST COAST AUSTRALIA POSITIVE-IMPACT TRAVEL

CLIMATE CHANGE & TRAVEL

It's impossible to ignore the impact we have when travelling, and the importance of making changes where we can. Lonely Planet urges all travellers to engage with their travel carbon footprint. There are many carbon calculators online that allow travellers to estimate the carbon emissions generated by their journey; try resurgence.org/resources/carbon-calculator.html. Many airlines and booking sites offer travellers the option of offsetting the impact of greenhouse gas emissions by contributing to climate-friendly initiatives around the world. We continue to offset the carbon footprint of all Lonely Planet staff travel, while recognising this is a mitigation more than a solution.

RESOURCES
waitoc.com
indigenousartcode.org
dpaw.wa.gov.au
ecotourism.org.au

UNIQUE & LOCAL WAYS TO STAY

Perth, the South West and Broome have by far the largest and most varied selection of places to stay. Elsewhere, your options are likely limited to motels, caravan parks and possibly an in-town apartment or B&B. In some areas which receive large numbers of tourists, such as Exmouth, the Ningaloo Reef or Broome, you may also find a resort or two.

HOW MUCH FOR A

Unpowered camp site
A$30/site

2-bed apartment
A$150–200

Motel
from A$120–200 per double room

ELLINNUR BAKARUDIN/SHUTTERSTOCK ©

THE AUSSIE MOTEL

The roadside motel is an Aussie classic imported from the US. Most are serviceable and without a whole lot of character but fine for the night. Others rise above their humble origins. All have en suite bathrooms and some have a swimming pool.

CARAVAN PARKS

The caravan park is a quintessentially Australian travel experience. If you're towing your own caravan or driving a campervan, you'll have a choice of powered or unpowered sites. Most caravan parks also have camp sites for those with their own tent, and some have on-site caravans for rent. The better ones have lots of shade, a swimming pool and children's playground. They're great places to meet other travellers, including Australia's transitory army of grey nomads who stay for weeks on end before moving on. Bookings are essential in high season.

GLAMPING

You don't find them in many places, but some camps have safari-style glamping tents. These have large en suite, permanent tents with proper beds, room enough to walk around in, sometimes an outdoor shower, and a private deck. They're a growing trend, but for now you'll find them in places such as Bridgetown, Balingup, Woody Island, the Kimberley, Cape Range National Park and Karijini National Park (pictured left).

NICK RAINS/GETTY IMAGES ©

FREEDOM CAMPING

A whole world of legend swirls around the Australian cattle station, and Western Australia certainly has its fair share of vast, working stations. In those that still operate as working commercial cattle stations, cattle roam across areas that are sometimes larger than some small European countries. In a small number of these, it's possible to stay overnight and catch a glimpse of a much-loved Australian way of life.

Accommodation varies from shared accommodation in converted former shearers' quarters to more luxurious quarters in the homesteads that once (or still) formed the headquarters around which station life revolved.

Some offer camping areas, usually close to the main homestead. If you're lucky, some also offer activities that showcase the daily life of the station, including, at certain times of the year, the mustering (corralling) of cattle in preparation for transport to the cities and export markets (pictured). You might also see at work jackaroos and jillaroos, skilled young horsemen and horsewomen who shepherd the cattle into holding pens, among other tasks.

You'll find station stays scattered across the northern half of the state, but they're especially common in the Kimberley, close to Shark Bay, along the Ningaloo Coast, and in some outback areas.

BOOKING

Advance booking is always recommended. In Perth, you'll always find something year-round, but book as early as you can for the central and northern coasts from June to September. Many places in the north also close entirely out of season.

Camps Australia (campsaustraliawide.com) A handy app with maps and information about campgrounds across Australia. Also try **Go Camping** (gocampingaustralia.com).

Caravan parks If you're doing a lot of caravanning or camping, consider joining one of the chain organisations, such as Big 4 Holiday Parks, Discovery Holiday Parks or Top Tourist Parks, which offer member discounts.

Farmstay Camping Australia (farmstaycampingaustralia.com.au) For station stays.

FAMILY FRIENDLY?

All across West Coast Australia, every town has at least one caravan park as well as motels, many with a swimming pool. Rooms or cabins often have interconnecting rooms that are ideal for families.

ESSENTIAL NUTS & BOLTS

PUBLIC TOILETS
The **National Public Toilet Map** (toiletmap.gov.au) has public toilet locations, including disabled-access toilets.

PHONE COVERAGE
Telstra has the widest mobile (cell) phone coverage, covering most of the coast and hinterland. There's no coverage in most of the outback or the Kimberley.

GOODS & SERVICES TAX REFUND
You may be eligible for a refund of the GST component of large purchases. To find out more about the Tourist Refund Scheme visit Australia Border Force (abf.gov.au).

FAST FACTS

Time Zone
GMT+8 hrs

Country Code
61

Electricity
230V/50Hz

GOOD TO KNOW

The legal drinking age is 18.

Australia has a three-prong socket (it is different to the British one). Bring an adaptor.

Australia uses the metric system.

All visitors to Australia need a visa, except New Zealanders. For more information and to apply online, visit homeaffairs.cgove.au.

ACCESSIBLE TRAVEL

Air travel Qantas offers discounted economy fares to people who have high-support needs, as well as to the carer travelling with them. Guide dogs travel free on Qantas, Jetstar, Virgin Australia and their affiliated carriers. WA's major airports have dedicated parking spaces, wheelchair access to terminals, and skychairs to convey passengers onto planes via air bridges. Most smaller airports also have accessible toilets.

Public transport Western Australia's suburban rail networks and the vast majority of urban buses are wheelchair accessible. Guide dogs and hearing dogs are permitted on all public transport.

Accommodation Legislation requires that new accommodation meets accessibility standards for mobility-impaired travellers. Many older establishments still lag behind.

Sights & attractions Many attractions, including many national parks, provide access for those with limited mobility. A number of sites also address the needs of visitors with visual or aural impairments.

Tour operators Discrimination by tourism operators is illegal. Ask each operator what's possible.

Lonely Planet covers a whole range of accessible travel issues. Visit lonelyplanet.com/articles/category/accessible-travel to find out more.

ALCOHOL
Check whether alcohol restrictions apply when visiting remote communities. You may be breaking the law if you have booze in your vehicle.

SMOKING
Smoking is banned from all indoor public spaces, and in some outdoor spaces where crowds congregate.

EMERGENCY APP
The Emergency+ (emergencyapp. triplezero.gov. au) app helps to locate people in an emergency. It's especially recommended for bushwalkers.

FAMILY TRAVEL

Sight & attractions Swimming with whale sharks, learning more about dolphins in Bunbury or Monkey Mia, and spotting humpacks at Albany or Ningaloo.

Supplies Baby formula, disposable nappies and kid-friendly food can be found in most major towns.

Child car seats Car safety seats are available from car-rental companies.

Concession Child concessions (and family rates) often apply to accommodation, tours, admission fees and transport.

Child-friendly meals Most cafes, pubs and restaurants offer children's menus.

GREETINGS
Usually a simple 'G'day', smile or nod suffices when passing people. Shake hands with men or women when meeting for the first time. In Aboriginal communities, direct eye contact can be considered overbearing. Be respectful, wait to be acknowledged and respond in a like manner.

PHOTOGRAPHY
For Aboriginal Australians, photography can be highly intrusive, especially when camera-toting travellers arrive in remote communities. Photographing cultural places, practices and images, sites of significance and ceremonies may not be welcomed. Respect is essential.

LGBTIQ+ TRAVELLERS

PrideFEST (pridewa.com.au) This 10-day festival runs in Perth in November, culminating in the Pride Parade.

Gay Perth (gaytravel.com/gay-guides/perth/gay-scene) Get the lowdown on Perth's small but dynamic gay bar, restaurant and entertainment scene.

LGBTIQ+-friendly? Like all Australian cities, Perth is LGBTIQ+-friendly, although attitudes tend to be more conservative in rural areas, especially in remote communities.

Gay marriage Same-sex marriages have been legally recognised in Australia since 2017.

Index